Lisa Saad

Author Megan Norris pictured with Cindy Gambino
at the dam in Winchelsea, Victoria where Robert
Farquharson left Jai, Tyler and Bailey to drown.

Journalist Megan Norris has a portfolio that covers some of the most
high-profile and horrific crimes in Australia. Her special interest in
women and children who are victims of violent crime has resulted in
a number of TV appearances as a media commentator on notorious
murder and missing persons cases. Megan is a former winner of the
EVA (Eliminating Violence Against Women) awards.

www.megannorris.com

LOOK WHAT YOU MADE ME DO

FATHERS WHO KILL

MEGAN NORRIS

echo

echo

Echo Publishing
A division of Bonnier Publishing Australia
534 Church Street, Richmond
Victoria Australia 3121
www.echopublishing.com.au

First published 2016

Printed in Australia at Griffin Press
Only wood grown from sustainable regrowth forests is used in the
manufacture of paper found in this book.

Edited by Linda Funnell
Cover design by Luke Causby, Blue Cork
Front cover image: Don Smith / Alamy
Page design and typesetting by Shaun Jury

Typeset in ITC New Baskerville and Klinic Slab

National Library of Australia Cataloguing-in-Publication entry (pbk)
    Creator: Norris, Megan, author.
    Title: Look what you made me do : fathers who kill / Megan Norris.
    ISBN: 9781760061838 (paperback)
    ISBN: 9781760061852 (ebook : epub)
    ISBN: 9781760061845 (ebook : mobi)
    Subjects: Filicide–Australia–Case studies.
    Children–Crimes against–Case studies.
    Marital conflict–Australia.
    Father and child–Australia.
    Family violence–Australia.
    Victims of family violence–Australia.
    Homicide–Australia–Case studies.
    Dewey Number: 364.152083

🐦 @echo_publishing
📷 @echo_publishing
📘 facebook.com/echopublishingAU

In memory of Kelly East, Jessie and Patrick Dalton, Jai, Tyler and Bailey Farquharson, Jack, Maddie and Bon Bell, Yazmina Acar, Darcey Freeman, and Marilyn and Sebastian Kongsom. And all the other innocents who have been used as weapons to punish their mothers.

Contents

INTRODUCTION
'Paybk u slut'

Prominent Melbourne criminologist Judy Wright once told me that when women were asked to nominate the worst possible thing a partner could do to them, their answers were always the same. Far more horrifying than having acid thrown in your face, or being set on fire to suffer a lifetime of disfigurement or a horrible death, women uniformly said that the most agonising punishment a spouse or former partner could possibly inflict on them would be to murder their children.

Nothing could ever top the crime of filicide (the murder of a child under the age of 18 by a parent), explained Judy; not when that crime was motivated by spite and an overriding desire to pay a woman back for ending a relationship. Surviving with the guilt, knowing that her children had been killed to punish her, was the worst kind of suffering any mother could imagine.

Tragically, studies in Australia reveal that 85 per cent of all child homicides are carried out by a parent. In 2014, a ground-breaking statistical overview of the 'tragic phenomena of filicide' in the United States revealed that over the past three decades, American parents committed filicide approximately 500 times each year. Worryingly, supporting research from around the world shows the majority of those offenders are the victims' biological fathers.

Determining motives for filicide is difficult and complex. However, in her 2012 discussion paper 'Just Say Goodbye', Dr Debbie Kirkwood, a renowned researcher in this area, says that records from the 2010 Annual Report from the National Homicide Prevention

Monitoring Program revealed that 35 per cent of all child murders recorded in Australia between 1997 and 2008 had been triggered by the collapse of a relationship.

International filicide studies have identified different categories for child murder, not including the killing of newborn babies, known as neonaticide. Dr Kirkwood cites a 1969 study conducted by US psychiatrist Dr Phillip Resnick, who identified five different types of child murder:

Altruistic — when a parent murders a child to protect it from real or imagined suffering.

Acutely psychotic — the parent who kills under the influence of a severe mental illness or in the grip of a psychotic episode.

Unwanted child — killings where the children are obstacles in a parent's life.

Fatal abuse murder — resulting from maltreatment or neglect.

Spousal revenge murder — killing a child to punish its mother. Dr Kirkwood says her own research for the Domestic Violence Resource Centre Victoria shows that younger children are more at risk of fatal abuse or accidental death, and that these types of killings are more likely to be perpetrated by mothers.

But she says retaliatory filicides, or spousal revenge murders, are different. Purposeful or intentional murders tend to be committed against older children and are crimes borne out of a specific intention to kill. They are crimes of revenge in which children are used by an aggrieved partner to punish a current or former spouse.

Dr Kirkwood points out that while there are documented cases where mothers have also murdered their children out of revenge, international studies into retaliatory filicides have consistently shown that most child revenge killings are perpetrated by men. In such killings there is likely to be a history of violence towards the intimate partner or other family members, while mothers who kill their own children have often been the victims of family violence.

In 2015 Professor Myrna Dawson, Chair of Public Policy and Criminal Justice at the University of Guelph in Canada and a member of the International Homicide Research Working Group, conducted one of the most extensive reviews of filicide ever undertaken. Studying Statistics Canada data covering more than 50 years of family homicides nationally, she discovered that between 1961 and 2011 at least 1612 Canadian children had been killed by a parent. Again, she found the majority of offenders were biological fathers, who were more likely than offending mothers to take their own lives after the crime.

What is telling, says Professor Dawson, is that statistics since 1991 showed there had been more reports of domestic violence leading up to these crimes, and that killer fathers were far more likely to be motivated by feelings of jealousy and a desire for revenge than mothers who killed their own offspring.

The fact that males are more likely to kill their children has also been supported by a groundbreaking UK study published in August 2013 in the *Howard Journal of Criminal Justice* by researchers from the University of Birmingham. After trawling through newspaper cuttings of cases of family homicides which occurred between 1980 and 2012, the research team identified four different types of killer whom they coined the family 'annihilator'. Professor David Wilson, director of the university's Centre of Applied Criminology and one of the study's three authors, explained that prior to this study, family annihilators had received little attention as a separate category of killer; previously these types of family killers had been viewed as 'spree' killers or serial murderers — offenders who had simply 'snapped' and gone on to murder their families. But this was not necessarily the case.

The most common characteristic of familicides was that 60 per cent of all family annihilators were male and that the crime was on the rise. Over half of the family homicides the researchers examined had been committed in the first decade of the millennium. And most of the offenders were men in their thirties, while 10 per cent were younger and the oldest offender was 59.

In England, the trigger time for the family annihilator appeared to be the northern-hemisphere-summer school holiday period when fathers had more access to their children. The UK study also found that around half of all family murders take place at the weekend, particularly on a Sunday. Research conducted by the Australian institute of Criminology confirms that Sunday is the most dangerous day of the week for children, probably because this is when the majority of youngsters are returning from weekend access visits with their fathers. Most murders occur during the afternoon and early evening, and younger children, under the age of one, are at most risk of being killed.

Like the UK study, Australian studies have found that family annihilators commonly attempt suicide after killing their families. This quashes the long-held theory that such offenders were inclined to seek a stand-off with authorities, resulting in 'suicide by cop', which is commonly the case in spree killings.

But what was also obvious in the UK study was that fathers who killed their families were not necessarily unhappy or frustrated dads with failed lives. Research showed that some family annihilators had had successful careers before they murdered and over 70 per cent were gainfully employed in occupations ranging from postmen and truck drivers to surgeons and marketing moguls.

Stabbings and carbon-monoxide poisoning were found to be the most common methods of murder and the majority of family murders took place in the home.

Through interviews with relatives and suicide notes presented to coroner's courts, the research team also examined the motivations of family annihilators. Family break-up was found to be the most common trigger, accounting for 66 per cent of the killings, though other domestic factors also came into play, such as a father's access to his children. And there were other contributing issues such as financial woes, honour killings and mental illness. By analysing the motivations for these murders and examining common traits, the team identified four different types of family annihilator: anomic, disappointed, self-righteous and paranoid.

'While these may overlap,' explained Professor Wilson, 'they all go beyond the traditional ideas of the revenge or altruistic murderers.'

Anomic killers are those killers who draw a link between their families and the economy. This type of offender perceives his family to be the result of his own economic success and a showcase for his hard-earned achievements. Once a killer perceives himself to be an economic failure, his family no longer serves this function and becomes disposable.

The disappointed annihilator believes his family has let him down or has behaved in a way that has ruined his fantasy of an ideal family life. He may be disappointed that his children do not want to follow his traditional, cultural or religious beliefs.

Self-righteous killers are those who blame their partners for the breakdown of the family, for their own violence and, later on, for the crime itself. This type of father will often phone his estranged partner before the murder to explain what he is about to do. For men like these, their status as the family breadwinner is pivotal to their notion of an ideal family.

The paranoid killer is the offender who perceives some external threat to his family. It could be the legal system, or social services, or some other external agency that he believes is against him and wants to take his children away. In these cases murdering his family might be motivated by a warped desire to protect them.

What is interesting about this research is that in each of the crimes, masculinity and perceptions of power form a background to the murders. Professor Wilson explained that the researchers believed the father's role in his family was central to his notions of masculinity and that such crimes were often his last attempt to perform a powerful manly role. He said it was important when looking at such crimes to consider the role that gender played, since it was mostly men who were responsible for them.

The international studies that found a strong connection between domestic violence and child and family murders are supported by more recent studies conducted by the Australian Institute of Criminology in Canberra.

In May 2015 Tracey Cussen and Willow Bryant released an update of an earlier study on family homicides conducted by researchers Jenny Mouzos and Catherine Rushforth. In their initial 2003 study, Mouzos and Rushforth had examined data spanning a 13-year period from 1 July 1989 to 30 June 2002. Their research revealed that, on average, 129 victims lost their lives each year in Australia in a domestic/family violence homicide. These figures made up between 32 and 47 per cent of all homicides reported annually across Australia.

Cussen and Bryant studied data from the National Homicide Monitoring Program Report, which includes information collected from state and territory police regarding all murders and manslaughters (except for death by culpable driving), along with data collected from the National Coronial Information Systems (NCIS), and found that of the 2631 homicide incidents documented over a 10-year period up until 30 June 2012, a staggering 41 per cent were family homicides.

Intimate partners made up 23 per cent of all homicide victims recorded by the NHMP; more than half of them were female and had experienced domestic violence. Worryingly, children made up the second most frequent group of victims in family homicides. Again, females were most likely to be victims of filicide and intimate partner murders. Cussen and Bryant further noted that over 23 weeks of monitoring family homicides, stabbing was consistently the most common cause of death and that the suicide of the perpetrator was more common after a filicide or family murder.

What is particularly alarming is that in a third of all these cases a protection order had been taken out by the intimate partner against the offender.

*

The findings come as no surprise to Australian anti-family-violence campaigner and author Rebecca Poulson, CEO of the Poulson Family Trust, a charity established in the wake of the murder of her family in order to save the lives of other children at risk of family violence.

In September 2003, on the day Rebecca turned 33, her Thai-born brother-in-law Phithak (Neung) Kongsom stabbed his two small children. Marilyn was four and her brother Sebastian, 23 months.

They were killed in a frenzied knife attack that also claimed the life of her elderly father. Sixty-year-old former college principal Peter Poulson died in the driveway of his home in New South Wales while courageously trying to protect his much-loved grandchildren from their embittered father's bloody revenge attack.

Kongsom had left a suicide note in which he threatened to destroy his estranged wife, Ingrid, and her entire family.

That afternoon Rebecca's younger sister, Ingrid, had arrived at her father's home with the police. She was being driven home in a police car after reporting a serious breach of an apprehended violence order (AVO) she had been granted to protect her from her ex-husband's ongoing violence. Detectives pulled onto the driveway where they interrupted the killer father who was in the throes of stabbing his mortally wounded son. Kongsom was shot by a police officer, but subsequently died of his own self-inflicted knife wounds. His children died at the scene along with their grandfather.

If the notion of an apparently loving father killing his own flesh and blood simply to exact a terrible lasting punishment on his former partner seems unfathomable, Rebecca Poulson has a straightforward explanation.

'It's about revenge,' she told me simply. 'Their desire for revenge is greater than their love for their own children.'

Why fathers are driven to kill their own children remains a widely misunderstood and hotly debated topic. But while the media continues to describe such crimes as 'senseless' and beyond understanding, the countless heartbreaking discussions I have had with surviving mothers and almost 40 years of covering courts have given me some insight into the nature of retaliatory homicides.

As the name suggests, spousal revenge murders are indeed a crime spawned by spite. They are malevolent, horrifying crimes that have their genesis in the overriding desire to pay a woman back for ending an untenable, sometimes abusive relationship.

For an estranged partner with a brooding grudge, the germinating fantasy of paying back a former spouse by taking her life often loses its lustre in the cold light of day. A wife's death alone will never be enough for an angry, controlling man whose sense of power and masculinity is eroded when his partner exercises her right to end their relationship. After the separation, the husband may have flirted with the idea of killing himself, intending his estranged spouse to torment herself after his death with the guilt of what he perceives *she* has done to him. But the prospect of ending his own life suddenly seems less appealing to a bitter ex when he realises his former wife has found a new man and appears to be moving on with her life. It's unlikely that a newly independent woman with a bright future ahead of her would be grieving for too long, so the murder–suicide fantasy takes a U-turn. For a bitter, angry husband hell-bent on inflicting a more enduring pain, the focus slowly shifts to his own children.

When Neung Kongsom's hopes of rekindling his failed marriage to Ingrid Poulson faded, he left her a message threatening to end his own life and take her with him. Similarly, 10 years earlier in Western Australia, simmering father Kevin East sent his estranged partner Michelle Steck his last will and testament, and Melbourne father Ramazan Acar also made repeated threats to kill himself when he realised his battered wife had left him for good.

But like other vengeful men, they quickly discovered there was a more effective way of inflicting a paralysing grief on their estranged partners.

Kongsom was well aware of the lasting nature of the agony he was about to inflict when he penned a second suicide note, this time telling his estranged wife he was poised to destroy her and her family. Sadly, in September 2003, little Marilyn Kongsom and her brother Sebastian became the tools for him to inflict unspeakable suffering on their mother.

Ramazan Acar's daughter Yazmina was looking forward to her third birthday when his suicidal fantasies turned to murder. In November 2010, after threatening to stab himself to death, he abducted and stabbed his little girl to death instead, dumping her body in an outer Melbourne suburb.

Disgruntled father Kevin East kidnapped his three-year-old

daughter Kelly, sparking a nationwide manhunt. A few weeks later, in January 1994, their bodies were found in East's abandoned car, which had been camouflaged and left in isolated bush in Western Australia. Father and daughter both died of carbon monoxide poisoning from exhaust fumes. So did Jack, Maddie and Bon Bell, who died in June 2008 when their father, Gary Bell, rigged two hose pipes from the exhaust into the family car, poisoning himself and his family.

Four years before, former One Nation candidate Jayson Dalton suffocated himself and his two young children — Jessie, aged 19 months, and three-month-old Patrick — during an access visit. Two days before the murder–suicide he had lost a bitter custody battle with his former partner, Dionne.

But just as the UK study revealed, none of these murders resulted from 'snap' decisions. As the stories in this book illustrate, all showed an element of forethought and, in most cases, some sort of threat had preceded each murder.

While Kongsom's suicide note left little doubt about his payback motive, Jayson Dalton's final message to his estranged wife, sent from the marital home in Brisbane, was a little more ambiguous. He told Dionne darkly that he had loved her and had been prepared to do anything for her until now. Later, in a cryptic phone call to his father just before the murder–suicide, he said ominously that he and his children were about to take 'a long sleep'.

In his suicide note, Gary Bell remained true to his narcissistic personality and only thought about himself. He took the extra step of leaving a chilling tape recorded message on his wife's camera, for her to find after he was gone. With the prospect of a prison sentence hanging over him for his latest brutal attack on his wife Karen, he claimed grandiosely that he couldn't live without his children, and they could not live without him.

Kevin East was more spiteful, taunting his estranged wife, Michelle Steck. On the day he vanished in November 1993, the simmering father posted Michelle a tape recording of songs that were significant to her. But by the time Michelle opened them, East and their little girl were already dead. East went a step further: he left a death journal sadistically recording Kelly's final moments to add to her grieving mother's agony.

Kelly's murder had not been a snap decision. Some weeks beforehand, little Kelly had returned from a visit to her father complaining that she had been frightened when Daddy held a pillow over her face while she ate a biscuit. The tot said she had not been able to breathe or swallow with the pillow on her face. But when an alarmed Michelle told her lawyer, she was stunned to be informed that the word of a toddler would not stand up in court. Supervised access continued, and it was while on a supposedly supervised visit that Kelly was abducted and killed.

Bearing out the UK study that revealed that 'self-righteous' style offenders were more likely to contact former partners and announce their intention to kill their family, Ramazan Acar warned his estranged partner, Rachelle D'Argent, in a menacing Facebook post just hours after abducting his daughter: 'Bout to kil ma kid.'

His motivation was clearly revenge.

'Paybk u slut,' he later added.

In January 2009, Melbourne father of three Arthur Freeman telephoned his former wife Peta Barnes from the approaches of the city's Westgate Bridge with his own chilling warning.

'Say goodbye to your children,' he told the shocked mother. Moments later, he threw his only daughter, Darcey, aged four, off the bridge to her death.

Killer father Robert Farquharson was not foolish enough to make any phone threats or send any messages that would have alerted his former wife, Cindy Gambino, to his dark intentions. Instead, he shared his callous murder fantasy with his closest friend, never dreaming his mate Gregory King would ever tell anyone. Three months before murdering his children in June 2005, he told King about a dream he'd had involving a car accident. In the dream he had escaped but his three young sons did not. It involved a dam and took place on a 'special day', like Father's Day, when he would be the last one to see the children alive. His mate was stunned when he learned that on Father's Day that September, the Farquharsons' car had indeed plunged into a dam near rural Winchelsea and that his mate's three boys, Jai, Tyler and Bailey, had all drowned. Just as Farquharson had predicted in his supposed dream, only he had survived.

Like the other disgruntled fathers in this book, Robert Farquharson had not been happy about the breakdown of his relationship. He was angry about the division of the family finances and resented his former partner, Cindy, driving around town in the 'good' car, while he drove around in the 'shit' one. Farquharson was also furious about the new man in Cindy's life and the fact that she was moving on.

'Nobody does that to me and gets away with it,' he told his good friend Gregory King.

Like some of the other fathers in this book, Farquharson had earlier expressed suicidal thoughts, though his former wife was unaware of this. While there was no phone call to alert Cindy Gambino ahead of the murder plan, she was the only person Farquharson wanted to speak to when he swam away leaving his three sons to drown. Refusing repeated offers of help from two good Samaritans who stopped on the highway that night, Farquharson's only request was for a lift back to Winchelsea, so he could tell his former wife in person that their children were dead.

Andrew Tinney SC, the crown prosecutor in Farquharson's second trial, would later say this was his 'delicious reward' for his crime, as it allowed him to see first-hand the pain he had caused to his children's mother.

Later, he milked the system for all it was worth, dragging the shattered mother through two trials and two failed appeals until his last-ditch bid to take his case to the High Court in Canberra was finally thrown out. But in the dock of the Victorian Supreme Court in Melbourne, Farquharson had a front-row seat as he watched the distraught mother reliving her worst nightmare as she gave evidence.

The tragedy in this case, as in all the stories in this book, is that the Farquharson children were simply collateral damage in a retaliatory crime that was not aimed at them at all. Their mothers were always the real targets, their children simply the weapons used to inflict lasting pain by a man whose fundamental obligation had been to love, nurture and protect them.

What is interesting in every case is that each of the killer fathers had expressed fear at the prospect of 'losing' their children and having reduced roles in the youngsters' lives because of custody arrangements. But as Dr Debbie Kirkwood told me, it defies logic that fathers who complain about not seeing enough of their children should then want to kill them.

What should be noted is that while it's been suggested that fathers are driven to kill their own children because of unfair court rulings and reduced access, in too many cases fathers have used their access to murder their children.

In 2011 Australian murder–suicide expert Dr Carolyn Harris Johnson of Curtin University in Western Australia studied a number of murder–suicide cases in which fathers had murdered after a relationship breakdown. In every case, the father had used his access time to kill his children.

Dr Harris Johnson, a social worker who worked with offenders in mens prisons in WA, published her findings in her book, *Come with Daddy*, and concluded that custody issues were not the main reason fathers murdered their children. The biggest motivation was to punish former partners for leaving. Her findings came at a time when the organisation Dads in Distress was receiving around 5000 calls a year, mostly from fathers reporting problems with the Child Support Agency such as restricted access to their children or dealing with AVOs taken out by former partners.

Dr Harris Johnson identified the kind of fathers who kill in such situations as having a 'proprietorial attitude' towards women and children. When a relationship ends, they are unable to relinquish the control they previously had over the family. Often they are pathologically jealous and when it becomes clear their wives will not be returning to them, they turn ugly.

Killing their children is a final act of power and control. These vengeful perpetrators are inclined to let their wives survive to ensure they experience the pain and grief of losing their children.

Yet while studies consistently show that a controlling man with a history of violence is behind most cases of family homicide, women's fears are often dismissed or minimised. In her book *Killing Love*, survivor Rebecca Poulson calls it the 'big brush-off'. She says the focus needs to be on finding ways to better protect women and children at risk.

At some stage during their failed relationships, each of the fathers I have looked at has been violent or abusive, though sometimes their abuse appears to have been of a more insidious emotional nature and was only identified as family violence in hindsight. This more subtle abuse includes put-downs, name-calling, refusing to help with the children or share the workload, restricting money and socialising, isolating the partner from family and friends, stalking, harassment, threats and shoving. Yet even those fathers the authorities knew had been physically violent to their partners were not considered a danger to their children.

The police were aware of the domestic violence perpetrated by Kongsom, East, Dalton, Bell and Acar. All five fathers had repeatedly breached AVOs and continued to harass, threaten and intimidate their partners. Kongsom breached his AVO four times on the day it was served, and 19 times in less than a month before he finally killed his children and father-in-law.

Acar's appearance at his former partner's home on the night he abducted and murdered their daughter constituted his twenty-eighth breach of the intervention order that Rachelle D'Argent had taken out to protect herself and her daughter. And Kevin East flouted his AVO almost by the day, only to be given a ticking off and released without charge. When New South Wales father Gary Bell was served with an AVO and charged with assaulting his partner, Karen Bell, it was the second time he had been arrested for attacking her. Hours after Karen was forced to leave the family home to save herself, Gary Bell killed his children. Jack, Maddie and Bon Bell's bodies were found beside Bell in his four-wheel drive at the family's remote New South Wales farm five days later.

Both Gary Bell and Ramazan Acar were facing possible terms of imprisonment for violence towards their partners at the time they murdered their children. Jayson Dalton, who tried to intimidate his fleeing wife into returning to him, was also facing possible charges for breaching his intervention order at the time he murdered his children. Interestingly, each of these men blamed their partners for the violence that had led to the AVOs. The brutal Jayson Dalton repeatedly told his battered wife throughout their marriage that his violence was all her fault — if only Dionne had done things properly, the way he liked them, he ranted. It was a case of 'look what you made me do'.

Yet despite these alarming histories of domestic violence and the escalating violence after separation, inquests into the deaths of most of the children mentioned in this book found that their murders could not have been predicted or prevented.

The day after Karen Bell was granted an AVO, New South Wales police alerted the Department of Community Services that there were children involved in the violent relationship. But because the children's names were not included on the AVO, Karen was forced to leave her marital home without them. When she rang police begging them to remove the children from her violent husband, she was told that without their names on the order, there was nothing more they could do. Within hours, the children were dead.

Ingrid Poulson also contacted police after Kongsom refused to allow her to leave with their daughter after an access visit and threatened to kill himself in front of his family. Four police officers later escorted Ingrid back to her ex-husband's apartment, only to wait outside while she went in alone to retrieve her daughter from her ex, who had earlier been armed with a knife.

Similarly, after her separation from her erratic angry husband, Arthur Philip Freeman, Melbourne mother Peta Barnes told her GP that she was worried he might harm their three children in order to hurt her. Despite rules relating to mandatory reporting of children at risk, the GP did not pass on these concerns to Protective Services. The family doctor would later tell an inquest into the little girl's death that he was aware the authorities and lawyers were already involved with the family and trusted that they would have intervened if required. But in the end nobody considered that a law-abiding computer geek like Arthur Freeman posed any real threat to his children. A few months later, in January 2009, little Darcey Freeman was dead in a tragedy witnessed by her brothers aged six and two.

While the inquest found there had been no way to predict such a terrible crime, the warning signs had been there. Just weeks before Darcey was murdered, Freeman told a relative that his former wife would 'regret it' if he lost his custody battle for his children. Two days after Freeman's access was reduced, he murdered his daughter; the conversation returned to haunt the relative who had not fully understood what Freeman had meant.

'The signs are always there,' Michelle Steck told me recently. 'But even when they are in your face, and you wave flags in other people's faces, nobody seems to want to know. Even after our separation, and the police found my ex living in my roof space, they let him use my shower before they arrested him, and he was never charged. They set him free and he was back again next day, harassing and threatening me again. If he had been charged, or punished for breaching his AVO, my little girl might have been alive today.' After Kelly's murder, Michelle Steck embarked on a crusade for change.

'I went to Canberra where I banged on doors, calling upon the decision-makers to amend the laws which were failing mothers like me,' says Michelle. 'They slammed them in my face.'

But Michelle remained vocal about the laws relating to AVOs, which she said were not worth the paper they were written on unless they were enforced and followed up by the courts with punitive consequences.

'I told anyone who would listen that unless something was done to protect mothers like me, there would be more innocent casualties like Kelly in the future,' she told me. 'But nobody was listening; it just wasn't sexy politics at the time.

'Domestic violence has never been a glamorous or popular subject. And I predicted all those years ago that it was going to take a very public murder involving some celebrity's child, or some high-profile person's family, to get this issue into the public's consciousness and get those changes happening.'

Tragically, it took the very public murder of eleven-year-old Melbourne boy Luke Batty on 12 February 2014, and the grief of another mother, to make the legislators and decision-makers take notice.

Luke Batty died on a suburban playing field after being attacked by his father, Greg Anderson, aged 54. His murder has etched itself into Australia's public consciousness. At the time Anderson was estranged from the boy's mother, who had taken out an AVO against him due to the longstanding history of domestic violence. Anderson was shot by police at the scene and later died in hospital from his injuries.

As with the stories of the other children in this book, a coroner found that despite Anderson's prior history of violence towards Luke's mother, Rosie, he had never been violent to his son.

Victorian State Coroner Ian Gray told the inquest in Melbourne in 2015 that because of this, there was no 'risk assessment tool' that could have accurately predicted whether a parent was likely to commit filicide.

'No person or agency could have reasonably been expected to foresee Mr Anderson would be that rare perpetrator and Luke that rare victim of a violent filicide.' The coroner accepted that Anderson may have been suffering from a delusional disorder at the time of the murder.

Michelle Steck recalls seeing Rosie Batty on the TV news and reliving her own worst nightmare.

'I remember watching that poor woman, knowing the journey that lay ahead of her, and wondering why it had to come to this,' she said.

But Rosie Batty was determined to make sure she was a voice for her son and other children like him caught up in the cycle of domestic violence. She campaigned tirelessly to lift the lid on domestic violence and raise awareness, determined to ensure that the issue became everyone's business.

In January 2015 Rosie Batty was voted Australian of the Year. It was a prestigious but hard-earned award for the influential anti-violence campaigner.

'The subject of domestic violence certainly appears to have gathered more momentum in the past 12 months,' reflects Rebecca Poulson. 'But you can't help wondering what will happen now Rosie Batty is no longer Australian of the Year. I only hope the good work will continue and that this issue continues to stay where it belongs, in the public eye.'

Between July 2007 and June 2010, a staggering 338 Australian children were victims of homicide, with children under the age of one still at greatest risk.

In September 2015, while I was working on this book, two more Australian children and two other mothers died in four separate crimes of family violence.

On 7 September, a Brisbane father was arrested on Queensland's Gold Coast and charged with the murder of his six-year-old daughter, who had been found dead in her bed at the family's home in the northern Brisbane suburb of Kedron. He has since been charged with the attempted murder of his eight-year-old daughter too. At the time of writing he is awaiting trial.

On 24 September, a 31-year-old man was charged with the murder of his stepdaughter, whose body had been discovered in her bedroom in the Hunter Valley, New South Wales.

During the same month, two mothers lost their lives. On the Gold Coast, Tara Brown was allegedly bashed to death by her former partner Lionel Patea, who has since been charged with her murder.

Two days later, Queensland mother of four Karina Lock was pursued by her estranged husband Stephen Lock into a packed Gold Coast McDonald's store. As diners looked on in horror, Lock grabbed his former wife in a headlock and coolly put a gun to her head and pulled the trigger. Minutes later, he turned his gun on himself. Despite frantic attempts to revive Mrs Lock, she died at the scene. Her critically injured ex-husband was taken to hospital under police guard, where he died shortly afterwards.

Mrs Lock, a devout Jehovah's Witness, had endured years of

...e at the hands of her brutal husband, and just months earlier had sold the family home in Maryborough in Central Queensland to begin a new life with her teenage daughter on the Gold Coast.

In the days after these murders made news, the *Courier Mail* reported that the number of calls for help to DV Connect, an organisation supporting women living with domestic violence in Queensland, had more than doubled. Operators working 24 hours a day, seven days a week handled more than 400 reports from women seeking help and advice every day in the aftermath of these crimes.

In response, the crisis service for women in Queensland moved its Red Rose Tribute from Brisbane to Southport Court House, joining Tara Brown's relatives and friends in a silent protest and placing roses at the front door of the court.

It was a black month in Queensland, which ended with a ray of light when the new prime minister, Malcolm Turnbull, announced a $100 million package of measures to protect victims of domestic and family violence.

'We need to elevate the issue to our national consciousness and make it clear that domestic, family or sexual violence is unacceptable in any circumstances,' he told the media.

On White Ribbon Day 2015, hot on the heels of Rosie Batty's campaign to encourage Australians to say no to violence, the federal government launched another initiative to 'break the cycle' of domestic violence and change community attitudes towards violence against women and children. The announcement came as damning research surfaced revealing that 78 women had already died that year through domestic and sexual violence — which equates to two women being murdered in Australia every week.

The Prime Minister said that parents, fathers and grandparents had a huge responsibility to teach their sons to grow up respecting their mothers and sisters. His comments came as the report revealed that victims continued to be blamed for domestic violence. Australians have been conditioned from a very young age to downplay the gravity of what is now recognised as a serious community issue. The 2013 *Young Australians' Attitudes Towards Violence Against Women* report, a study aimed at determining changing community attitudes among the younger generation, yielded some alarming findings. Of the 1923 Australians aged 16 to 24 surveyed, most thought it was OK to be violent towards a woman, providing you were sorry afterwards.

Over half the young men surveyed thought it was acceptable to track a partner with an electronic device without her consent, as did 40 per cent of young women. More worrying still, two in five young people agreed rape resulted from men not being able to control their sexual urges. And one in five agreed women say no to sex when they really mean yes. Some blamed the victims for the violence committed against them.

Sadly, this is not a new emerging trend but an entrenched attitude. And it exists in older age groups, not just among Australia's younger generation. Many of the women whose stories are included in this book have described the subtle and not-so-subtle blaming they have had to endure since losing their children.

Some have been blamed for not leaving violent husbands; others have been blamed for leaving them. One ABC viewer, after seeing Ingrid Poulson speaking on TV about her family's murders, contacted the show's website asking why on earth she hadn't left Kongsom the second he showed his true colours. Another male viewer wrote that the segment was a 'load of crap' and ranted about women using children as 'hostages' to punish their former partners when relationships broke down. That 'crap', Ingrid Poulson later pointed out in a White Ribbon speech in 2011, was the murder of her two children and her father.

She is not the only survivor to have experienced blame. Cindy Gambino was confronted in a supermarket after she appeared on *Sixty Minutes* saying she still believed her children's drowning deaths were accidental and that her former husband was innocent. I had organised that story, and had written it for the show's sister magazine, *Woman's Day*. It was obvious to me at that time that the only way Cindy was surviving was by clinging to a deep denial about the murders. To have acknowledged her children's deaths for the crimes they actually were, would have destroyed her. It would be almost five years before

Cindy came to accept that Robert Farquharson really had murdered their children to punish her. But after the show, a complete stranger bailed her up and angrily told her she was a 'stupid' woman for believing her husband's account of events. Cindy, already dosed on antidepressants, retreated home in tears, where she continued to receive hate mail from other judgemental people. Judgements like these, she said, only compounded her deep grief. She had been victimised once by Farquharson, now it seemed that everyone else was punishing her too. Cindy lost friends and withdrew as her children's murders cast a stain on the tiny town of Winchelsea, where even today locals remain reluctant to talk about the crime. Cindy is a social leper in a community where she continues to feel blamed for the crime committed against her.

And she is not alone. A woman in an online chat room, responding to a newspaper story about the murder of little Yazmina D'Argent, also blamed the murdered girl's mother for the crime perpetrated by her vengeful ex-partner. She angrily demanded to know what on earth Rachelle D'Argent was thinking when she allowed her former partner, a man she was terrified of, to take their daughter for a ride in his car that night.

The blame game continues. Another mother's estranged husband shot his two children dead as they slept beside her in bed before turning the gun on himself. During the attack she received serious shotgun wounds to her leg, before the disgruntled father turned his gun on himself. Afterwards the injured mother's leg had to be amputated. A woman observing the injured mother limping on her new prosthetic leg asked her pointedly:

'What did you do to him, for him to do this to you?'

The mother replied: 'I was simply breathing.'

It is judgements like these that constitute secondary victimisation of mothers who have already tormented themselves with the 'what ifs' and 'if onlys'. What is interesting is that the 'blamers' tend to be other mothers.

'We are all judged, and we are all judged differently,' Ingrid Poulson told a White Ribbon gathering in 2011.

Until the murder of her children and her father, Ingrid said she had always been an average person with a face that 'blended in'. But the story of her husband's crime was not average; it was huge. And it put her in the public eye where every aspect of her life and her character was suddenly being scrutinised by the media and strangers.

The experience was eye-opening for Ingrid, who told the White Ribbon supporters that she had no doubt that if her family had been killed by a falling tree, her life would not have been examined in such a public and critical way.

What was most astonishing, she said, was that the focus was not on the crime, nor the man behind it, but had become her: what she looked like, what she wore, how she presented and whether she was educated or not. In truth, what she looked like, what she wore, or what she did or said was irrelevant. It wasn't about her at all.

'It's always about him,' she said.

Yet people tended to look for ways to make themselves different from her; nobody wanted to be her. Ingrid said she felt that by making themselves different, they seemed to be reassuring themselves that what had happened to her could not happen to them.

But instead of looking for differences, she said people should be looking at the similarities. Statistically, one of the biggest commonalities in these crimes was simply being female. Being a woman means you are far more likely to be the victim of a violent crime.

In early 2016 there were 950 000 AVOs current across the country. The majority had been taken out by women against their intimate partners.

Two of the country's biggest corporate giants, Target and NAB, have since announced paid leave for women living with family violence, and in Queensland, Premier Annastacia Palaszczuk has announced paid leave for government workers battling domestic violence. The announcements were timely, given that every three hours in Australia a woman is admitted to hospital with injuries inflicted by a current or former partner. This is just the tip of the iceberg, as these are only the cases that are reported. There are many other invisible victims out there who are not reporting assaults and not presenting at hospitals and doctors' surgeries, but remain trapped in the cycle of violence.

Around this time I paused to watch another story unfolding on the news: a father had driven his car off a pier with his two small children inside in another apparent murder–suicide. According to people who knew the father, there had been no hint of the impending tragedy until he posted a suicide message on his Facebook page very early that morning. He had been a 'top bloke', the press declared, running a phone number for Lifeline. It later emerged that a firearm had been found in the car when it was recovered from the water, and that all three bodies had suffered shotgun wounds. The discovery prompted South Australian police to issue a media statement saying that while the investigation was ongoing, issues of mental health and family violence would be among the evidence presented to the coroner.

I pondered this as I signed Rebecca Poulson's Facebook petition calling for the changes her family had demanded over a decade ago. In spite of the slow cultural shift in police attitudes to domestic violence, the mandatory reporting of children at risk, the tweaking of stalking legislation, and the automatic inclusion of children's names on AVOs granted to abused mothers, there was clearly a great deal of work still to be done.

In her petition, Rebecca Poulson, now an author and inspirational speaker, urged Australia's Prime Minister Malcolm Turnbull, the New South Wales Premier Michael Baird, the New South Wales Police Commissioner Andrew Scipione and the New South Wales Police Minister Troy Grant to implement immediate changes that may spare other women her family's heartache.

'What happened to my family can still happen today and it breaks my heart,' she says.

One of the most significant changes she is calling for is immediate prison sentences for violent men who breach intimate-partner AVOs.

Other suggestions for change include greater public awareness, with media running the 1800 RESPECT number in every story about domestic violence, and giving more coverage to stories about women who have lost their lives as a result of it. She also says there is a need to educate police about domestic violence procedures, and more training in how to follow them.

She says few officers, if any, receive any real training in how to handle domestic violence after they leave the academy, or are even familiar with the procedures. The officers handling her sister's case had not even read the reports and did not know the violent background to the relationship when she reported Kongsom's breaches of his AVO.

Rebecca is also calling for mandatory police follow up of all AVOs, even in those cases where women decide to withdraw their complaints. And she highlights the need to see domestic violence education in all Australian schools to educate students who are living with family violence so that they know it is wrong and can access help.

Her petition also calls upon the New South Wales Department of Community Services to allocate more case workers to children at risk of family violence and for the government to immediately reopen the emergency shelters the Abbott Government closed, in order to provide safe places for women and children escaping the cycle of violence.

As Rebecca points out, women still make up the biggest single group of all homeless Australians. And since more than half of all women in violent relationships have children in their care, their children are homeless, too.

The petition attracted more than 1200 signatures in just three days. By February 2016 more than 27 816 names had been added.

*

A month after I signed Rebecca Poulson's petition, Australia's first Royal Commission into Family Violence delivered its findings to the Victorian Government. The Commission made 227 groundbreaking recommendations aimed at stemming the epidemic of domestic violence across the state. Commissioner Marcia Neave said there needed to be a 'transformation' to address the failings of a system in crisis.

The Victorian Royal Commission grew from a 2014 election promise made by Victorian Premier Daniel Andrews to Rosie Batty in the wake of her son's murder. The Royal Commission wrapped up in October 2015 following months of wideranging consultation with victims of family violence, the police, and support agencies.

Echoing Rebecca Poulson's calls for greater education, the commission said it believed the key to change lay in teaching young Australians about respectful, healthy relationships. The commissioner recommended that mandatory classes be implemented in all schools so that youngsters could tell the difference between a healthy, respectful relationship and an unacceptable, abusive and potentially dangerous one. The commission's Respectful Relationships Education program is now set to become the flagship of the Victorian Government's Family Violence Prevention Strategy.

Other recommendations made by the commission include the formation of support hubs throughout Victoria, where specialists in family violence will be available to refer clients on to appropriate support services. These would include intervention programs for violent perpetrators and counselling services for women and children caught up in the cycle of violence.

The commission further recommended the establishment of a central information point, based on the British and South Australian models, where information from police, courts and correctional facilities can be channelled for risk-assessment purposes and to ensure that violent offenders are more closely monitored by the police and the courts in future.

In another trailblazing first, the Commission wants Victorian police to trial body cameras on call-outs relating to family violence. Cameras will make it easier for officers in the front line to collect evidence, and cut down on unnecessary paperwork associated with domestic violence complaints. It also wants to see specialist family violence courts established across Victoria over the next five years to deal solely with domestic violence and the criminal and civil matters arising from such complaints. Family Violence Courts should have upgraded security to afford greater protection to victims of abuse, sparing complainants the anguish of coming into contact with their abusers during the court process.

Commenting on the recommendations, the Chief Executive Officer of Domestic Violence Victoria, Fiona McCormack, told news outlets the commission had 'got it right', though its success would depend on how the recommendations were implemented 'and to what extent. We have got the Premier talking about this issue in a way that provides leadership,' she told journalists.

The recommendations made by the Royal Commission prompted debate, which led anti-violence campaigners in neighbouring New South Wales to demand greater resources to tackle domestic violence there too. The ABC reported that Dr Andreia Schineanu, an expert in family violence studies from Charles Sturt University, felt there was insufficient funding to address family violence on a national level, let alone to prevent it. Dr Schineanu argued that the lack of crisis accommodation for women was now a widespread contributor to the problem of homelessness, since funding cuts had closed women's refuges. The federal government had recently slashed funding for this sector, and now needed to respond to the situation as a matter of urgency.

Dr Schineanu went on to say that even though the prime minister had restored some of the funding that had been cut, it was still 'nowhere near enough'. Future budgets needed to allocate resources for specialist family violence services in order to address a long-term national problem. The Victorian Royal Commission's recommendations needed to be applied around Australia. The recommendations gave new hope, she observed, because they focussed on a longer-term solution to the current crisis.

Days after the Royal Commission's Report was tabled in parliament, the ABC revealed that Australian police were responding to 657 reports of domestic violence every day. That equals a new complaint every two minutes. By the time you have finished reading this chapter, police will have responded to at least 20 new reports of family violence.

Based on data collected from police in every state and territory, these figures mean that by the end of the year a staggering 239 846 incidents of family violence will be handled by front-line officers around the country.

These statistics come hot on the heels of the third annual report of the New South Wales Domestic Violence Death Review Team. That report, published in 2015, analysed data collected between 2000 and 2010 and revealed that during that 10-year period, 238 homicides had occurred in New South Wales alone as a result of domestic violence. Over half of the murder victims were women; 55 were children. More chilling, 96 per cent of those children had been killed by a parent.

The convenor of the review team, New South Wales State Coroner Michael Barnes, told the ABC that the figures made 'disturbing reading', particularly since 60 per cent of the homicides were intimate partner murders and that most of the women killed had been the victims of domestic violence. Interestingly, while 29 of the 35 male victims had been murdered by a current or former partner, almost all had been the abuser in the relationship. Not one of the murdered women had been the abuser and most of the homicides had occurred after a recent separation, or during the separation process.

Mirroring the recommendations in Rebecca Poulson's petition, the review team called for better recruitment and training of police, stating that more care needed to be taken by officers when gathering evidence in cases of family violence. It further recommended that Family and Community Services should be notified about any domestic-violence complaints where children were living with a violent perpetrator.

By 12 April, when I finished writing this introduction, researchers from the feminist group Destroy the Joint's 'Counting Dead Women' Facebook initiative estimated that 22 Australian women had been murdered in the first four months of 2016. By 6 June ten more women had been murdered. They continue to add new names to the depressing Facebook register, which grows every day.

*

Domestic violence is dangerous. For the 13 little children whose stories are in this book, it proved to be deadly. But as Rebecca Poulson says, there are often red flags in such cases, which means some deaths, at least, may be preventable in future.

'But police need to implement a procedure *now* that stops women living with violence from being brushed off or not believed when she approaches them for help,' Rebecca says impatiently. 'Because brush-off can equal death.'

CHAPTER 1

'You're going to pay for your actions for a long time.'

The story of Michelle Steck and Kelly East

Michelle Steck studied her three-year-old daughter's worried face as she sat quietly in her pyjamas in front of the television, clinging to her favourite Roger Ramjet toy. It was November 1993, and while Kelly had previously returned from her access visits with her dad happy and animated, after this particular stopover the little girl was so subdued that her mother's gut instinct told her something was terribly wrong.

Since Michelle's turbulent separation from her violent partner, Kevin East, in January 1993, she had grown increasingly concerned about his access to their two small children, Kelly and 16-month-old Wesley.

After she ended the relationship, Michelle and the children had moved from their former family home in the Perth suburb of Forest Field to the small West Australian coal mining town of Collie, in the heart of jarrah timber country in Western Australia's Darling Range, almost 60 kilometres east of Bunbury.

But East, who was 11 years Michelle's senior, had flatly refused to accept that the troubled relationship was over. When it became clear his estranged partner would not be returning, he became so angry and erratic that the 24-year-old mother had been forced to cancel his access, alarmed that he was too unstable to care for two small children on his own.

For a while East paid a local woman to drive him each weekend from his home in Rockingham to Collie to collect his children. But even the presence of a female driver on the journey did little to reassure their worried mother, who was still concerned about her toddlers spending time alone with East.

By September 1993 his fragile mental health was obviously deteriorating, though East appeared to have little insight into Michelle's decision to stop the children's access visits. He was furious about the situation and projected his anger onto Michelle, blaming her for everything, just as he had done during their abusive relationship. As far as East was concerned, she was deliberately withholding the children to punish him.

In this adversarial frame of mind, Kevin East took legal action claiming he was being emotionally blackmailed by a woman who was manipulating the system out of revenge. The hard-up single mother, unable to afford a lawyer, was forced to represent herself. The warring parents were subsequently referred to a counsellor who, overlooking the violent history of the relationship, suggested this was a matter that could be amicably resolved through mediation.

At mediation, Michelle argued that East's erratic behaviour posed an unacceptable risk to her children and insisted that access should not be resumed. She also reasoned that at 16 months old, Wesley needed his mum and was too young to cope with being separated from her for the overnight stays East was now demanding. The mediator agreed that Wesley was too young to be with his father overnight, and accepted Michelle's proposal that East should have his son for daytime access only. But because Kelly was older and had formed a stronger bond with her father, it was decided that overnight access should be resumed for her.

Despite Michelle's misgivings, she reluctantly agreed that access could begin again on alternate weekends and that Kelly alone would be allowed to stay over. But, in a legal first, the mediator upheld the young mother's argument that East's access visits with his children should be supervised by an appropriate adult.

Supervised access was a coup for Michelle, who felt reassured knowing a third party would be around to keep an eye on things. But her relief was short-lived when it was proposed that East's parents would be the supervising adults. Michelle knew from her own experience that her former partner was a controlling personality who was used to barking orders, not following them. He was a narcissist who resented being told what to do and Michelle doubted her in-laws had the ability to effectively supervise their son, who would simply do as he liked with his children. Despite her protests, Michelle was advised that the supervision clause offered a good compromise and that it was important she followed the rules and cooperated.

'The law's an ass,' Michelle grudgingly told the mediator as she left that day.

But if Michelle Steck felt uneasy about the new access arrangements, her ex-partner was positively furious. He stomped angrily out of mediation, livid that he was to be supervised with his own children.

The overnight access resumed in October 1993. As agreed, Michelle dropped her children off on alternate Saturday mornings and Wesley was returned in the early evening, leaving Kelly on an overnight stay with her father at her paternal grandparents' home. By November 1993 the visits appeared to be going smoothly enough with Kelly generally arriving home the following day, chatting happily about everything she had done with her father.

But on her latest access visit in late November, the tot had returned looking pale and silent and her worried mother wanted to know why.

'What's happened, Kel?' pressed Michelle, completely unprepared for what she was about to hear.

Kelly eyed her mother and fidgeted nervously.

'Daddy put a pillow over my mouth,' said the little girl, staring up at her mother, her blue eyes clouded with fear.

'I was eating my biscuit ... I couldn't breathe.'

In her own child-like way, Kelly went on to describe her father pressing a pillow on her face while she choked on a cookie. Kelly told her mother that she had not been able to swallow and wanted her daddy to stop. East had finally lifted the pillow from her face and she had been able to breathe again. But the little girl looked frightened as she related what had happened.

Michelle's heart was pounding. In the months following the separation — a separation that East had not wanted — she had become accustomed to the barrage of menacing phone calls and death threats. The relationship had become so abusive that she had become desensitised, barely turning a hair when East threatened to kill her. But throughout the relationship, and in the 22 months since their separation, he had never exhibited any animosity towards his children or harmed them in any way. Until now, the target of East's violence and threats had always been Michelle alone.

After a sleepless night, the panic-stricken mother telephoned her solicitor and made an appointment to see him. In his office, Michelle related the terrifying experience her tiny daughter had described the previous evening.

'He put a pillow over her face, for Christ's sake,' Michelle gasped. 'He was trying to smother her ... She can't go there any more, he's bloody dangerous.'

The lawyer listened, fiddling with his bow tie, apparently unconcerned.

'You have to tell the court,' said Michelle, still shaken.

She was astonished when the lawyer explained that there was little he could do. At just three years old, Kelly was considered too young to be reliable, or to give evidence about the alleged smothering. And since Michelle had not been present to witness the incident herself, she could not give evidence on her daughter's behalf. Michelle couldn't believe her ears.

'No court will rely upon the evidence of a three-year-old girl,' said the lawyer, showing her the door.

'So you mean we just have to wait until he does something worse, then?' replied Michelle, stunned.

She had no doubt from the fear on Kelly's face, and the innocent manner in which the little girl had described the chilling scene, that East must have been toying with the idea of smothering his own child. It wasn't the sort of thing any three-year-old would make up, she pointed out.

'Out of the mouths of babes,' said Michelle. The lawyer

sympathised, but he repeated there was nothing more he could do. Michelle left the office bewildered, unable to comprehend that a child at risk was not allowed a voice in a legal system that prevented anyone else speaking for her.

That conversation haunts Michelle Steck to this day.

*

Michelle was a vibrant, independent teenager when she first met Kevin East in 1989 in a Perth city shopping centre. She was working in the accounting department of a major mining company in Perth, and had been enjoying a day out in the city with her girlfriend. The pair had been to an upmarket salon to have their hair done and were wandering around the shops with their smart new hairdos when they literally bumped into him.

Their chance encounter with the handsome older man led to an impromptu offer of lunch, and by the time the pretty 19-year-old joined East at a table in one of the shopping centre's cafes, she was completely bowled over. At 31 years old, East was more experienced than the feisty teenager who had immediately caught his eye. Over lunch, East revealed that he was recently divorced from his first wife, a former model and hairdresser. She had broken his heart, he told Michelle. He had been in the process of helping her set up a new hairdressing salon when he discovered she was seeing another man. East admitted he had been so upset by the betrayal that he had 'gone a bit mental' and punched a few holes in the wall in his distress. The violent reaction was natural enough for a man who loved his wife so much, he explained.

Michelle sipped her coffee wondering why anyone would be foolish enough to cheat on such a charming, charismatic, fit-looking bloke. The impeccably dressed East had a good job as a computer electronics engineer. He was an intelligent and handsome man who spoke with such authority that Michelle could not imagine finding anyone more eligible on the singles scene. Swept up in the moment, the dazzled young woman saw only the positive traits in this confident man, and the implications of his own admission that he possessed a violent temper didn't register on this first romantic encounter.

Later, reflecting on that first meeting, Michelle realised the entire conversation had revolved around East. The only thing he had asked Michelle about herself was his peculiar chat-up line.

'So ... what sort of car do you drive?' East had inquired, describing his own preference for luxury four-wheel drives. In retrospect, Michelle felt it was an odd sort of question. She wasn't sure why it mattered what sort of car she drove, or if she drove at all. But as she would soon discover, public image was important to the flashy-dressing, status-driven Kevin East.

Missing the warning signs, Michelle left her lunch date with East's phone number, completely smitten.

There were more romantic dates and, after a whirlwind romance, the couple moved in together. Not long after, they bought their first home in the popular Perth suburb of Forest Field, where the relationship continued to flourish.

The busy, upwardly mobile pair worked long hours as they forged their respective careers. They ate out most nights at one of their favourite city haunts and socialised with friends at weekends, each enjoying their financial freedom and their independence.

But things took a dark turn when East began to exhibit an irrational jealous streak. Michelle was stunned when, at a work function, he accused one of her bosses of showing inappropriate interest in her, and challenged the man to a fight in the car park. Michelle was so humiliated that she subsequently resigned and left the job she loved. But East never apologised for his jealous outburst. It was as if he was entitled to do whatever he liked.

Seven months into the relationship, Michelle discovered she was pregnant. East was delighted at the prospect of becoming a father, and Michelle, who wanted nothing more than to be a mother, couldn't have been happier. She worked up until two weeks before the baby was due, busying herself with preparing a nursery. Kevin East was by her side when Michelle gave birth to their daughter Kelly on

19 April 1990 and appeared every bit the proud father as he drove his wife and new baby home from hospital.

But by the time Kelly was six months old the happy fairytale was fading fast. Michelle doted on her new baby and was reluctant to leave her daughter in the care of strangers in order to return to the workforce. This became a bone of contention between the new parents, with East complaining bitterly that they could not afford to live on his wage alone. As the weeks passed, he began to pressure Michelle to find a childcare place for Kelly so that she could resume work in the city. But Michelle, who was still breastfeeding, flatly refused. As far as she was concerned, Kelly was too young at six months to be separated from her mother. Work would just have to wait, she reasoned, hoping that her partner would understand. He never did.

While Kevin East was happy enough to show off his delightful daughter, behind closed doors he was not the hands-on father an exhausted young mother might have hoped for. And there was something about his public displays of fatherly pride that left her feeling most uneasy. It was as if Kelly was his own little show pony, a pretty new accessory to be admired and shown off.

East revelled in the compliments of friends and relatives who cooed over the pretty tot in her pram, but behind closed doors he was not so eager to help with the daily care of the tiny baby. During the week he worked long hours and was happy to leave the nappy changing, bath times and feeding routines to Michelle. At weekends he overcompensated with lots of cuddles and spoiling. But he appeared to lose interest quickly and as Kelly grew into an adorable toddler, the irrational jealousy Michelle had glimpsed in the early days of the relationship returned.

When Kelly was a few months old, East's younger sister, Maureen, celebrated her twenty-first birthday. She threw a big family party at her parents' home in the hills outside Perth and relatives flew in from the UK to join the celebrations. The new parents decided to take their baby along, knowing that East's sister Linda would be at the family celebration. Linda had also recently had a baby, and the two young mothers chatted happily in the lounge room where East's British cousins were showing off their holiday snapshots. Kevin East watched in annoyance as his de facto wife joined in the conversation. Even at 21, Michelle had travelled Australia extensively and had lots of stories to share about her adventures. But East, darkly observing the holiday chatter, appeared to resent the brief attention his partner's contribution to the discussion was generating. He finally lost his temper and stormed into the bedroom where he deliberately woke his sleeping daughter in a bid to break up the conversation. The discussion ended abruptly when East summonsed Michelle to attend to her crying baby. While Michelle tried to settle the distressed tot down, East began to berate her, accusing her of flirting with one of his relatives.

The hostility did not end there. When Michelle and Linda sat up later breastfeeding their respective infants, East became enraged all over again. He followed Michelle into a bedroom where she was putting the sleeping baby back into her cot and accused her of flirting again, this time with Linda's husband Tony. His brother-in-law, who was in the process of putting his own infant son to bed, was as mortified by the accusation as Michelle, and retreated from the bedroom in embarrassment. A huge argument followed and the night was ruined for the bewildered young mother, who spent the remainder of the party in tears. Nobody had any idea where East's irrational accusation had come from, and he never apologised for spoiling his sister's birthday party or for upsetting everyone.

As the months passed, Michelle observed a distinct shift in the balance of power in her relationship. With East now the sole earner in the family, she had become completely dependent on him. The independence she had once relished seemed to be disappearing before her eyes.

Michelle resented having to ask her partner for every cent, and having to explain her sparse household spending. It seemed she was now expected to justify everything she did. But as far as East was concerned, he was the breadwinner and, since he controlled the purse strings, he held the power.

East became more possessive and controlling than ever. In the early days of the relationship he had been in the habit of calling Michelle at work every morning to inquire about her day. Later, he would call her again during the afternoon for an update. At first Michelle felt flattered that she had found such a caring and attentive partner. But now that she was housebound and had a small baby to attend to, these constant calls throughout the day were not only irritating, they felt intrusive too.

East seemed to call her at the most inconvenient times, demanding to know what she was doing, who she was speaking to and who had called.

If she failed to answer the phone immediately, East demanded an explanation. When Michelle explained that she was busy changing or feeding the baby, and couldn't just drop what she was doing to take the call, he became angry and even more demanding. When Michelle complained that his constant phone calls were intrusive and intimidating, East told her that his repeated calls showed how much he cared about her.

But Michelle felt she was under constant surveillance and that, even from a distance, East was watching and directing her every move.

If Michelle wanted to go out with the baby, she had to justify the outing. When she told East she had made plans to visit her family, he allocated her a time frame for the journey, calling Michelle before she left home and again when she reached her destination. He said this was the only way he could ensure she was where she claimed she would be.

If Michelle was caught up in traffic and did not arrive at her destination on time, East wanted to know why it had taken her so long, and where she had been in the interim. To the bewildered young woman, it seemed he now wanted to be in charge of every-thing — even the traffic.

Later, Michelle discovered that before he left for work each morning, he had begun noting the odometer reading on her vehicle. This allowed him to keep close tabs on her daily movements while he was at work. If she left the house in the car without asking him first, or forgot to tell him she had been somewhere, he would soon know when he checked the odometer. Blazing arguments followed and soon Michelle was unable to drive to the milk bar without his permission. With every new argument, Michelle's confidence began to plummet.

One morning Michelle was busy with the baby when East called on one of his morning check-up calls, demanding to know what she was doing. This time, Michelle had had enough. Hanging up the phone, she hurriedly packed a small suitcase and strapped Kelly into her baby capsule. Then she headed off towards her mother's home in Collie, determined to end the relationship.

When East telephoned again at lunchtime and Michelle failed to pick up, he immediately guessed where she would be. Flying into a rage, East immediately telephoned his mother-in-law's home, demanding to know if she was there. He was so intimidating that by the time Michelle finally arrived in Collie, her family were anxiously waiting on the doorstep, afraid of what might happen next.

'It's always sad to see families breaking up,' said Michelle's mother as they sat in the kitchen trying to second-guess East's next move. Her mother's remark, along with the countless phone calls from East promising to change and begging Michelle to return, saw her slowly change her mind. Perhaps this show of defiance had taught him a lesson, she reasoned as she drove back to Perth the following day. Her hopes were short lived.

By the time their son Wesley was born in May 1992, Michelle was feeling suffocated. Her life was no longer her own and she found herself wondering how long she could survive in such a stifling relationship. But while Michelle was unhappy, East appeared to enjoy the powerful hold he had over his partner. He was a man who liked being in charge.

Soon, the emotional mind games turned physical. When Kelly and Wesley were very small, Michelle's younger sister, Natasha, then in her early teens, arrived from Collie for a visit.

Excited at the prospect of seeing her sister, Michelle drove to the bus station to collect her. But when they arrived home, East became furious and demanded to know why he had not been consulted about the teenager's visit. To Michelle's horror and embarrassment, he flew into such a rage that he hurled Natasha's suitcase from one end of the room to the other and threw a large ceramic container at her. He then attacked the terrified young mother in front of her horrified sibling and beat her severely. Natasha was so frightened that she fled from the house and telephoned her mother to come and collect her. Michelle's shocked mother drove from Collie to Perth, a round trip of more than 360 kilometres, arriving at 2 a.m. to collect her traumatised teenager. She was horrified by the violence Natasha had witnessed and was frightened for her older daughter. But Michelle maintained that East had never before been violent towards her and refused to return to Collie with them.

On another occasion when Michelle's mother arrived in Forest Field unannounced, East hit the roof again. Michelle and her mother had been sipping tea in the kitchen when he arrived home from work and exploded at the unexpected visitor. He demanded to know why his mother-in-law was in his house and told Michelle it was inconvenient and that she should have asked his permission. Michelle was angry and stood up for herself. This was her mother, she pointed out. Surely she did not require his permission to have her own mother in their home. East responded by stomping off into Kelly's bedroom where he promptly woke his sleeping daughter. Then he ordered Michelle to deal with the screaming infant.

Over time, Michelle began to sense that East's behaviour towards her family was a deliberate ploy to isolate her from the people she cared most about.

When Michelle's 86-year-old grandmother moved from Sydney to live in Perth and be closer to her granddaughter and great-grandchildren, she was horrified by East's abuse. On her first night at Michelle's house she was so enraged by what she saw that she immediately packed her bags and left. Before she did, the straight-talking older woman had a word of advice for Michelle.

'If you've got any sense you will leave here with me,' she said. 'The best thing you can do is get away from this arsehole. He's no good.'

The older woman's words resonated with Michelle as the restrictions and rules began to grow and she found herself feeling more isolated than ever. Over time friends dropped off and relatives became cautious about arriving unexpectedly. Michelle was slowly losing contact with anyone who might provide her with a reality check on her dangerous relationship.

While East continued to monitor Michelle's every waking moment, his own growing absences from the family home left his partner wondering if he might be having an affair himself. Things finally came to a head when she discovered him on the phone, masturbating as he engaged in steamy sex talk with his new woman on the other end of the line.

For some months Michelle had been mulling over her grand-mother's warning. She had long recognised that the relationship was toxic, but without access to funds Michelle had no idea where she would go, and no money to leave with. In desperation she had begun stashing $5 notes underneath the carpet in the living room.

The phone-sex session was the final straw for the exhausted young mother, who decided enough was enough. A major argument followed and in December 1992 Michelle told her de facto she was leaving. East, watching her pack her few belongings, was furious. He stormed out of the room and returned with a length of rope. While her babies screamed in fright, he proceeded to tie their hysterical mother up with the rope, tying a gag around her mouth to stifle her screams while they sobbed and clung to her. Oblivious to his children's distress, East then began to kick his bound captive from one side of the room to the other, the terrified tots screaming their lungs out the entire time. Eventually, he stormed out of the house, leaving Michelle hogtied and bleeding on the floor.

Little Kelly spent hours sobbing and clinging to her mother's tethered body. It was three hours before East finally returned to the house. He appeared more subdued and apologised to a shaken Michelle for his behaviour. He then helped to untie his badly bruised and traumatised partner. But any doubts Michelle had had about leaving him disappeared that night. She had glimpsed the real East and there was no going back.

On New Year's Day 1993 Michelle limped away from her house with her two small children, determined to get as far away as possible. As she left, East raged, 'You don't have the right to pack up and leave. You're going to have to pay for your actions for a long time.'

A few months later, Michelle moved to Collie. Michelle thought it would be the perfect place to make a fresh start, close to her family, with her young children.

But despite his brutal attack, East refused to accept that the relationship was over, and treated the separation as something temporary. He had not been impressed when he discovered his de facto partner was intending to move to Collie. Still harbouring hopes of a reconciliation, he offered to help with the move, and Michelle, wanting the break to be as trouble-free as possible, reluctantly accepted his offer.

East even offered to help with some rewiring and minor renovations at the older-style property, which the hard-up single mother gratefully accepted. But Kevin East, an electronics expert, had his own agenda, and used the opportunity to install some hidden listening devices, including bugging her telephone, that would allow him to continue monitoring Michelle. Now he would know who she was talking to and what they were talking about, even from a distance.

As well as keeping his estranged partner under 24-hour surveillance, East repeatedly drove out to Collie where he began to treat Michelle's new home as his own. Despite their separation, he was breezing in whenever he felt like it. When Michelle rejected East's constant pleas for a reconciliation, he flew into a rage and repeatedly threatened to get her. Michelle now knew what he was capable of, and when he turned up on her doorstep unannounced, she was afraid of turning him away. Walking on eggshells left Michelle drained and battle-weary and on some occasions it was easier to let him in, or give into his demands for sex, than deal with yet another argument.

But later, standing under the hot shower, no amount of scrubbing was enough to erase the dirty feeling when he left. When East finally realised that a reconciliation was not going to happen, his phone calls and threats became more menacing than ever.

By mid-1993, it was clear to Michelle that her former partner was unravelling physically as well as mentally.

During their relationship East had always been particular about his appearance. He had been extremely health-conscious, always watching what he ate and paying meticulous attention to his personal hygiene. Kevin East was the most immaculately dressed man she had ever known and his hours of gym work had given him a toned physique he was proud of.

Friends of Michelle's who caught a glimpse of him around Collie had been amazed by his carefully groomed appearance and affable manner. To those who did not know him, Kevin East appeared to be a friendly, harmless sort of guy — nothing remotely like the crazy and violent control freak who was monitoring Michelle's every move and making her life hell. Michelle was dismayed; it seemed as though East had everyone fooled.

When they had eventually gone to mediation over his access to the children, Michelle's friend Tracey was astonished by the charming, smartly dressed man who strode past her in the lobby.

'My God, is that your former partner?' she asked Michelle. 'He looks more like a lawyer than the real lawyers in here.'

But despite his public appearance, behind the scenes East continued to be a domestic terrorist.

By mid-1993 he was turning up in Michelle's street at all hours of the day and night. His formerly smart appearance now gave way to a more dishevelled, unkempt look as he took to watching her house from the vacant block across the road. Sometimes he spied on her for hours on end, emerging only to yell abuse at the top of his voice while swigging from a bottle of Jack Daniels. At some stage he created a crude, concealed camp on the empty block, which enabled him to observe his estranged partner up close. As well as monitoring her every movement from his makeshift den, he was still listening to all Michelle's conversations via his covert bugging devices.

But throughout 1993 the mother of two had no idea her home had been bugged or that East had taken up temporary residence across the road. He was spending so much time in Collie that he even rented a post office box for his mail. When Michelle heard the drunken rants coming from across the road, she assumed he had just turned up again, never dreaming that he had just emerged from his hidey-hole and had been monitoring her the entire time.

On the many occasions that she reported the disturbances to the police, they simply arrived and moved the unravelling father on without pressing charges. The officers told the flustered young mother they didn't like involving themselves 'in domestics'.

The harassment campaign was slowly taking its toll on Michelle. In September 1993, when East again threatened to 'get her', she told him: 'Go ahead and do whatever you need to do ... Just get yourself better and leave me alone.'

But as October arrived, East's declining mental health and his deteriorating physical appearance were giving Michelle grave concern. He appeared to have stopped caring about himself, or anything else. When he turned up on her doorstep shouting abuse, she noticed he was unshaven and his formerly immaculate clothes were unwashed and dirty. Suspecting this was all a cry for help, Michelle urged him again to seek professional counselling.

'I'm not paying 160 bucks for a shrink to listen to me pour my heart out ... Anyway, they need more help than I do,' East snarled.

By October 1993 East was sporting a large tattoo bearing Kelly's name. Until now he had always frowned on people with body art, and his astonished former partner was more convinced than ever that he was falling apart. When his behaviour became publicly disruptive, the police either escorted him out of town, or locked him up briefly to allow him to cool his heels.

But nothing deterred East, and since he was never charged with anything, he was never held accountable for his outrageous stalking. Michelle felt utterly dismayed. The lack of police action simply enabled him and he was doing exactly as he pleased. Even when the issue of access was resolved at mediation, with an agreement that East would be supervised by his parents, he blatantly ignored the supervision clause and took the children wherever he wanted on his own.

Just as Michelle suspected, his parents struggled to police the access visits. The incident Kelly had described to her mother, of her father placing a pillow over her face, had occurred on one of his supposedly supervised visits.

Around the time of the pillow incident, there was a bizarre turn of events that left Michelle stunned and seriously frightened.

Michelle was about to go shopping and had just strapped her two toddlers into their child restraints in the car when she realised she had forgotten her handbag and had returned to the house to get it. As she opened her front door, she heard the distinct sound of the toilet flushing in the bathroom. In that split second she realised that someone else was in her house. She strongly suspected that this 'someone' was Kevin East.

Not wishing to alert him to her presence, Michelle made her way quietly out of the house, locking the door behind her. Then she drove at speed to the Collie police station.

'My ex-husband has broken into my house and is hiding in my roof space,' the frightened mother told the desk sergeant. Michelle hurriedly explained that over the past two weeks she had become aware of dull thudding sounds in her ceiling at night. The sounds appeared to be coming from the roof space and she had initially suspected she might have possums or rats in her ceiling. With two small children to care for, she had been worried that if the native animals nibbled through her electrical wires, she faced the real possibility of a house fire. She had planned to call a pest expert but had not yet done so. Now she realised the pest that had taken up residence in her roof space was her ex-partner.

Michelle shuddered as she wondered how long East had been hiding in her house, spying on her like some silent voyeur. The police, who had repeatedly attended disturbances at Michelle's home, drove out again to investigate the new complaint.

Opening the trapdoor into the ceiling, the officers found East hiding in the darkness. It was hot in the confined space, and it was clear from the foul smell and the scattered food wrappers and drink cans that he had been up there for weeks. The police dragged the unkempt father out of the roof and into the daylight where he was arrested. But East appeared completely unfazed.

'Do you mind if I have a shower?' he asked the officers politely. The uniformed officers studied the foul-smelling offender with sympathetic faces. They almost felt sorry for the guy. How desperate must this young dad be to be hiding in his ex-partner's roof? The least they could do was allow him to clean himself up before piling him into the back of the divisional van and locking him in the cells at the police station.

'OK,' they nodded. 'Have a shower, but be quick, you're under arrest.'

When Michelle was informed that her ex had indeed taken up residence in her roof, she felt violated and furious. She was more alarmed when the police revealed that their search had uncovered the listening devices he had covertly installed when she moved in. Michelle could not believe that the police had allowed her intruder to use her shower before taking him into custody. The authorities' half-hearted reaction to this disturbing new development simply defied belief.

But in an era when stalking legislation was yet to be introduced and when East's previous offences had been written off as 'domestics', Michelle doubted anything would happen to him this time either.

Her hunch was right. East made a brief appearance before the Collie Magistrates' Court the following morning where the police filed no charges. Instead, his victim took out a restraining order to protect herself and her two small children. East, it transpired, had been hiding in her roof for a number of weeks, watching her constantly, creeping down while she was out to use her toilet, take a shower and grab some food. If he was prepared to do this, thought Michelle, God knows what he might do next. East was released from custody with a slap on the wrist, the police remarking as they watched him go, that he seemed like 'such a nice guy'. The whole scenario left Michelle incredulous.

'How nice is a guy, when nearly a year after you separate, he breaks into my home and hides in my roof, where he has installed listening devices, so that he can watch my every move in between harassing and threatening me?' she fumed. Why on earth was this blatant break-in still a domestic when she had ended her relationship with the offender, and was now living an independent life in a different town?

'If this had been a stranger in my roof, watching me and installing listening devices without my permission, you'd have him locked up and charged in a heartbeat,' she said.

To Michelle Steck's dismay, East was back on the streets of Collie, free to harass her all over again.

Amid the stress and the chaos, Michelle had made a decision to reclaim control over her life. A few months earlier she had found herself a bar job at Collie's Victoria Hotel, determined to use her income to furnish her home, buy her children Christmas presents and live independently. She had also decided to return to study with a view to becoming a teacher. On Sunday 17 November she drove to the nearby university to sit an entry test for mature age students. But the trauma and the years of worry were taking their toll.

As Michelle sat at the desk, filling out the answers, she noticed the test paper in front of her turning pink and then green. She was so alarmed that she later made an appointment to see her doctor. The concerned GP explained that the visual symptoms she'd described were consistent with extreme long-term stress.

Just before East was sprung hiding in her roof, Michelle had started seeing a new man. She had met Gerard Pullen at the local hotel where she worked. What had begun innocently enough as a lift home for one of the punters soon became a romance when Gerard asked her out on a date. When Michelle discovered her home had been bugged and that East had taken up residence in her roof space, she had no doubt he would have been well aware of her study plans and the new man in her life.

Ironically, by then East had formed a new relationship with

another woman. Michelle had been taken aback when the woman telephoned her out of the blue one night, telling her all about a child she had lost. It was a bizarre conversation, Michelle thought, hanging up. Still, she was relieved to hear that East was seeing someone else and hoped it might take the pressure off her. She was wrong.

Within days of being dragged out of her roof space, East flew into an uncontrolled rage about the new man in Michelle's life. He turned up outside her home screaming abuse and Gerard was forced to restrain the furious father from climbing onto the roof. Michelle watched in amazement as East proceeded to wrap himself in plastic on her front doorstep and started slashing his wrists. The police were called and he was taken away again. Again the disturbance was viewed as another 'domestic' and no charges were laid. The next day East was back on the vacant block, yelling insults and screaming abuse at Michelle, all the while swigging alcohol from a bottle.

A few days later, Michelle opened the mail and was alarmed to discover that East had posted her his last will and testament. Then she heard from some of the locals that he had been seen in the hotel where she worked, openly smoking a joint of marijuana, flashing his new tattoo and yelling abuse at anyone who looked sideways at him.

This out-of-control drinking and flagrant drug use, in addition to his tattoo, was so out of character that Michelle was convinced he was in self-destructive mode. Whether he was distancing himself from the evaporating Kevin East, she wasn't sure. But at around this time she discovered that he had been using an entirely different name. It was as though the old disciplined East had vanished and had been replaced by a new persona who did not care about anything.

More ominously, shortly after the smothering incident Michelle's heavily pregnant sister Tina opened a card from her former brother-in-law congratulating her on her baby news. This was great, wrote East; the new baby would replace the ones the family were about to lose.

*

At around 9.30 a.m. on Saturday 11 December 1993, Michelle drove Kelly and Wesley to Soldier Park in Collie to meet their father for his supervised weekend access visit. On the journey, a teary and highly anxious Michelle observed Kelly playing with her toy Roger Ramjet. The little girl, sensing her mother's anxiety told her: 'Don't worry, Mum.'

At the drop-off point, Michelle kissed her children goodbye and put on a brave face.

'See ya, Kel,' she smiled, waving as East drove away with their children.

Kelly was three and a half years old, and Wesley was just 16 months.

At 5 p.m. Michelle's sister Natasha drove to the park to collect Wesley from his father. East handed Wesley back with his nappy bag and took off. His mother later realised that the bag had been returned without any of his spare clothes, which was odd. More worrying, there had been no-one in the car supervising East at the drop-off.

The following afternoon, Michelle drove to the same park to collect Kelly. Five o'clock came and went and Michelle felt her anxiety rising. There was no sign of East's silver Nissan Navara or their daughter. She rushed home in a panic and telephoned the Collie police.

Trying to keep calm, Michelle explained that East had taken her little girl on an access visit but had failed to return her. She briefly detailed his erratic behaviour, and reminded the officer how he had been found hiding in her roof a couple of weeks earlier. But despite her apparently calm demeanour, the young mother was jumping out of her skin.

Until now there had been only one occasion when East had failed to return Kelly on time. It was not long after their separation and Michelle and the children had still been living in Perth. When East failed to turn up at 5 p.m. as arranged, the worried mother had contacted the local police asking them to help locate her estranged partner. Then she telephoned her sister-in-law, Linda, who appeared to share her concerns. Linda told Michelle her brother had left hours earlier with Kelly, in plenty of time to make the handover. Linda was convinced he and Kelly must have been involved in an accident and was out of her mind with worry. Two hours later, East turned up with his daughter, offering no apology or explanation and scoffing dismissively that it was all a fuss about nothing. Michelle suspected he had enjoyed his sadistic game and the anguish it caused her.

Since then he had become so much more unpredictable, and with the smothering incident and the sick congratulations card still fresh in her mind, Michelle wasn't sure what he might do.

'I don't trust him one bit,' Michelle told the police, trying to hold it all together. But they seemed strangely unconcerned as she hung up the phone. Michelle would later learn that her determination to sound rational and calm had worked against her. The police later told her that she had appeared so calm that they hadn't taken her concerns seriously. But Michelle had not wanted to sound like a hysterical mother, convinced the police might have treated her like some crazy woman who was simply overreacting because her child was late coming home. Ironically, she hadn't sounded distressed enough.

At home the clock was ticking and Michelle's panic was rising. An hour after returning from the park, she rang East's parents.

'Where is my daughter?' she screeched down the phone.

East's parents sounded unconcerned. 'They went to the beach,' said his mother.

Michelle was livid. 'Aren't you supposed to be supervising?'

She insisted that East had gone missing with Kelly. His parents called her a liar and refused to listen. Their son would never hurt his own daughter.

At some time after 10.30 p.m. Michelle telephoned the Collie police again, updating them on the situation. This time the panic in her voice was unmistakable and two uniformed officers were immediately dispatched to an address that was now familiar with them.

At 11 p.m. the police were taking notes when Michelle's phone rang. It was Kevin East.

Michelle demanded to know where Kelly was. 'Too late — the police are here,' she told him angrily.

He hung up, saying nothing.

Fearful for her daughter, Michelle called her new boyfriend, who immediately drove over to her house. Gerard offered to stay until Kelly was safely returned.

At 3.15 a.m. Michelle sat bolt upright in her bed, suddenly and inexplicably overwhelmed with emotion. She heard her own voice screaming hysterically across the darkness. 'She's gone, she's gone.'

The distraught mother leapt from the bed and began dashing from room to room in a state of total meltdown. Her baby had gone, she screamed. She just knew it.

Not sure what to do, Gerard telephoned Michelle's mother. She arrived on the doorstep shortly afterwards with Natasha. Their attempts to reassure Michelle fell on deaf ears. Nothing anyone said could take away this dreadful knowing. Sitting silently over a hot drink in the kitchen, Michelle felt a strange emptiness creeping over her that she could not explain, but which would make sense to her later on.

The days that followed were a nightmare. Five days after Kelly went missing, Michelle attended the Bunbury Magistrates Court where she was granted an order enabling police in every state to apprehend the fugitive father and return Kelly to her mother.

'It's ridiculous,' Michelle told her mother. 'If a stranger had taken off with Kelly, the police could arrest the person who took her on sight. But when that person is the child's father, they need a court order to do it.'

Arriving home from court that Friday afternoon, Michelle was stunned to find a package in her letterbox addressed in East's handwriting. The postmark showed it had been posted the weekend he disappeared with Kelly. Inside was a tape of the rock band Guns N' Roses' tracks 'Sweet Child of Mine' and 'My Michelle'. He also included a rambling tape accusing her of stuffing up his life, and made the veiled threat that she was going to pay for it.

Michelle felt sick to her stomach. This was typical of East, a meticulous planner who was always writing lists of things he needed to do and recording seemingly minute details on bits of paper. These songs were ominous and listening to them, she felt more fearful than ever.

On the same day that Kevin East mailed his ominous tapes and ranting message, he had posted a second envelope to the *West Australian* newspaper. In it was a handwritten letter, in which he complained bitterly about the way women screwed over separated fathers. As far as he was concerned, women came out of relationships with everything, while fathers like himself emerged with nothing.

Michelle was mortified when excerpts of the letters appeared in the newspaper the following week. They painted a biased picture of the separation and were filled with East's lies. To add to Michelle's public humiliation, an enraged East had gone to the trouble of posting some private snapshots to her employer. In the photographs she was heavily pregnant and partially dressed, while other snapshots showed her breastfeeding her infant son. These photographs also arrived in the days after East vanished with Kelly. Michelle only learned about them when someone from work alerted her, trying to make light of what was intended to be a public violation. But for a mother with a missing child, she had bigger things to worry about than a handful of embarrassing photos and a barrage of lies in the press.

While Michelle harboured a glimmer of a hope that East might return their daughter in time for Christmas, with each passing day she felt more hopeless and despairing. During the countdown to Christmas 1993, she collected the gifts she had put on lay-by at Big W for her two small children. Among the presents she had chosen was a collection of the cartoon character figurines that Kelly loved so much. The little girl had lots of them, which she liked to place in her giant fairytale castle, moving them around the various rooms as she played. Michelle knew the tot would love these new figurines for her collection.

Kelly was such a delightful little soul, thought her mother. She was affectionate and well behaved, and she was very smart. She hated lollies and turned her nose up at the sugar-loaded fizzy drinks other children seemed to like. Instead, Kelly liked to sit in the supermarket trolley nibbling on small cherry tomatoes and drinking fruit juice.

Michelle had handstitched a quilt for her daughter based on a Ken Done print. The quilt was Kelly's favourite thing and she loved it on her bed. But now Kelly's bed was empty and only her father knew where she was.

As the West Australian police launched a nationwide hunt for the missing toddler and her fugitive father, the distressed mother appeared on the national news, where she appealed for her little girl's safe return.

'I'm scared that the slightest thing might upset him and he might decide to do something silly,' she told viewers through her tears. 'I just want him to bring Kelly home.'

Michelle Steck's agony was palpable as she addressed the runaway dad directly.

'Don't be silly. Don't kill her,' she pleaded.

Each time Kelly's face flashed on the TV news as the police appealed for information, her brother Wesley screamed like a small wounded animal. He spent days toddling from room to room on wobbly legs, bewildered and sobbing as he repeatedly called for the big sister he adored. It tore his mother's already broken heart into a million tiny pieces. Even at such a young age, he knew what grief felt like, his stricken mother observed.

Christmas came and went with no news of Kelly and no contact from East. Michelle spent a bleak Christmas with her family, wishing the day away. Everyone was solemn; nobody felt like eating lunch or opening gifts. There was nothing to celebrate with Kelly still missing. The cartoon figurines Michelle had lovingly wrapped remained unopened beneath the Christmas tree. Even in her pain, Michelle noted the lack of phone calls from her in-laws.

While Michelle harboured hopes that East might be hiding out with friends, or holed up in some remote hotel somewhere with Kelly, the detectives on the case were not so optimistic. Among the many tape recordings, letters and photographs East had mailed the weekend he disappeared was a particularly chilling tape he had posted to his own family. The contents of that tape were so disturbing that seasoned investigators had not shared the information with the missing child's mother. The gist of East's final message to his family was that he intended to carve his name in history — as a killer.

What nobody knew as Australia entered a new year was that when East hung up the phone on that fateful Sunday night in December, Kelly's fate was already sealed. Aware the police were after him, he had sped off on a 200-kilometre drive along the Brookton Highway and onto the Great Southern Highway. As East approached the small community of Beverley, he'd turned off the highway and driven his car down a remote road into dense bush. Deep in the bush, he had pulled over and carefully buried his vehicle under a pile of branches and leaves, making it almost impossible to find.

In the dark solitude of the early hours of the Monday morning, East attached a length of hose to his exhaust and directed it through a window into his car. Then he carefully closed the windows and turned on the ignition, watching in silence as his little girl slowly succumbed to the poisonous carbon monoxide pouring into the car. Ever the meticulous planner, East kept a chilling 'death journal' in which he recorded the last harrowing moments of his daughter's passing. It was his final ghastly legacy for her mother to find. When his daughter had taken her last breath, East gassed himself.

At the very moment that Michelle had sat bolt upright in her bed in Collie, screaming into the darkness that her little girl had gone, Kelly had left the world. East's notation of 3.15 a.m. confirmed the exact time of her death.

On 10 January, just over a month after East's disappearance, a bushwalker hiking along the remote track stumbled upon the four-wheel drive carefully hidden beneath the branches and leaves. Peering inside, the walker made the grim discovery the police had been dreading. Inside lay Kelly and her vengeful father.

Beside Kelly lay her favourite Roger Ramjet toy and her father's hideous journal. Hardened detectives poring over its contents were so traumatised by what they read that many of them required counselling afterwards. East's words left them in no doubt of his motive: he had committed the ultimate act of family violence to punish Michelle Steck, the true target of his festering rage, for ending their relationship. He wanted her to suffer for the rest of her life. Sadly, the little girl who had trusted him to keep her safe had been used as a weapon against her mother. Kelly was the innocent casualty in her father's quest for vengeance.

In the early hours police officers made their way back to the house in Collie where they had attended so many domestic disturbances in the past. No charges had been brought then, and no charges ever would be laid against Kevin East, who had eluded justice by taking his own life. The police may not have involved themselves in 'family matters' before now, but this was one 'domestic' nobody could ignore.

In the small hours of the morning, Michelle Steck's agonised screams penetrated the air. For years to come, she would recall the single continuous primal howl reverberating around the empty streets of Collie that summer night. Michelle's sobs woke Wesley from his sleep, and he instinctively began to howl at the top of his lungs, aware that something was terribly wrong. The news she had been dreading for weeks plunged her into an ocean of suffering that Kevin East intended would last her entire life.

Michelle wanted to see the journal the police had found; she needed to know what had ignited the ticking time bomb her ex-partner had become. She also needed to be certain that the little girl the police had found inside that car really was her beautiful daughter.

But the experienced homicide detectives who had already read the journal had found the diary more confronting than the chilling crime scene itself. Many of these officers were fathers with families. They gently advised her not to read East's vengeful words.

'Don't go there,' said one seasoned detective. The diary was filled with malevolence intended only to add to Michelle's suffering.

'Don't give him that … Don't let him win,' said the officer. 'Some things are better not known.'

It was sound advice, and despite her many unanswered questions, Michelle reluctantly agreed she would not read the journal. She would cherish the happier memories she had of a little girl who would never grow up.

'The outcome is the same,' she told her family. But for years to come her dreams were haunted by images of Kelly's final moments in that car. Michelle's imagination ran wild as she tormented herself with this troubling question: was it possible that her threat about the police had finally tipped East over the edge and driven him to murder?

'I often wondered if I hadn't told him the police were at the house, if Kelly might still be alive today,' she told me.

In the end, Michelle decided the blame was not hers to shoulder. That was what East would have wanted. After years of blaming her for everything, he would have wanted their daughter's death to be her fault too.

The cold reality was that East had already been contemplating something dark when he'd placed a pillow over Kelly's tiny face on the access visit two weeks earlier. And the idea of murder was almost certainly germinating when he posted his worrying card to his pregnant sister-in-law. He was unravelling then, so perhaps his daughter's death was inevitable.

But there was no doubt in Michelle's mind that the system had enabled her daughter's murder: a flawed legal system that did not allow a three year old to tell a court that her father had tried to smother her, but allowed access to continue with a supervision clause that was not worth the paper it was written on.

Kelly's funeral was held on 13 January in Collie's tiny St Bridget's Catholic church, beside the small local school. While Michelle did not know it at the time, the West Australian police force had paid for the little girl's remains to be returned to the town where her mother had attempted to build a new life for her family.

It was a crime that had stunned the small community. Even the woman who ran the local undertaker's was so distressed by her latest charge that she took the trouble to call in on the bereaved mother to offer comfort. Jobs involving children were always particularly painful, but senseless losses like this touched even those who were used to dealing with death.

The tiny tot who had brought so much joy to her mother's life was buried with her favourite Roger Ramjet toy and the figurines she loved. Her mother stood quietly beside the grave, holding the hand of the local priest, Father Leo, and bravely fighting back tears.

She had not been allowed to view her daughter's body or to hold her one last time to kiss her goodbye. In her shock and denial Michelle couldn't help wondering if the tiny body she had just lowered into the ground was her little girl at all. What had she actually buried?

Because East had so carefully hidden the car, Kelly had been out in the summer heat for weeks. Her mother now tortured herself wondering whether all of Kelly had been recovered from that camouflaged tomb and was now lying in the cold earth. Or, worse — had she accidentally buried something of the disturbed and angry dad who had snuffed out her life? These thoughts continue to torment Michelle to this day.

The young mum scoured the wreaths and flowers for cards or messages from East's side of the family. She had been branded a liar by his parents who refused to believe their son might be capable of harming his own flesh and blood; she had been blamed for the demise of their relationship and for denying her children access to their father. Now she blamed East's parents for failing to properly supervise his access visits with Kelly. If only they had followed the mediator's instructions, she told herself, her beautiful little girl might still be alive and she would not be staring at a hole in the ground. She vowed if she found a single card or flower, or worse still, an apology, she would tear them to shreds. Michelle needn't have worried. There were no condolences from Kevin East's family.

Similarly, there was no word from her in-laws about his funeral, which took place during the third week of January, just days after Michelle buried Kelly. Michelle learned he had been buried in Karrakatta Cemetery in Perth when her in-laws dispatched their accountant to her home with a message.

'They would like to talk to you,' he ventured cautiously.

Michelle was enraged.

'If they come here they will be looking down the barrel of a gun,' she fumed. She didn't even have a gun. But she was in shock and her grief was giving way to anger.

Michelle told the messenger she wanted nothing more to do with a family that had betrayed her and warned them never to cross her doorstep. Her son would have no part of their lives, she vowed, and shortly afterwards she changed Wesley's last name.

The months ahead were agony. Shortly after the funeral, the police visited Michelle and handed her a selection of photographs of Kelly that she had never seen before. They were photographs of the smiling little girl pushing a mini trolley stacked with toys around a local shopping mall. Sickeningly, this joyful event had been captured by East on his final access visit with his daughter. Kelly would never get to play with the gifts her father had showered on her. A day after taking those happy snapshots, East murdered his daughter and the photographs were among the evidence collected by the police.

Just after Kelly's funeral, Michelle's heavily pregnant sister gave birth to a baby. The baby's arrival was overshadowed by Kelly's murder and was a painful reminder of all that Michelle had lost. The grieving mother robotically bathed and cuddled her own precious son, grateful that Wesley had been too young for the overnight stay that would surely have claimed his life too. But her heart broke a little bit more every time he scoured the house calling Kelly's name.

As Wesley grew, his big sister's absence would be keenly felt at every birthday and Christmas. Every milestone he celebrated would be overshadowed by a loss that scarred his life forever too.

His mother sobbed herself to sleep each night, reliving the nightmare, trying to console herself with the thought that Kelly would have felt no pain. She would have left this world peacefully in her sleep, unaware that her father had taken her life away.

For Kelly there would be no school, no graduation or boyfriends, no learner's licence or weddings or babies. For her mother, the absence of these milestones ensured she'd always remember her loss, just as East intended.

Shortly after Kelly's funeral, Michelle was sitting at the kitchen table with her friend Tracey when she was overcome with fury.

After their separation, East had sent his children letters, complete with drawings and little stick figures, hearts and kisses. Michelle snatched them all up and piled them onto a baking tray and set them on fire. She began cutting his face out of every family photograph, tossing the images of him onto the bonfire in her kitchen. She sipped her wine and watched his face melt in the flames, the purging releasing some of the free-floating anger she hadn't known what to do with.

Five weeks after Kelly died, Michelle Steck forced herself back to study, determined that East would not destroy her. The relationship with Gerard continued to gather momentum. When she announced her plans to marry, her family advised against it. 'This is not the time,' said her mother. But she felt they were grieving and not coping either, and was not prepared to listen.

Even her priest, Father Leo, told her that he felt she was in such grief that she was not yet ready for a new relationship. But Michelle, who was undergoing intensive therapy and not in a good headspace, was not listening. She was married in September 1994. Sadly, the warnings proved correct and the marriage born in grief did not flourish.

In March 1995 Michelle gave birth to a son, Blake, followed by a daughter, Shayley, the following year. Her fifth child, Kordel, was born in on 18 April 2000, the day before what would have been Kelly's tenth birthday. A spiritual child, Kordel grew up insisting he felt the closest to the big sister he would never know. Being born so close to Kelly's birthday made him the 'special' child in his mother's brood of children.

But despite the love of four beautiful children, the distance between Michelle and her new husband was widening with every passing year. She sensed that Gerard struggled to support her or understand her pain, and the growing tension between herself and her in-laws became too much.

As Michelle discovered, her journey was a lonely one. It was impossibly painful living with the knowledge that her child had died simply to punish her. Her own mother, desperately trying to make sense of the senseless, once remarked: 'Poor Kevin, he was just crying out for help, and self-destructing.'

The throwaway remark made her daughter's blood boil. 'How can you stand there and say that to me?' fumed Michelle. Did this mean she was to blame for everything wrong with East's life? He had certainly blamed her during their abusive marriage, telling her repeatedly that she was the cause of all that was wrong in his life; that everything was her fault. But then he'd also told her that she had no right to leave, and that she would pay for it for a long time. She hadn't understood what he'd really meant when he made that threat. Since Kelly's murder those words haunted her.

In the months after the murder, Michelle's family regularly pondered the prospect that East had indeed been in the grip of a mental breakdown. But this angered the target of his vengeful rage. Michelle argued that whether he was mentally ill or not, he knew it was wrong to murder his own child; he did it anyway because he wanted to punish her and make sure she suffered forever. He had acted out of pure revenge and left behind his hideous diary to add to her anguish.

'It is not depression or some disorder that drives vengeful men to kill their children,' she said. 'It's a choice. He knew exactly what he was doing when he hid in my roof, when he blew that joint in the pub and he knew what he was doing to me, and to Kelly and Wes, and he didn't give a damn!'

As far as Michelle was concerned, no medical explanation could ever justify such heinous crimes.

Almost one year to the day after Kelly's murder, Michelle received a letter in the post from the coroner's court, telling her what she already knew: that her daughter had died from carbon monoxide poisoning. The poor timing and the cold, clinical nature of the letter paralysed Michelle, who was already bracing herself for the anniversary of Kelly's death.

*

After Kelly's murder, Michelle became a mother on a mission. Determined to make her daughter's life count for something, she studied and gained employment. While she had refused to bow to East's demands to return to work when Kelly had been a newborn, this time she chose to take on a job when her daughter Shayley was just six months old.

Having too many plates in the air at once became Michelle's way of dealing with her grief and fighting back. Juggling a job and four children kept her focused and busy. She said it was better than 'following the path of the magic pill'. Despite her courage, she spent many black days crying for hours on end, telling herself that all the work and all the purpose in the world changed nothing.

'I mastered the art of putting ice cubes on my puffy eyes, which often resembled golf balls after hours of crying myself silly,' she told me. 'You do whatever it takes to get through. There were many occasions when I drove past the local psychiatric hospital not far from my home, reminding myself there was no point in being depressed. Ending up there because I felt hopelessly sad wasn't fair on the people I loved and would give Kevin all that he hoped to achieve through his crime. He wanted me on my knees, and I couldn't let him win.' That thought kept her going when she felt like giving up.

After Kelly's death Michelle assumed a role at a community centre in Collie. She formed a bereavement group and found comfort helping other mothers dealing with the pain of losing a child. While none of the mothers in her group at that time had lost a child through murder, Michelle related to being in a room with people who understood how empty and desolate it felt to lose someone you loved. Over time, the group expanded to provide support to anyone dealing with bereavement.

Michelle went on to become an advocate for survivors of family violence and a vocal anti-domestic-violence campaigner. Her personal experience as the survivor of family violence, and more significantly her insight into the dynamics of domestic violence, prompted her to set up a support group for survivors. She offered support in a non-judgemental environment, helping women to make positive changes to their lives.

Her newfound profile led her into local politics. She felt that the small changes she could make at the coalface of local politics might lead to bigger changes at a state and possibly federal level.

In 2002 Michelle was voted onto the Collie Council, and three years later she became a member of the Bunbury Council, where she championed a number of community issues. One of her major objectives was to generate awareness about the issues facing the survivors of intimate-partner violence. She firmly believed that greater understanding could help change the attitudes of the community and the police to domestic violence. It should not be viewed as a private family matter that was none of their business, she argued. As far as Michelle was concerned, that attitude had contributed to her daughter's murder. Domestic violence ought to have been everybody's business.

In 2003 Michelle Steck was the keynote speaker at an anti-family-violence rally in a park outside the West Australian Supreme Court. The event was supported by celebrities like Nicole Kidman, a national magazine and Channel Seven, who filmed the sea of red bodies and life-size cut-outs of mothers and children representing the casualties of domestic violence that filled the park.

Michelle took the stage in a carefully chosen Armani suit, which she slowly peeled off to reveal a singlet screaming 'Domestic Violence — Australia says NO'.

She wanted to illustrate the fact that family violence crosses cultural, social and economic boundaries; that the women she had supported included the wives and partners of police officers, doctors, surgeons and barristers. She said that behind closed doors, anyone can be a casualty of intimate-partner violence. Her speech received resounding applause, and women later came forward to share their own stories.

'Mostly they just wanted to touch me,' recalls Michelle. 'They knew I understood what it felt like to be a survivor.'

At another rally, Michelle met another survivor. Perth mother

Ann O'Neill's two children had been murdered by her estranged husband, Norm O'Neill, in 1994. He had broken into her home late one night and fatally shot their children — Kyle, aged six, and Laetisha, four — before firing at her leg. He left her alive to suffer the knowledge that their children were murdered to punish her. Then he turned the gun on himself. Ann was forced to have her leg amputated and spent years recovering from the tragedy.

'From the moment I met Ann, I realised who she was,' said Michelle. 'We both had the same cautious demeanour as we approached. But we did not cry, we just put our arms around each other, saying nothing. We knew instinctively what each of us was going through. Some things don't need to be said to be known.'

Michelle Steck's crusade took her to Canberra, to the seat of federal government. On the way she lobbied politicians and hoped to draw attention to the issue and suggest ways family violence could be tackled at a national level. To Michelle, what was needed was a total overhaul of the legal system that had failed her and continued to short-change women and children.

'I spoke to a very prominent woman, a chief of staff with five degrees who held a very high-profile parliamentary position, who patronisingly told me this was not how things were done,' recalled Michelle. 'Nobody wanted to hear what I had to say, or learn from the sorts of mistakes that had cost Kelly her life. Doors slammed in my face wherever I went because at that stage the issue of domestic violence just wasn't considered "sexy politics". I left Canberra feeling utterly deflated, convinced that there would be an epidemic of children being murdered by their fathers to punish women like me unless someone recognised that these crimes were the ultimate in domestic violence and that the legal system needed changing to stop it from happening again.'

Michelle predicted that it would probably take the murder of a celebrity's child by its father, or some other very public murder of a child before anyone really paid attention. Sadly her warnings proved correct, though it would take more than two decades and many more deaths before the message was finally heard.

It was the public murder of 11-year-old Luke Batty, whose father killed him on a Melbourne cricket field in 2014, that turned the public spotlight onto this formerly taboo subject and sparked a national debate.

'My heart goes out to poor Rosemary Batty, because if anyone had been prepared to listen to me all those years ago, perhaps her little boy might have been alive today,' says Michelle. She has lost count of the number of children murdered by vengeful fathers before the message finally reached Canberra and politicians threw their weight behind the anti-violence campaign.

'The worst of it is, there are so many of us mums walking in Rosie Batty's shoes,' says Michelle. 'And we've been out there campaigning for changes and canvassing these issues for so many years without anybody really listening.'

However, Michelle believes things are moving in the right direction, though there is still a lot of work to be done.

'For years, losing Kelly consumed my every thought; it was a bottomless pit which consumed my entire being, just as Kevin intended it to. He was right when he said I would suffer for a long time because I have and I still do. It was meant to be a suffering that lasts a lifetime, a living hell, and it really is.'

Michelle blames that endless suffering on the collapse of her second relationship, which ended in 2007.

'We didn't stand a chance; I wasn't really in this marriage from day one, I was hurting so much,' she admits frankly. 'I married in grief which was so deep that it was impossible for other people to relate to, and the distance only widened it until it cost me my marriage and I walked away from it, a single mother of four children.'

She says the pain of her daughter's murder also cast a shadow over the lives of all her younger children, not just Wesley, who was spared Kelly's fate simply because he was too young to stay overnight with his father. Michelle says her three younger children, born after the murder, feel the loss as keenly as she does. Every time there is a birthday, a Christmas, a Mother's Day or some other significant event, there is always someone missing.

'There is forever an empty hole and I believe this will continue as long as the family unit exists,' says Michelle.

When people ask her how many children she has, the question inevitably paralyses her. She wants to answer 'five', but then she would have to explain, aware of the impact her revelation would have on some well-meaning stranger who would no doubt wish they had never asked. She finds it kinder, and easier, to simply say she is the mother of four children, a response which always leaves her with the sense that she is somehow betraying the memory of the little blonde tot who was taken from her.

It was Kelly's memory that spurned Michelle to be a keynote speaker at Perth's May Day rally in 2009. The event, which was replicated in every state in Australia, opened with the raising of a clothesline bearing a row of little red clothes and cardboard cut-outs representing the many young casualties who die each year in Australia when family violence turns deadly.

Now part of a national association comprising journalists, legal experts, parents, academics, domestic violence workers, men's anti-violence groups and health professionals, this feisty Perth mother remains committed to her crusade to address the failures of the system which cost her daughter her life.

'If I can spare one other mother the painful journey I am on, then I will be satisfied,' she says. But the dilemma remains how to legislate against a dangerous father like East. All the warning signs were there in his behaviour, yet when Michelle reported the smothering incident to her lawyer, nothing could be done.

To Michelle, the system still only appears to care about the law when it should care about the families at risk and the men who pose a danger to their partners and children.

'It may be black and white when it comes to the system, but when it comes to families and emotion, it's all damn grey,' she says. Reflecting on her own experience, she says that East's relentless abuse had increased her own tolerance to a point where she was immune to his threats.

'But when men say they are going to pay you back for leaving, what the authorities should be asking is how exactly they intend to pay you back.'

And while it is important that disgruntled men know where to go to seek help when relationships collapse, the real problem is that until violent men actually commit a crime, it's nothing more than a waiting game.

'For a dangerous father, intent on committing a serious violent crime, I don't believe there's a court in the land that can protect women from it, or legislate against it,' Michelle ponders.

In the end, the whole point of revenge murders is to cause lifelong suffering.

'Kevin wanted me to suffer for my whole lifetime,' she says. 'That's why I can't let him win.'

Today, Michelle Steck has built a new life with a former political rival who she once threatened to 'cut off at the knees' during an election campaign. She shares her time with the former West Australian minister, living between a home in Bunbury and their 300-acre farm and vineyard in the Ferguson Valley. She continues to lobby for change and raise awareness.

Each year on Kelly's birthday, at Christmas, and on the anniversary of her murder, Michelle makes the pilgrimage to the small graveyard in Collie where she places flowers and a new figurine on her daughter's grave.

'My partner hates me going,' she says sadly, 'because I lose three or four days every time I go; the pain is so deep that the ground seems to open up and swallow me alive. I never go home the same.'

Michelle recalls an emotional telephone call from a woman whose partner had been jailed for life for murdering their children. The woman told Michelle that for years her family had been telling her she had to forgive her former husband for his dreadful crime. Michelle took a deep breath. She had no idea how agonising it would be, knowing that the partner who robbed you of the most precious thing in your life was still alive, healthy and breathing.

'Why do you have to forgive him?' replied Michelle. 'Who says?'

The woman on the other end of the line burst into tears.

'I don't want to forgive him,' she said, sounding relieved. 'He killed my children so I would suffer forever.'

Michelle Steck understands the anguish only too well. In 2011, Kelly would have been 21. It was one of the toughest years of Michelle's life. She has battled depression and often finds herself wondering what might have been.

'I'm travelling a road I wouldn't have chosen, but I have no choice ... I have to keep moving forward, and I do,' she says.

'You tell yourself these bastards won't win, but in the end they do. They take away the most important thing in your life and they know it. What more can they do to top that?'

CHAPTER 2

'If you'd done as you were told it wouldn't have happened.'

The story of Dionne Fehring, Patrick and Jessie Dalton

A dark sense of foreboding hung over newly separated mother Dionne Dalton as she stood in silent contemplation at the dawn Anzac parade in April 2004. Gazing into the clouds above Currumbin, the 33-year-old Queensland mother of two felt a cold shiver race down her spine as the eerie red plume from a low-flying plane cast a surreal glow across the skies. Dionne caught her breath and watched uneasily as the red vapour trail spilled through the clouds. It was as if the morning sun itself was weeping tears of blood.

To Dionne, standing silently in the crowd that morning on 25 April, it felt like a terrible omen. And in a single split second, everything that had been so good about the new day felt suddenly and inexplicably wrong.

Just a few weeks earlier, on 4 March, the panicking young wife had arrived on her mother's doorstep in Tallebudgera on Queensland's Gold Coast. She'd made a spur-of-the-moment decision to escape from her violent marriage to former One Nation candidate Jayson Dalton. During the afternoon she had received a menacing phone call from Dalton, who had called her from work to check up on her and warned darkly that 'tonight's the night — it's on'.

After three years of emotional torture and brutal beatings, Dalton hadn't needed to elaborate. His petrified wife knew only too well that the apprehended violence order she had recently been granted to protect her from her husband's violence would not be worth the paper it was written on when he finally arrived home. For months she had known that if she remained in this relationship, Dalton would undoubtedly kill her. In her panic, Dionne decided to fast-track the escape plan she had been hatching over the past few weeks.

'Just come down here,' her worried mother, Julie Wherritt, had urged from her home on the Gold Coast when she heard her daughter's frightened voice on the end of the phone. Hanging up, Dionne grabbed her baby son Patrick's nappy bag and bundled him hurriedly into his capsule in the back of her car. Then she raced to the local day care centre to collect her 17-month-old daughter Jessie, strapping the tot into her car restraints in the back seat beside her brother. Dionne half expected to see Dalton's work van screech up outside the centre to halt her escape plan. He controlled her so completely it was as if he knew what she was thinking.

But with no sign of Dalton or his van, Dionne checked her rear-view mirror and raced towards the Pacific Motorway and headed south towards the Gold Coast where her mother was anxiously waiting.

Dionne's instinct had been right: her 33-year-old husband, Jayson, was not far behind her. After his threatening phone call, he had leapt into the company's work van and rushed home, becoming enraged to discover his wife and children had gone. In three years of marriage, Dalton had systematically extinguished all of his wife's friendships and he knew there were few places left for her to hide.

Jayson Dalton put his foot down and sped down the motorway after her, aware that her mum's home was her only likely refuge. As he drove, he repeatedly called his wife's mobile phone. Dionne jumped every time the phone rang, too terrified to answer, knowing Dalton would be ringing to intimidate her into returning with the children. But there was no going back. A later check of the phone records revealed Dalton had made 76 calls to his wife's phone by the time she had reached her mother's home.

For months Dionne had realised that if she stayed, she would pay with her life. Dalton had already twice breached the apprehended violence order the police had taken out on her behalf. She could only imagine what he would do now he realised she was intent on leaving him.

In Tallebudgera, Dionne was handing Patrick over to her mother when Dalton's van screeched onto the driveway behind her. The terrified women rushed into the house with the children and hurried to lock all the doors. Inside, Dionne's younger sister, Tammy, was already on the phone to the police. But the women had overlooked the side door into the garage. Seizing his chance, Dalton burst through it and hovered menacingly in the passageway, his face white with anger.

'This is your son,' the frightened grandmother gently reminded him, pointing to the baby in her arms. But Dalton was only interested in his wife. He lunged at Dionne and his mother-in-law sprang defiantly in between them, blocking his path to her cowering daughter.

'The police are on their way,' she warned him. But Dalton's rage had reached boiling point. Unable to get at Dionne, he threw a punch at her mother instead, catching the shocked grandmother on the hand as she tightened her grip on the crying baby.

Her warning about the imminent arrival of the police had the sobering effect Julie had hoped for. Aware he was about to be arrested for yet another breach of his intervention order, Dalton raced outside. Seeing the keys in the ignition, he leapt into his wife's car, hurriedly started the engine and sped off. Even in the heat of the moment, Dalton's escape showed an element of calculated foresight. He would have known that by taking the car with the child seats, his wife would be grounded. Unlike his work van, the family car was automatic. Dionne could not drive a manual vehicle, which meant he would know exactly where to find her when he was ready to make his move.

But his next move came from left field. Instead of returning to his mother-in-law's home as Dionne and the police anticipated, Dalton began legal action. He embarked on a bitter custody battle for the two children, knowing the prospect of losing them would bring their mother into line.

Two days before Anzac Day, Jayson Dalton finally lost his bid for shared custody of the children. The court awarded full custody of

Jessie and Patrick to his former wife and Dalton was granted weekend access only. He was ordered to return the children to their mother on the afternoon of Anzac Day.

The custody triumph had been a source of enormous relief to Dionne and her family. She had spent the Anzac weekend rushing around buying cots and converting her mother's spare bedroom into a nursery for her children. Jessie and Patrick were to be returned to her care at 4 p.m. that sunny Sunday afternoon outside the Southport police station. Dionne had specifically chosen the police station as the handover place. Not only was it neutral ground, it was the safest place she could think of. She suspected that if Dalton had been enraged over her leaving, he would be livid now he'd lost custody. Losing the children meant he had lost all control over his wife, who would not be returning to the relationship.

Standing in the crowds on Anzac Day, Dionne checked her watch again. In a few hours the children would be back and a new, more peaceful life was about to begin. Yet there was something about the blood-red trail greeting the dawn that left her feeling uneasy, and her growing anxiety continued to build as she and her mother made their way home from the parade that morning.

'There's nothing to worry about,' Julie soothed, handing her daughter the Sunday papers. 'You won; they'll be back this afternoon.' Dionne wasn't so sure. At 8.30 a.m. she felt even more unsettled as she turned the pages of the *Sunday Mail* and found herself reading an article about angels. The story claimed that even though people we love may no longer walk among us, angels are always by our side. The story resonated with her strangely and she folded the paper and found herself suddenly wishing the day away.

At around 3 p.m. Dionne again checked the little cot her mum had helped her assemble for Patrick and sat on the pretty child's bed she had made up for Jessie. By now she felt so anxious she could barely breathe.

At 3.50 p.m. Dionne and her mother waited outside the Southport police station for the children's arrival. She scanned the street for signs of her estranged husband's car, feeling more anxious than ever.

Four o'clock came and went and there was no sign of Dalton or her children. Her mother, observing Dionne's pale face, told her to relax.

'Give him another five minutes ... he'll be here,' Julie reassured her.

The entire weekend had been such a waiting game, thought Julie, checking her watch again. At just after 4 p.m. Dionne couldn't stand it any longer. She dashed to the door of the police station and pressed the buzzer. When nobody answered she dashed around to the side of the station, screaming, 'Something's happened'. An officer appeared and listened as the breathless mother related her story to him. Her husband was an abusive man who did not care for the rules. He had already breached his intervention order on three occasions, and had not turned up with her children after losing a custody battle. She was panicking. The policeman shared her concerns. He picked up the phone to alert the Federal Police.

'He's probably done a runner,' the officer remarked sombrely.

In her panic, Dionne telephoned their business partner, who had been aware of her plans to leave her abusive marriage. He had been shocked when Dionne had told him what had been going on behind closed doors, and had sworn not to breathe a word. Now he shared Dionne's concerns for her children, as he revealed he had not heard a single word from Dalton over the weekend. He offered to call Dalton's father, Michael, who had been helping him to care for Jessie and Patrick over the five weeks that the custody issue was being debated in the courts. Dionne's heart sank when this colleague rang back a few moments later to explain that the children's grandfather, a returned serviceman, had gone to spend the long weekend at a Vietnam veterans reunion in Mount Isa and had not been supervising his son's access at Dionne's former marital home. Dionne's body began to shake as she realised that her children had spent the weekend alone with her angry, bitter husband.

Upon hearing this news, Dionne telephoned Senior Sergeant Brian Kelly in Brisbane. The officer had attended a violent domestic incident at her marital home in Kelvin Grove Road, Kelvin Grove a few months earlier and had been so alarmed by Dalton's escalating anger that he had advised Dionne it was time to consider her options.

'You need to get out,' Kelly had warned.

From the police station in Brisbane, the seasoned policeman now shared Dionne's concerns for her children's safety. Kelly responded by dispatching a patrol car to Kelvin Grove to check on Dalton and the children. Back on the Gold Coast, Dionne and her mother anxiously returned home to wait for news. But as the clock ticked, Dionne's fear was building. She grabbed her mother's car keys.

'I have to go home,' she said. But she was in no state to drive anywhere.

'I'll drive,' her stepfather offered.

Shortly after the car pulled out of her driveway, Julie Wherritt felt compelled to check her computer. She caught her breath as a new email popped into her inbox, its disturbing subject line leaping out at her. The sender was Jayson Dalton, the son-in-law she had never liked, and the subject line said ominously, 'Goodbye Dionne'. The email had been sent at 8.30 that morning, the precise time Dionne had been reading the newspaper article about angels walking among us.

Dalton's email stated:

I wish we had not gone through this. I was being fair the whole way through. I believe the children have been truly affected and you know Jessie adores me. I love you more than I can say, and had forgiven you up until Friday. Lots of love from us all, Jayson, Jessie and Patrick.

Disturbed by the email, Julie telephoned Senior Constable Kelly again and told him about this new development. In her panic, she missed the loaded silence on the other end of the line.

When she paused, Kelly said gently, 'The children are gone.'

'Gone?' gasped Julie blankly. 'Where have they gone? Are they sleeping?'

The officer took a deep breath and struggled to find the right words.

'They're all dead,' he said. The rest of the conversation would forever remain a blur for the devastated grandmother as she tried to process the enormity of what she was hearing.

'No, they're not dead,' Julie wept. But her thoughts were already on her own baby — Dionne would be arriving at Kelvin Grove at any moment. Somebody had to warn her, she told Kelly.

'Dionne's phone's flat,' explained Kelly. He had already tried to contact her. There was nothing he could do to spare Dionne every mother's worst fear.

'Oh God,' Julie sobbed. 'Make sure there's an ambulance for my daughter.'

At 10 p.m. on the evening of Anzac Day 2004, Dionne Dalton drove headlong into a nightmare.

Her stepfather was driving over the crest of Kelvin Grove Road when Dionne first noticed the flashing blue lights up ahead. All the way from the Gold Coast she'd repeatedly reassured herself that everything would be OK. But those flashing blue lights confirmed the nagging feeling she had had all morning and everything around her now spun like a ghastly slow-motion slide show.

Somewhere in the distance, Dionne was aware that her stepfather was pulling over. She sluggishly observed the police roadblocks and the crime-scene tape ahead, sectioning off the road. There were police cars outside her former home, which Dionne now realised was lit up like a fairyland. She noted ambulances in the street and a news crew. The crew's cameras had been trained on her front porch, and now turned towards her. The cameras continued to roll as the ashen-faced woman leapt from the car and bolted across four lanes of traffic towards her own front steps.

It was a moment that Dionne would relive for many years to come. She describes it as a dreadful dream-like scene in which she felt herself disconnecting from her physical body and hovering over the chaotic events below as a silent spectator. She watched, mute with shock, as the crumpled woman below collapsed on the road while emergency lights flashed around her. She numbly registered being held by strangers as the warm sensation of urine seeped through her clothes, leaving her overwhelmed by the stench of her own distress. And all the time, the cameras continued to capture the hideous unfolding drama as Dionne asked, in an unfamiliar choking voice: 'Are they alive?'

Glances were exchanged among the throng that had gathered around her. Finally a stranger's voice responded with the answer nobody wanted to give. They were all dead.

It was a surreal moment. The details blurred into one another, to be recalled in agonising detail later as flashbacks gripped her. She would relive the sound of her own strangled sobs as she pleaded with the paramedics to cover her with a sheet. She didn't want to see herself in some freak show on the TV news.

Tragically, the gut-wrenching scene did find its way onto the news. And from her hospital bed at the Royal Brisbane and Women's Hospital, Dionne realised that the blood-red tears that had dripped from the sky above her that morning had been a haunting premonition of things to come.

Later she would learn that at the moment she had stared into the dawn sky, her former husband had been snuffing out the life of her baby son. Twenty-five minutes later, he suffocated her little girl, callously posing Jessie's lifeless body beside her baby brother on the marital bed they had once shared.

An autopsy would later reveal that Dalton had drugged both children before murdering them. And in a macabre twist, Dalton had taken the additional step of theatrically staging the crime scene to add to his wife's pain. Before his own suicide, he took the trouble to slip Dionne's wedding ring onto the little girl's finger and to place nearby other special items of jewellery he had brought his wife during their turbulent marriage. Dalton had also scribbled the times of the children's deaths on the wall above their heads. Patrick had died at exactly 3.05 a.m., aged just 12 weeks. The infant had not lived long enough to say 'mum' or hold a spoon to feed himself. Jessie, aged 19 months, had died at 3.30 a.m.

After the carefully executed murders, the killer dad had sat at his computer and callously tapped out the goodbye email to his estranged wife, which he'd sent at 8.30 a.m. At some stage after sending the email he had telephoned his father, Michael, saying cryptically that he and the children were about to take a 'long sleep'. Then he positioned himself on the bed between the bodies of his dead children and suffocated himself with a plastic bag, the same way he'd killed Jessie and Patrick.

Near Dalton's computer the police would find a newspaper article about another father who had murdered his family before burning down his family home. A subsequent check by IT experts would reveal that while Dionne had been preparing a nursery for her children's arrival, their enraged father had spent his weekend researching various methods of suicide. By the time he drew his last breath, Dalton had already inflicted the ultimate act of family violence on his battered wife. Dionne's broken bones would mend and her bruises would finally fade, but this final wound was so deep, it would span a lifetime and never heal.

While Dionne Dalton lay sedated in hospital, her ordeal was being replayed on the national news. The following morning, the nation's newspapers posed the question: how could a father who apparently loved his own children be driven to murder them? And what sort of a judicial system would allow this to happen when all the warning signs were clearly there?

Jayson Dalton's history of depression and violence towards his wife was well documented. His contempt for the law, in particular the efforts of the police to protect Dionne from his anger, was well known to authorities and his close family. He had openly flouted the apprehended violence order the police had taken out on his wife's behalf, with no concern for the consequences. As far as he was concerned, the order was a useless piece of paper; his wife and his children were his property, chattels to do with as he pleased.

This was a time when the reform of the Family Court system was a high priority on the Queensland Government's agenda, and when abused women were being urged to report family violence and authorities were being urged to take these complaints seriously. But by the time anyone listened to Dionne Dalton, it was too late to save her children.

*

Dionne was a confident, independent 28-year-old divorcee in late 1999 when she first met Jayson Dalton through an internet chat site. They had their first date on 19 December, and she had been most impressed when Dalton, a charismatic and charming man, told her he could not wait to meet her family. Not too many men would be eager to join a family gathering so early in the relationship, she observed. This could only get better. Yet a thoughtless throwaway remark on their second date offered a small but disturbing insight into Dalton's true nature.

'You were not my first choice,' he told his new girlfriend tactlessly. 'But you were the next best thing.'

Caught up in the headiness of the new romance, Dionne dismissed the cruel remark. She was already smitten by this attentive, strong man, a former parliamentary candidate. In her mind, Dionne had found her very own Mr Right. By the time she glimpsed the dark, explosive and dangerous persona lurking beneath Dalton's suave facade, it was too late.

Dalton was an only child who was eight years old when his parents separated. At first he lived with his mother in Queensland, where he exhibited some serious anger issues. By high school, his anger was escalating and, after an ugly incident involving a female teacher, Dalton was finally expelled.

While the exact nature of the events leading to his expulsion remains sketchy, his cousin Valerie Dalton later told *Four Corners* it was widely believed he had threatened the teacher. After this Dalton went to live with his father in Mount Isa. When his dad enrolled him at a new school, he specifically requested that his son only be taught by male teachers to avoid any future 'trouble'.

What is telling about this request is that it is evident that even as a young man, Jayson Dalton had an issue with women. It appears that his aggression towards women escalated with age, though his mates in Mount Isa would remember him as 'one of the lads' and a bit of a 'larrikin'.

But Dionne was unaware of all this when, just eight weeks after their first date, Dalton moved into the old weatherboard house she'd bought in the popular Brisbane suburb of Kelvin Grove. As far as she was concerned, she'd found the man she wanted to spend the rest of her life with. She shared Dalton's drive and ambition. In Dionne's mind, they were a perfect match.

When Dalton's stepmother, Evelyn Dalton, was first introduced to the new girl in her stepson's life, she was so impressed she told him she believed he had 'hit the jackpot'. Dionne was Dalton's first serious girlfriend and to his family it seemed that for the first time in his life he was truly happy. He'd found a woman he adored and, as Evelyn observed, he seemed very proud of his new girlfriend.

Within six months the whirlwind romance had yielded a marriage proposal. Dalton, the romantic, got down on one knee and asked Dionne to marry him. Dionne was smitten by her new man's charm. He had put in a huge effort around the house she owned, and she firmly believed that she had finally found someone who appreciated her.

But shortly before their wedding in 2001, a worrying incident occurred that left the bride-to-be feeling shocked and nervous. Days before their nuptials the couple were driving to a local motel to collect Dalton's father and stepmother, who had just arrived from Western Australia for the wedding. A squabble erupted over something so minor that Dionne later struggled to recall it. But Dalton exploded, flying into such a rage that he punched the car windscreen with his fist, shattering it.

His fiancée was stunned by the outburst, as was Dalton's stepmother, who commented on the smashed windscreen as she climbed into the car. When Evelyn asked the couple if someone had thrown a rock at the car, Dalton sheepishly accepted responsibility, confessing he had put his fist through it.

'Oh,' said Evelyn, as amazed as Dionne had been. And nobody mentioned the subject again.

But while Dionne was troubled by the outburst, their wedding was just three days away. There had been no previous violence and she concluded this was a one-off, hoping that once they were married Dalton would feel more secure about the relationship and things would calm down.

The windscreen was long forgotten by the time they exchanged wedding vows in September 2001. But among the smiling well-wishers in the congregation, one guest was struggling to celebrate.

From the moment she'd first met Jayson Dalton, Dionne's mother Julie had not liked him. He was a controlling man, she thought, who appeared to dominate her daughter and manipulate everyone around him. As far as Julie could see, he was a man who liked having everything his own way; a perfectionist who appeared to be possessive of his new bride and resentful of her family. As the family grew to know Dalton, they found him obsessive and just as resentful of her long-term friendships and even her working relationships.

Julie's initial uneasiness had grown when Dalton hijacked the all-women trip to choose bridesmaids' dresses. The women were amazed when he joined them, telling them what colour and style of dresses to choose, and later instructing them how he wanted them to wear their hair. His mother-in-law's gut feeling that Dalton was a dominating, controlling man was confirmed at the wedding when the groom sidelined her and ignored her for the entire day.

After the wedding, Dionne's mother took an overseas holiday. When she returned, her newly married daughter appeared more distant, and soon what had been regular contact with her family dwindled as Dalton sought to monopolise her every move. He systematically extinguished his new wife's friendships, particularly those with more outgoing girlfriends who might want to take her to pubs or restaurants. Dalton said he saw no need for an independent social life outside of the marriage, which quickly became all-consuming. As he repeatedly told his new wife, he was the one who cared about her and helped her, and he expected that same devotion from her.

'You only get married once,' he said. 'And for me, it's for life.'

Privately, Dionne's family and friends suspected he resented Dionne having any kind of friendship that might allow her some perspective about the increasingly one-sided nature of the relationship and her new husband's hold over her. Allowing different perspectives into his wife's life would have undermined his power over her and he discouraged any kind of a social life outside of himself.

Soon the newlyweds were doing everything together. They even ran together as independent candidates in the 2001 Queensland State Elections for the seat of Brisbane Central against Premier Peter Beattie.

It was ironic that as part of that election campaign Dalton supported a tougher stance on crime and promoted his position on the Crime Stoppers Committee. Two years earlier, as the One Nation Candidate for the federal seat of Kennedy, he'd campaigned against family violence, calling for family law reform and changes to the Child Support Agency. His campaign saw him polling more than 12,000 votes. But his image as a staunch family man was not what it seemed, and by the time Dionne discovered she was pregnant, four months into the marriage, the rot had already begun to set in.

Jayson Dalton was thrilled at the prospect of becoming a father. But as Dionne's pregnancy began to progress, so did the expectant father's controlling behaviour. Now she was socially isolated from both her family and friends, Dalton began to abuse and belittle his pregnant wife. While he played the doting family man outside the house, behind closed doors he was cruel and crude and had no problem insulting Dionne in front of his own family. His female relatives were as shocked by his foul language as his wife, who bore the brunt of his abuse.

Aware of Dionne's distaste for profanities, Dalton swore at her constantly. Even his ordinary daily conversations were soon peppered with the 'f' and 'c' words. Dionne, uncomfortable with her husband's volatile temper and upset by his dirty mouth, made up her mind to do everything she could to please him. She determined to head off trouble by keeping him sweet, though nothing seemed to make any difference. Everything was always wrong and it was always her fault.

In the midst of the pregnancy, Dalton suddenly decided to start a new joint business venture. He opened a hardware business, selling door handles, locks and similar products, claiming grandiosely that the store would stock the biggest collection of door handles in Australia. His pregnant wife would run the business, he decided, while he continued his own work in the mining industry.

With a baby on the way, Dionne was too tired to argue. She reminded herself it was a good thing to be married to an ambitious man and went along with the enterprise.

But as the weeks passed, Dalton's hair-trigger rages became more frequent and every second word was 'fuck'. He accused Dionne of lying to him, and ordered her to seek counselling for her 'problem'. But the counselling backfired when it became clear to the therapist that this supposedly 'problem' wife was an abused woman who had been resorting to white lies to protect herself from her husband's rages. When Dalton asked his wife if she had performed a particular chore that she had forgotten, Dionne would pretend she had done it because she was afraid of the repercussions if she admitted she had overlooked it. Later she would dash around the house to try and complete the task before her husband discovered the lie. It was a cat-and-mouse game that she always seemed to lose, she told the therapist. When it became apparent that Dionne was not the problem, Dalton put a stop to her counselling, claiming she was taking too much time off work.

The exhausted expectant mother worked in the fledgling family business until the day she went into labour, though she didn't plan it that way. Her husband had become a hard taskmaster who interfered in the daily running of the business. He was soon checking every figure and every order, and became so demanding that Dionne felt like a slave.

Apart from the long hours on her feet at work, Dionne was responsible for all the household chores. She seemed to spend her days answering to him at work, and cooking, cleaning, washing and ironing for a tyrant that could never be pleased.

One day, after a huge argument, Dionne became so upset that she went into early labour. Dalton drove Dionne to the hospital where doctors induced her. They expressed their concerns about the impact her stressed-out state might have on her unborn child.

Dionne's baby daughter, Jessie Caitlin Dalton, was born the following day on 12 September 2002, and Dalton apologised profusely for the angry outburst that had brought on his wife's early labour.

From the moment Jessie was born, Dalton appeared to be besotted with his baby daughter. Dionne was on a high, praying as she cuddled her tiny girl that her arrival would bring some calm into their lives. But the new mother had barely begun to bond with her baby before her husband began pressuring her to leave hospital and return to work.

Jessie was just one week old when Dionne reluctantly placed her in her baby capsule and took her to the hardware store, where Dalton insisted she work three days each week. Exhausted and still recovering from the birth, Dionne felt more stressed out than ever.

Now, as well as running the business and doing all the household chores, she had a new baby to tend to. This was not how she had imagined motherhood to be. Dionne wanted to be like the other new mums who proudly pushed their prams to parks or clinic appointments. Instead, she was exhausted, working full-time, nursing a baby and functioning on autopilot. Worse still, at home and at work, the emotional abuse was escalating.

Now, as well as calling her a liar and screaming profanities at her, Dalton began spitting on his wife. He timed Dionne as she mashed his potatoes, rounding on her if he found lumps in them and hurling the plate of food against the wall. He demanded that she lay his clothes out every morning just the way he liked them and lost it if she did it incorrectly.

Dalton inspected the floors after his wife mopped them and raged if they were not done to his satisfaction. When his waistline began to expand from Dionne's delicious home-cooked meals, he blamed her for that too.

'You're feeding me too much!' he seethed.

Soon the derogatory put-downs covered everything from her poor parenting skills to her role as a wife.

When Dalton was fired from his job shortly after Jessie's birth, he decided to join his worn-out wife in the family business full-time. Almost overnight, the young mother's only respite from her abusive marriage came to an abrupt halt. Now, as well as berating her and controlling her every move at home, he was doing it at work too. There was no escaping his tyranny and Dionne's life became a living hell, under close surveillance at work and at home.

The nightmare grew, and it wasn't just Dionne who copped his wrath. In less than two years, 17 staff came and went, the steady stream of resignations a result of Dalton's verbal abuse and threats.

Things finally reached a head at home after a particularly heated argument turned physical and Dalton hit his shocked wife for the first time.

'Why did you hit me?' Dionne asked, in tears. 'What did I do to deserve that?'

Dalton's eyes flashed angrily. 'You didn't do as you were told,' he snarled, unapologetic. 'If you had done as you were told, it wouldn't have happened.'

'But I didn't do anything wrong,' replied Dionne, bewildered. 'I only did what I was supposed to do.'

Dalton looked furious. 'You didn't do it the way I wanted it done!' he snapped.

After that, the slapping around became a disturbing new feature of the relationship. When the sharp slaps turned to powerful punches, Dionne's low confidence hit rock bottom. Dalton showed no remorse for his violence. Instead, he told his injured wife that if she only did things 'properly', he wouldn't have to lose his temper. Dionne tried harder but nothing made any difference.

Interestingly, Dalton was not out of control during these violent explosions. If anything, it seemed to his wife that he was even more in control. He seemed to enjoy her distress as he beat her, carefully directing every blow at her arms, legs and torso — places where bruises would not be noticed, or could be easily hidden.

Jayson Dalton's public image was very important to him and he certainly didn't want customers seeing his wife sporting a black eye or a bruised face. Customers and suppliers who thought he was a lovely, affable sort of guy would have formed a very different opinion of him if they'd seen what he was really capable of.

While Dalton showed little remorse for his actions, blaming his battered wife for her own victimisation, Dionne hid her bruises, ashamed of what was happening to her.

When Jessie was a few months old, Dionne begged her husband to allow her to reduce her workload to concentrate on their daughter. He refused. By now her growing baby needed more stimulation than her time-pressed mother could offer in a workplace environment where her workload had become unrealistic. Reluctantly, Dionne bowed to Dalton's pressure and relinquished her little girl to day care.

But even Jessie became a weapon for her father, who skilfully used her to control her terrified mother. When the tot cried out at night, Dalton sadistically locked the distressed mother in their bedroom and refused to allow her to comfort her crying baby. By the time he relented and let Dionne out, Jessie had become so upset that she had vomited all over herself.

Dalton's mind games and torment also extended to his daughter. When Jessie started walking, she showed a talent for singing and dancing and would often perform her favourite little dance for her proud parents. When Dalton began to order her to dance on demand, Jessie, who had witnessed her father's explosive assaults on her mother, stubbornly refused. She was already afraid of her father's temper, and as the violence against her mother escalated, she began to hide in her room, terrified of him.

On occasions when his anger turned physical, the toddler would scream in fright. To subdue Jessie's hysterical screams, Dalton gripped the little girl tightly and blew directly into her face until she stopped.

Jessie became a possession to control. When her hair began to grow, Dalton refused to allow Dionne to take the child for a haircut, insisting on cutting Jessie's baby hair himself. Throughout the haircut Jessie screamed and hit herself in the face with her tiny fists in protest.

Even before she was able to walk she had learnt to protect her mother from her father's violence. When arguments turned physical, Jessie would scuttle across the room and cling to her cowering mother's legs. As small as she was, she quickly learned that Daddy would not continue to hurt her mummy if she was clinging to her. Later Dionne would reflect that what Dalton was doing to Jessie was every bit as violent as the physical beatings she was suffering.

By April 2003, Dalton's family had become well aware of his violence towards his wife. His stepmother Evelyn, visiting Queensland for Jessie's christening, noticed the kaleidoscope of bruises on her daughter-in-law's arms and asked Dionne how she had sustained the injuries. Feeling ashamed and embarrassed, Dionne explained what had been going on. Evelyn's concern was evident; these things never got better, she warned. They only got worse.

When Dionne retired to bed that night, Evelyn confronted her stepson, warning him that if he didn't stop he would lose everything that mattered to him. Dalton made no effort to deny his violence, but despite the admonishment, nothing changed.

In April 2003 Dionne conceived their second child. The date is etched in her memory because the baby was conceived in a Melbourne hotel room during a business trip. An argument had erupted in the hotel after Dionne refused to have sex with her husband. She had asked Dalton why he imagined she wanted to be intimate with a partner who beat her black and blue. The refusal sparked a deep festering sulk that finally erupted into a savage beating.

Later, as Dionne lay nursing her injuries on the bed, Dalton brutally raped her. At the time, Jessie was sleeping beside the bed in her cot and her mother, terrified the tot might wake and witness the attack, endured the harrowing assault in silence.

A few days later, it was Mother's Day and Dalton handed his wife a card from their daughter, capturing the precious milestone on his video camera. Observing his depressed wife's tears as she thanked her little girl for her thoughtfulness, Dalton remarked, 'Oh, Mummy's crying now ... Why? What did she say, Mummy?'

Dionne stifled a sob. 'I can't read it because I'll cry again,' she responded.

'You'll cry again?' pressed Dalton, obtusely. 'Did it say something ... that Jessie can't wait until she can say that she loves you all by herself?'

'That's right,' Dionne agreed, crying for herself and her daughter.

While no mention was ever made of the violent rape, workers at Jessie's childcare centre were shocked when Dionne suddenly told them about the violence that had been taking place at home. When Dalton discovered that the childcare workers knew his secret, he immediately pulled Jessie out of the centre and found her a new childcare place somewhere else. The beatings continued throughout Dionne's second pregnancy and on one occasion Dalton even punched his wife's emerging baby bump.

Things came to a head in November 2003, during one of his rages. Now heavily pregnant, Dionne had refused to get out of an armchair where she was cuddling Jessie on her lap.

Enraged by the uncharacteristic show of defiance, Dalton picked up the microwave and hurled it at Dionne with such force that it gouged chunks out of the floorboards.

Horrified that his reckless anger may have harmed Jessie, Dionne immediately called the police. But Dalton became so angry at the sight of the police on his doorstep that it took eight burly officers to drag him out of the family home. The alarming incident was witnessed by worried neighbours who emerged from their houses wondering what so many police cars were doing in their quiet suburban street. Dalton spent the night in the local watch-house and returned the following morning, apologetic and remorseful. Afterwards, he took to his bed for four days and refused to get up for work. Finally, after much pleading on Dionne's part, he agreed to attend anger-management sessions.

The police had been so concerned about the violent episode that they urged the frightened young wife to take out an intervention order to protect herself from her husband. But Dionne was too afraid of the consequences and refused. The police were not prepared to let this drop. They ended up taking out the order on her behalf and serving it on Dalton.

But even a court order was not enough to deter Dalton. Just before Christmas he erupted again. This time he was furious that his wife had left some washing on the line. In his rage he punched a hole in the French doors and hurled a broom like a spear at the back of his pregnant wife's head, striking her neck.

Realising that he was now likely to be arrested for breaching the apprehended violence order, Dalton snatched his little girl and drove off, leaving the child's hysterical mother screaming down the phone to the police. Dionne told the officers that her husband knew people in Mount Isa who would no doubt hide him and their little girl. If that happened, she sobbed, nobody would ever find Jessie.

'You've really got to do something,' the attending policeman told the tearful mother. 'Your husband's violence is escalating.'

Later, the police called Dalton on his mobile phone and warned him that unless he returned his daughter immediately, they would charge him with kidnapping. The prospect of being charged with kidnapping brought about a change of heart, and Dalton later returned his little girl. But because the kidnap and violent assault on Dionne constituted a breach of the earlier AVO, Jessie's name was added to the intervention order. Yet the order made no difference to Dalton, who became unstoppable. The next time he lost his temper, he made sure to rip the phone from the wall so that his wife could not call the police for help.

When Jayson's cousins Valerie and Mollie visited his home in January, Dionne was eight months pregnant. Her mother Julie had recently come to stay, and Dionne reluctantly told her all about the domestic violence. Her shocked mother told her she had to leave Dalton, and Dionne reluctantly agreed. But it would have to be planned, she said. She was worried about what would happen when she did.

On 24 January 2004, after a painful 12-hour labour, Dionne's son Patrick James Dalton was born at the Royal Brisbane and Women's Hospital. An hour after the baby's birth, Dalton studied his newborn son in his mother's arms.

'My God he's ugly,' he remarked cruelly. 'Are you sure he's mine?'

The proud new mother was shattered. Five days after she gave birth to Patrick, Dalton ordered the breastfeeding mother back to work. He was aware that Dionne had suffered a spinal complaint as a result of her recent pregnancy and was now wearing a back brace and in constant pain, but it made no difference. The new baby joined his sister in day care and their mother returned to work, more depressed than ever.

Dionne's mother, watching her exhausted daughter in her back brace struggling to climb the front steps of her weatherboard house while juggling shopping and two small children, was horrified.

'You need to be at home,' she observed.

But Dionne put on a brave face and shrugged it off. It had to be done, she said, utterly defeated.

In the weeks following Patrick's birth Dalton become so menacing that Dionne contemplated faking a supposedly fatal accident, in which she and the children escaped to a new life far away from him.

But she was so fearful and so lacking in confidence that leaving became as terrifying a prospect as staying. Dalton had repeatedly told her that marriage was for life and that he would never let her go. He had also threatened that if she ever tried to leave him, he would kill her and her entire family, beginning with her elderly grandparents. Though he'd never threatened to harm his children, Dionne now believed that it was inevitable that one day he would kill her.

One night, not long after Patrick was born, Dionne woke to find her husband fast asleep beside her. A dark thought crept over her. What if she held a pillow over his face, she thought, fleetingly considering smothering him in his sleep. But what would happen if he woke and she failed? Even if she was successful and managed to murder him, she would be caught and sent to jail. What would happen to her two small children then? There seemed to be no way out, and Dionne went back to sleep feeling more trapped than ever.

The beatings were growing progressively worse. Dionne went to work wearing warm turtleneck tops in the heat of summer to hide the bruises that covered her neck. When she asked Dalton's permission to visit her dying grandfather, he responded by bashing her, tying her up and locking her in their bedroom. On another occasion, she was beaten after her husband discovered she had been to church. The shop was now open seven days a week and the traumatised wife was at her wits' end.

In desperation Dionne organised counselling for her husband through the Vietnam vets' service and together they attended different therapists. But the therapy made no difference and Dalton's violence continued. When someone gave her husband seven firearms, the already fearful wife told herself it was just a matter of time.

Aware that her husband had hidden the firearms under the wardrobe floor, Dionne contacted Dalton's female therapist and explained that she was so afraid that she was considering leaving him.

'Do you think he's capable of shooting me?' Dionne ventured, afraid that she was becoming paranoid.

Confidentiality rules prevented the counsellor from confirming or denying anything Dalton might have intimated during their sessions, let alone commenting on his state of mind. After a tense silence, the counsellor simply told the frightened wife: 'Just follow your gut and do what you think is right.'

Feeling more afraid than ever, Dionne hung up, convinced her fate had been sealed.

In early March, while her husband was at work, Dionne secretly contacted a removalist and explained her predicament. She needed the move to be fast and secret, she said. Under no circumstances could her violent husband find out. The sympathetic manager told her any payment could wait until she and the children were safely out of harm's way.

Behind the scenes, Dionne made her plans to leave Dalton. She had decided upon the Anzac weekend, six weeks away, when he would be attending an industry trade show in Sydney. With him out of the house, she would be free to pack what she could and get out before he returned. At work, she confided her secret escape plans to their business partner, telling him for the first time what had been going on at home. The sympathetic associate offered to loan her the company car for her escape and promised not to breathe a word.

But the plan changed on 4 March 2004, the afternoon Dalton telephoned work and discovered that his wife had gone home early. Dalton immediately called his home to find out why.

'I didn't give you my permission to leave work early,' he fumed, refusing to listen to her explanation that she had been suffering a migraine and that Patrick had been too unwell after his vaccinations to attend day care.

That's when Dalton made his menacing threat, warning her 'tonight's the night' and that it was 'on'.

'It's going to happen,' he warned.

Dionne knew what was coming. These were the words Dalton spat before each beating. Aware of the hidden firearms, and convinced this beating was about to be her last, Dionne made the split-second decision to grab her children and run.

Jessie was so hungry that she screamed all the way down the freeway from Brisbane. Her distress was so great that her mother was forced to pull over into a McDonald's car park near Helensvale to grab Jessie some food and to feed her baby. Ironically, Dionne stopped at the same McDonald's that would later become a murder scene in 2015 when another furious husband fatally shot his former wife in front of shocked customers. This was the very fate Dionne feared as she fed her baby, knowing that her husband would be catching up, determined to thwart her escape.

When Jayson finally arrived at her mother's house, assaulting Julie and making off in the car, Dionne knew it was just a matter of time. Without her car she was grounded. She could not drive his manual work van and without the child seats she was a sitting duck.

Tammy had been on the phone to the police, who arrived at the same time as a taxi pulled onto Julie's driveway. It had been dispatched by Jayson Dalton, who had instructed the cab driver to order his wife to get in the car and return home with his children immediately. At the sight of the police, the cabbie drove away without his terrified cargo.

The police reassured the trembling young mother that Dalton's latest breach of the AVO meant he would be arrested and would spend the night in custody.

But as Dionne watched them drive away, she wondered what would happen when he was released. He would be angrier than ever and capable of anything.

The weekend that followed was the calm before the storm. Dionne walked her children to the local playground with her mum and watched in delight as Jessie enjoyed her first-ever swim in the local pool close to her grandmother's home. These were such normal activities for other families, though neither Dionne nor Jessie had ever experienced them before.

Over the coming days, Dionne contacted a solicitor who advised her to freeze her bank accounts and to immediately add her new baby's name to the intervention order. The existing order had been taken out before Patrick's birth and only covered herself and Jessie.

'Does Jayson have access to firearms?' the lawyer asked. Dionne's heart lurched as she recalled the hidden firearms. She spent another sleepless night, petrified about Dalton's reaction when he discovered his bank accounts had been frozen and that the police were about to be informed about the firearms. She guessed that when they searched the house for the guns, he would go ballistic and direct his anger at her.

On 10 March, police officers armed with a search warrant attended her former home in Kelvin Grove Road to look for Dalton's hidden stash of firearms. But they were nowhere to be found, and a complacent Dalton, watching the search, smugly denied ever having had any weapons. This was a fuss about nothing, he smirked. He was arrested just the same for breaching the AVO and taken to the police watch-house in Brisbane, where he was placed in custody. There, he faked a seizure, and was subsequently taken to a city hospital where he spent the night under police guard. But without the firearms, the police could not detain him. Dalton was released on bail on 11

March, leaving the police concerned for the safety of his wife, his children and her entire family.

'Get out of there now,' Senior Sergeant Brian Kelly instructed, ringing the terrified mother on the Gold Coast. 'If you don't have anywhere to go, we can find you a safe house,' he said. 'But you cannot stay there, you are not safe.'

Dionne's stricken mother called a relative who lived on a remote farm in rural Queensland, five hours drive from the Gold Coast. Then they bundled the children into the car with a few hurriedly packed belongings and began the long drive to the small isolated community of Dalby. There, on a side road, Julie's cousin Jenny waited nervously in her car, ready to lead them along the deserted road to her farm at Warra.

'Jayson won't ever find you here,' reassured Dionne's mother, as she tucked her sleeping grandchildren into bed.

But amid the relief, the terrifying events of the past few days were catching up with Dionne. The acute stress surrounding her frightening bid for freedom after four years of constant violence and torment had left her in a state of heightened fear and hypervigilance. The young mother had not slept for two nights and was in the grip of post traumatic stress disorder. Safely away from Dalton's violence, she began to experience horrific flashbacks. She was also berating herself for failing to do more to protect her children from their father's rage. Overwhelmed with guilt, fear and relief, Dionne's mental state began to unravel.

Twenty-four hours after arriving in Warra, Dionne's mother woke to find her daughter racing up and down in the paddock, sobbing and screaming.

'He's here, he's followed me,' Dionne sobbed, inconsolable and paranoid. Her mother held her tightly, but Dionne's mind was elsewhere. In this altered state she had become delusional. She began to ramble, telling her mother that doctors were coming to get her because they knew she was not well. Dionne's thoughts became so disordered and her words so incoherent that Julie called an ambulance.

Dionne was immediately admitted to Chinchilla Hospital while a bed was organised for her at the Acute Mental Health Unit at Toowoomba Hospital. After assessing the traumatised patient, a psychiatrist diagnosed Dionne with postnatal psychosis. He told her concerned family it was the most severe case of post traumatic stress he had ever witnessed in a victim of family violence.

'Dionne's life must have been a living hell,' observed the psychiatrist. 'You see this in prisoners who have been tortured.'

But while the patient lay heavily sedated in the safety of her hospital bed, back in Kelvin Grove it was Jayson Dalton who was now in combat mode. His wife's escape had challenged his powerful grip on the family and he was intent on reclaiming that power immediately. When he discovered that Dionne was in hospital suffering a breakdown and that his children were with his mother-in-law, he hit the roof. He wanted his kids back right now, he raged.

Dalton's cousin Valerie advised him gently that it would be very difficult for him to care for two little babies on his own. But Dalton wasn't listening.

'They will be with their mother or me ... nobody else!' he snapped. 'Julie does not have the right to them.'

On 16 March, Dionne's lawyer, Ros Byrne, received a fax informing her that Dalton was applying to the Family Court to have Jessie and Patrick returned to his care. She had less than 24 hours to prepare her case to fight the application.

The following morning, in a 14-minute hearing, Dalton's application was heard in his estranged wife's absence. Because Dionne was still in hospital and too unwell to make a sworn affidavit about Dalton's sustained brutality, there was only one brief mention alluding to the violent background of the relationship. Dionne's lawyer, who had only been able to chat to her client on the telephone, told the court there were 'domestic violence issues.'

As a result, the judge ruled that while the children's mother was unwell, the most logical person to care for them was their father. The judge granted an interim custody order and instructed that the children be immediately returned to Jayson Dalton.

The children's shattered grandmother, agonising over the prospect of this violent man caring for two small tots, asked Ros Byrne after the hearing, 'What would you do if these were your grandchildren?'

The lawyer's response was guarded. 'As an individual I don't know what I would do. But as a lawyer, my advice to you is to bring the children back because you don't want the police to become involved.'

Julie and Tammy subsequently collected the children from her cousin's farm, and drove them back to their father. On the return journey they called someone they knew at the Federal Police who confirmed the lawyer's advice to return the children. But he suggested they could try to persuade the judge to reconsider his order if they could make it back to the Family Court before the close of business. Julie drove at speed to Brisbane, arriving at the court with just minutes to spare.

At the brief hearing, Julie was informed she was not the party applying for the custody of the children. In desperation, she told the judge about the suffering and torment that had resulted in her daughter's hospitalisation. Jayson Dalton was dangerous, she warned. And he posed an immediate threat to his children.

The worried grandmother elaborated saying that while he appeared to love his daughter, Jessie, he had never bonded with his baby son. More disturbingly, the family were worried about Jayson's short fuse when it came to dealing with small children on his own. But while the judge accepted that Dalton had been hard on his wife, there was no evidence before the court to suggest he had been violent towards his children. The youngsters would have to remain with their father, at least until their mother was well again.

The children's aunt was furious, stating loudly that to leave the children in the care of an angry, violent father, amid a raging custody battle, would be a certain death sentence for her niece and nephew. Dalton had just lost control over a wife he had spent years trying to beat into submission, argued Tammy. The guy was a ticking time bomb and a danger to his own children.

'Congratulations,' Tammy raged, storming out of court. 'You have just condemned those children to death.'

The news was shattering for Dionne, whose fragile mental health remained a concern. Twelve days later, she was finally discharged from hospital, feeling more afraid than ever.

With the bank accounts now frozen, Dionne did not have the funds to mount an expensive legal battle. But a generous uncle, hearing about her dilemma, offered to cover her legal bills, even suggesting the name of a seasoned Family Court barrister whom he instructed to take up the fight on his niece's behalf.

Dionne's lawyers returned to the Family Court where they filed an urgent application seeking the immediate return of the two children to their mother. A date was set for 23 April, weeks away. Dionne was granted temporary access for the Easter holidays.

The distraught mother choked on her own tears as she observed the bewilderment and fear on her little daughter's face when the Easter holiday came to an end and she was forced to return to her father. Jessie left her mum, her little face white with fright, and Dionne felt helpless to protect her.

By now Dalton had joined MEND, a 12-week program for separated fathers, in a bid to turn his life around. But for Dionne, it was too little too late. With the new court hearing hanging over him, the unravelling father telephoned his own dad in Western Australia. Whatever Dalton told his father in that phone call remains a mystery, but Michael Dalton was concerned enough to call the Vietnam vets counselling service in Brisbane, saying his son was sick and needed to be admitted to hospital as an emergency. Nothing happened and Michael Dalton caught a plane to Brisbane to help his son care for his two small children.

It became clear to everyone that Dalton was no longer thinking rationally. He was angrier and more erratic than ever.

'I just want my wife and family back,' he told his relatives, bursting into tears and crying for up to 16 hours a day. He was no longer sleeping and had stopped taking the anti-depressants he had been prescribed by his doctor. Everyone was worried. Dalton's obvious sleep deprivation was very evident to the organisers of MEND, who noticed he was not coping. Evelyn was so concerned by her stepson's unravelling mental state that she penned a long letter explaining that Dalton — a man with a history of family violence — was fighting for the custody of his two young children. She pointed out that her stepson had twice breached apprehended violence orders yet his children remained in his primary care. She faxed the letter to the Coolangatta Police and to the main current affairs shows on Channels Nine and Seven. In it, she warned that unless something was done, the situation was destined to end in tragedy.

But Dalton's stepmother was unaware of the stringent reporting rules relating to coverage of cases before the Family Court. Strict rules prohibit the identification of any parties in any matters before the court involving children or custody issues. The case would not be reported until much later, and by then it was exactly the tragedy Evelyn Dalton had wanted her faxes to head off.

The next five weeks were a waiting game as Michael Dalton helped his son care for his children and the court case approached. There was no doubt that during this time Jessie and Patrick were loved and well cared for. Dalton took time off from work and splashed out on toys and clothing for his kids. He also spent money on his rising legal bills, convincing himself that no court would refuse his application for custody when he demonstrated he could care for his children so well.

But the pressure was building. His family noted with alarm that his extreme fatigue was now affecting his judgement and that his behaviour appeared to be growing more bizarre by the day.

During this period Dalton began to keep a journal, in which he obsessively recorded every detail about everything that was going on in his life. He meticulously noted the expressions of the people around him as they reacted to his conversations; he even noted the manner in which his family cuddled his children or played with his daughter.

Jayson Dalton became particularly vigilant about recording the details of all the phone calls concerning the children. More bizarrely, he took to carrying a small tape recorder around with him, which he carefully concealed under his clothes.

When his estranged wife was discharged from hospital and was granted access to the youngsters over Easter, the increasingly obsessive and paranoid dad waited outside the Southport police station with his hidden tape recorder. He told his cousin Valerie, who had gone with him to collect Jessie and Patrick, that he needed to have proof if Dionne made any threats or allegations against him.

Later, when they returned home with the children, Dalton repeatedly asked his cousin if she'd noticed the way Dionne had looked at him when she'd handed Patrick back; had she actually looked at him at all? What had she been thinking? he pondered, clearly paranoid. On the car journey back, he played his secret tape recording at least 20 times, listening intently as he replayed the brief conversation he had with his former wife. The following morning, his family noticed him listening to it all over again. He played it at least another 20 times.

The family also noticed that Dalton had taken to recording other strange details in his bizarre diary. He documented the number of mozzie bites on his daughter's body following her Easter access visit with her mum. And he grandly told everyone that he was by far the better parent.

Aware of Dionne's application for full custody of the children, he remained overly optimistic that his own application for shared custody would be successful. His cousins tried to warn him that this was not likely to be a realistic outcome. Sharing custody would make it difficult to create a settled, stable environment for the children who would be split between two homes, they said. They couldn't imagine the logistics of a father having his kids three days one week, and four days the next. The children wouldn't know where their home was. Worried that he was setting himself up for a bitter rejection, they reminded him that even if he lost, he would still have regular access to his children. But privately his cousins didn't believe Dalton had a strong case at all. With his lengthy history of family violence and breaching apprehended violence orders, the whole notion of shared custody was unrealistic to everyone but Jayson.

Dalton later abandoned his support group for separating dads, where other fathers on the program had observed his tiredness and depression. But while he remained optimistic about winning shared custody, to some observers it was clearly a case of wishful thinking on his part.

The case returned to court on 23 April, where allegations were made by each parent about the other's poor parenting. The judge was confused by Dalton's accusations that his former wife was a 'poor mother' who failed to properly look after her children, supposedly returning them from access visits in filthy nappies. This made no sense. If Dionne was such a dreadful mother, why wasn't he demanding full-time custody of his children? Since her discharge from hospital, Dionne had made a chilling 100-page statement graphically detailing the years of emotional torment and violence she'd suffered. She had included the chilling details of her brutal rape, and the mental abuse and vicious beatings that even included Dalton's past attempts to stab the family dog.

To the family's great relief, the judge ruled that Jessie and Patrick should be returned to their mother's full-time custody. Their disappointed father was instructed to return the children at 4 p.m. on the Sunday afternoon at the Southport police station. Dalton was furious.

But while Dionne and her family returned home discussing their plans to turn the spare room into a nursery for the children, a deflated Jayson Dalton made his way back to their children in Kelvin Grove more dejected than ever.

His cousins Mollie and Valerie Dalton, who had been caring for the youngsters, listened as he complained about the lost custody battle and how his good character had been muddied. At some time that morning he spoke to the founder of the separated fathers group, and told him about the failed custody bid. Then he rang his dad, who was in Mount Isa for the Vietnam veterans reunion that weekend.

During this conversation Dalton became so angry that his words were almost incoherent. He swore and ranted down the phone, saying the judge hadn't understood. Dionne was out to destroy him. Michael Dalton would later tell the police that his son 'just went berserk'.

When he put the phone down, Dalton snatched baby Patrick out of Mollie's arms and told her curtly, 'He's my son and I have the right to see him grow up. If they go to their mother I won't even see them on their birthdays and at Christmas.' He looked furious. 'They are my children,' he said.

He began to rant; someone else would one day be part of his children's lives; some stranger who knew nothing about them. Cautiously, the two women attempted to point out that things were not quite that bad. But Dalton would not hear it. Later, he produced his video camera and made a chilling home movie.

'We all love each other, don't we?' he drawled, cuddling his children on camera. 'We had bad news today about the courts, yeah … You're going to miss Daddy being around, aren't you?'

On the Saturday morning Dalton took some snapshots of his children, who spent the rest of the day alone with their father. The following morning, while Dionne watched the red vapour trail bleeding into the clouds over the Anzac Day parade, Dalton stared for the last time into the faces of his sleeping children. Then he coldly smothered the life out of them. After the murders he telephoned his father again, telling him cryptically that he and the children were about to take 'a long sleep together'. Then he sent his farewell email and lay on the bed beside his children's lifeless bodies, ending his own life the way he'd ended theirs.

It was growing dark in Brisbane when Valerie and Mollie Dalton made their way to Kelvin Grove Road. Despite their repeated telephone calls to Jayson, they'd been unable to raise a reply and neither had his father, his friends or the police. Everyone was worried.

They noticed that all the lights in the house were off and that Jayson's car was still parked on the driveway where it had been the previous afternoon. When he failed to answer the door, they rang

Michael Dalton, who immediately alerted the police, informing them about the worrying 'goodbye' phone call.

At some time after 6 p.m. police cars converged on the street, and a couple of uniformed officers made their way into the house. They found Dalton huddled with his children dead on the bed in the main bedroom. Ambulances were called: one for the children, another for their dead father, and one for the unsuspecting mother on her way from the Gold Coast to deal with the worst news of her life.

*

Jayson Dalton's funeral was a low-key affair. His wake was attended by a number of fathers from his separated-fathers group. Some of the fathers claimed the tragedy stemmed directly from the lack of equal rights for fathers who failed to get justice in a legal system that was heavily stacked in favour of mothers.

But Dionne, who had identified her children's lifeless bodies at her local morgue, wondered where the justice was for her murdered children. Tragically, Tammy's prediction to the court had proved horribly accurate. Jayson Dalton had been a ticking time bomb and a danger to his kids, but by taking his own life, he made sure he would never be held accountable for his hideous revenge crime.

In contrast to their father's small funeral, Jessie and Patrick's funeral was a packed affair. Ten days after the tragedy, more than 100 mourners turned out to say farewell to Dionne's two 'little cherub angels'. They watched in tears as the grief-stricken mother lifted two white doves out of heart-shaped boxes and kissed them before releasing them into the heavens over Allambe Gardens in Nerang. The doves symbolised the spirits of the two children. Pale-pink and baby-blue sashes were handed to mourners. Dionne, dressed all in white with her own pale-pink and baby-blue sashes around her neck, watched the birds disappear into the clouds. Her face was ashen as she studied the hearse filled with teddy bears where her children lay together in a single tiny white coffin. Dionne believed this was fitting; Jessie would take care of her baby brother in heaven.

As the coffin was lowered into the ground, Dionne sang 'Frère Jacques', the French children's folk song she had often sung to her babies. But while Dionne told the congregation she felt empty, she vowed her children's deaths would not be in vain. Urging the congregation to stand and observe a minute's silence for Domestic Violence Week and for other silent victims, she revealed her plans to set up a foundation to buy a small country farm that would provide a safe haven for domestic violence victims. She said she wanted it to be a place of solace. 'Where there are no bars and the smell of fresh air, and the sound of the wind whistling through the trees can lift the weight of stress from their shoulders, and the children can run and laugh without fear while they regain their strength.

'If someone had listened, our two babies would still be lighting the world today,' Dionne said sadly. She said she hoped her tragedy might help to change the decisions that resulted in little ones being returned to violent fathers when a mother was too sick or incapable of caring for her children.

On 16 August, Dionne and her mother appeared on *Four Corners*, speaking publicly about the events that had led to her children's murders. In the show, entitled 'Losing the Children,' presenter Liz Jackson said the story behind this terrible tragedy highlighted the confronting issues of domestic violence, and the dangers that often followed 'bitter battles for custody' in the wake of family violence.

In her first TV interview, newly appointed Family Court Chief Justice Dianna Bryant spoke about the tragedy of cases such as Dionne's and the challenges such cases presented to the family courts.

'If it happens, you go over the case and think, 'I did what I could. There was nothing to indicate this would happen,' but eventually, of course, it affects us. We're all human. I think it affects everybody. We all live in the shadow of this happening to us, unquestionably.'

The show revealed that since the murders of Jessie and Patrick Dalton, the Government had acknowledged a need for a reform of the system that had failed their mother. The call for reform was an issue the bereaved mother would continue to flag publicly in the months and years ahead.

The six months following her children's murders were unbearably empty. Despite intensive counselling, Dionne remained haunted by images of her babies' final harrowing moments. For weeks, her dreams were filled with visions of her babies in the morgue, or lying side by side in their coffin. In her darker moments she had flashbacks of her collapse in the street, when the smell of urine permeated her senses. She felt trapped in some ghastly nightmare. Each morning she would wake up only to find it was horribly real. Around her, the world continued to turn. But she moved through her life feeling numb.

For Dionne, what had happened was a final selfish act of revenge deliberately inflicted by a disturbed father. Dalton knew that taking away the two things that mattered more to her than anything was the most effective way of reclaiming his power and punishing her for ending their relationship.

But even in the darkest days, when she felt she had nothing left to live for, Dionne wasn't prepared to let her former husband win. He had already robbed her of two lives she wasn't about to let him claim another and destroy her. She found solace in her Christian faith, and with intensive counselling found the strength to keep going. There were lessons to be learned from her children's deaths, she reasoned. By telling her story and joining the fight against family violence that Dalton had once paid lip service to in his days as a parliamentary candidate, she hoped to make Jessie's and Patrick's brief lives count for something. She found that by publicly sharing her story, she could raise awareness among the police, the media and domestic violence organisations around the country. Better awareness, she reasoned, might highlight the glaring loopholes in a system that failed to protect vulnerable children.

Jessie's and Patrick's deaths would become the driving force in a campaign to raise awareness about the destruction caused by domestic violence, and Dionne would become a voice for other mothers and children at risk. Her new crusade helped Dionne refocus as the months passed.

In July 2004 Dionne joined forces with Senate candidate Hetty Johnston to launch a state-wide campaign to raise awareness about child protection issues in Australia. The campaign, entitled 'Next Step Canberra' stemmed from Hetty Johnson's election promise to ensure that children's voices were heard in Canberra. Until now, children had not been a national or political priority, the parliamentary candidate told Brisbane's *Sunday Mail.*

'Kids don't vote, but our children are important,' she said. 'There's nothing more important than our children.'

Hetty Johnson told the *Sunday Mail* that the failure of the system to protect Dionne's children was 'beyond comprehension'.

Dionne, using two baby shoes to symbolise her murdered children, made footprints on a canvas that campaigners later took around towns in Queensland as part of the campaign to give children a voice.

At around the same time, Dionne announced that she was instructing her lawyers to investigate the possibility of taking civil action over the alleged failure of the authorities to protect her two children. The likely targets included the Family Court itself, and possibly Queensland's Department of Child Safety, who were both warned the children were in danger. But this was not about blaming anyone, she explained. This was about ensuring that a tragedy like this did not happen to another mother. She could not even bring herself to blame her ex-husband for his hideous crime. With hindsight she now believed he must have been sick, suspecting strongly he may have suffered from bipolar disorder or some other mental affliction.

To really heal and move forward, Dionne decided it was important to forgive and let go of any blame.

As the first anniversary of her children's murders passed, Dionne felt stronger. Life was moving on for her. She was stunned to find that she had fallen pregnant from a short-term relationship that had since ended. Dionne was in the midst of her pregnancy in June 2005 when her mother persuaded her to post her profile on an internet dating site. But Dionne was cautious. She wasn't sure she could ever learn to trust another man, let alone date again.

That changed when Dionne met Sergeant Glen Fehring, a soldier serving at Brisbane's Enoggera Barracks, a few months later. Glen had been on an overseas tour of duty in April 2004 when Dionne's children were murdered by their father, and knew nothing of her painful past when he began exchanging emails with her. Three weeks later they met for the first time and, despite Dionne's initial wariness, the spark between them was undeniable.

As they got to know one another, Dionne nervously suggested that Glen should google her name to find out more about her. The seasoned soldier was lost for words when he read her story on his computer screen.

On Christmas Day 2005, Glen proposed to Dionne. Her son Sean Alexander was born two days later in the same birthing suite at the Royal Brisbane and Women's Hospital where she had given birth to Jessie and Patrick.

It was a bittersweet but precious moment for the delighted mother, whose joy was tainted by poignant memories of her other children's births. But Glen's reaction, as he nursed the baby he viewed as his own son, was in stark contrast to Dalton's spiteful words when he called his own newborn son 'ugly'. Their new baby boy was absolutely perfect in every way.

Still, amid the excitement surrounding Sean's birth, the soldier could not help sensing his partner's lack of elation compared to the other mothers as they showed off their newborns to the world.

Despite her pain, Dionne was besotted with her baby boy and delighted that she had been given another chance. But it was still agony knowing that Jessie and Patrick were not there to welcome their new baby brother or give him a first cuddle. Throughout her stay in hospital, Dionne said, she felt the presence of her little angels keenly. She finally went home convinced that Jessie and Patrick were smiling down on her, urging her to be happy again.

In September 2005, Dionne had been with Glen in Victoria to attend a family engagement party when she was confronted with the chilling news footage of a tragedy in which three children had died while on an access visit to their father. She felt sick to the stomach as she watched the images of Robert Farquharson's car being hauled from an icy dam in rural Winchelsea on Father's Day where his three little boys had drowned.

'When I heard those three little boys had drowned in their father's car, and only he had survived, I just knew,' she said. 'My heart was pounding and I turned to Glen and his mother, saying, "No way was this an accident. Just think about it. This guy's got his kids on an access visit for Father's Day and they all drown, but he makes it out. No way."'

She mulled over the footage for the rest of the night, the images plunging her back into her own nightmare.

When in 2012 Queensland father Jason Lees rode his bike off Brisbane's Story Bridge with his two-year-old secured in a child seat on the back, killing himself and his toddler Brad, Dionne found herself reliving her nightmare yet again.

Dionne said her heart broke for the child's mother, who would be tortured for the rest of her life. Each similar tragedy would be a reminder of the horror she had lived through, and continued to live through.

Dionne told Kate Kyriacou from *the Advertiser*, 'She'll be thinking, 'If only I hadn't said that, or done this; if only I'd done something different.' That's what I went through when my kids died, but at the end of the day it's just a terrible, terrible crime.'

Over the years, the never-ending torment Jayson Dalton intended for his former wife has continued. It only takes a trigger like the mention on the news of a new child murder and Dionne Fehring relives her own ordeal all over again. It is a ghastly recurring memory, she says. And sadly, as more cases fill the news, it keeps on happening.

In 2006, Dionne married her soulmate Glen Fehring and the couple went on to welcome another child: a daughter, Melissa. As the years have passed, Dionne says she has discovered a new kind of 'normal'. But it remains an ongoing journey for a mother who has required continuing psychiatric and psychological counselling to help her regain her trust in her own judgement and her confidence in her independent decisions.

Today, on the surface, Dionne Fehring's life is much like any other mother's. She does the school run, helps with homework, makes school lunches and enjoys her family. But she says a piece of the jigsaw of her life remains missing all these years later, and the pain never leaves.

'There are many times when I find myself thinking of all the things Jayson took away from me when he killed my children. I never had the chance to watch Jessie or Patrick start school; to buy Jessie her first bra or watch Patrick play his first game of football. His crime took away the pleasure and joy which goes with all these milestones. It still breaks my heart.'

In the past 11 years Dionne has suffered three nervous breakdowns. The trigger for her mental collapses generally occurs in the black abyss between 4 March — the day she fled from Jayson Dalton — and Mother's Day in May. This period, she says, yields the most agonising anniversaries, from Anzac Day and the anniversary of her children's murders, to their funerals and her first empty Mother's Day when she was a mother without children.

'Every year on Mother's Day my two little angels are absent reminders of a pain that continues to eat at my heart,' she says.

In Dionne's heart, she remains, even today, the mother of four beautiful angels: two daughters and two sons. And while there are only cards from her two living children, her husband has placed a seat in their garden bearing a plaque that honours her two lost babies.

In some ways Jayson Dalton's death is a relief to his former wife. She says she could not stand living with the knowledge that the man who had so callously killed their two children was still alive to watch her suffering.

'I cannot imagine, on top of such a deep loss, the constant agony of knowing he is still alive and breathing when your children are not,' Dionne reflects. This is the situation for mothers like Cindy Gambino, Peta Barnes and Rachelle D'Argent, whose killer exes now remain behind bars for their revenge crimes.

'Neither could I imagine the pain of having him playing the victim, grabbing all that attention in court and breathing the air you breathe when your kids have paid with their lives,' she says. Dionne is now an ambassador for the Gold Coast Domestic Violence Centre and an active anti-family violence campaigner. 'I have been able to move forward in my life. But how is it possible for those mothers to move forward with that added burden hanging over you? He's alive and your kids are dead. That really would be a life sentence.'

CHAPTER 3

'Nobody does that to me and gets away with it.'

The story of Cindy Gambino and Jai, Tyler and Bailey Farquharson

The unseasonably sunny morning of Father's Day 2005 brought families out of their homes in droves. All around Australia dads received gifts wrapped by small hands, before heading off with their kids to play ball games in picnic grounds or to drink beer with their own fathers at suburban backyard barbecues.

But for thousands of single dads like 38-year-old Robert Donald William Farquharson, access arrangements meant only a few quality hours with their children. These fathers had a lonely air as they supervised their children at fast-food outlets or called in on relatives with no plans of their own. They would do their best to celebrate Father's Day, but when it was over, they'd return their kids to homes they no longer shared, saying their goodbyes on the doorstep in time for bed and the new school week.

Ironically, Robert Farquharson had not been meant to have his three children, Jai, aged nine, Tyler, seven, and Bailey, two, on Sunday 4 September. The mutually agreed access arrangements he'd organised with his children's mum, Cindy Gambino, meant he had them every other weekend at his father's house, where he'd been living since their separation 10 months earlier. It wasn't his turn to have the boys until the following weekend, when they'd sleep over at Rob's dad's cramped house just around the corner from his former marital home in rural Winchelsea, Victoria.

Cindy knew that Farquharson's first Father's Day as a single dad might be difficult. When she realised that Father's Day fell on a weekend that he wouldn't normally see his children, she immediately offered to change the arrangements so he could spend this special day for dads with his kids. It was a decision she would deeply regret.

When the 35-year-old mother initially raised the subject, Farquharson told her he'd been rostered on to work on Father's Day morning. Earlier the previous week, he'd been sent home from work suffering from flu, and a throat and chest infection had left him with a troublesome cough. But he needed to make up the lost time because he was broke. It was agreed that Cindy would drop the boys off at their grandfather Don Farquharson's house in Esse Street at 3 p.m.

In their rush to leave the house that day, Jai somehow overlooked the back scratcher he'd bought for his dad from his primary school's Father's Day stall. His younger brother, Tyler, had remembered the giant bar of chocolate though, and hoped his father might share it with them. But Jai had been close to tears on the car ride to his Grandpa Farquharson's when he discovered he'd forgotten his precious gift for his dad.

His mother told him not to worry. She'd wrapped a set of saucepans and a framed photo she'd taken a few months earlier of the boys sitting on the sofa at the rental house she and their dad had once shared.

The portrait had been such a good one that she'd had it enlarged and framed, certain it would take pride of place in Rob's new house, if he ever got around to finding somewhere.

'You can give Dad the photo and saucepans, and surprise him with your back scratcher when he drops you back home later on,' Cindy suggested brightly.

Tragically, there would be no 'later on' for the three little Farquharson boys. Within hours, chilling images would dominate the national news of Farquharson's waterlogged car being hauled from the depths of an icy dam on the outskirts of Winchelsea, and Cindy's poignant snapshot of the three little boys lost would cast a shadow over the small community, for whom Father's Day would never be the same again.

What really happened in those final harrowing moments when Robert Donald William Farquharson's car suddenly veered off an isolated stretch of road and into the waters of a murky dam would become the contested ground of a controversial legal marathon. The case would ultimately divide the small town, which had been home to generations of Farquharsons and Gambinos.

What is known is that about 7.15 p.m. on that Sunday evening, as Farquharson drove his sleepy children westward along the Princes Highway from Geelong towards Colac, his old white Commodore VF Berlina suddenly and inexplicably careered across the deserted carriageway onto the opposite side of the road. From there, it crashed unseen through a post-and-wire fence and headed down a steep embankment, picking up speed as it travelled across a paddock, narrowly missing some trees and plunging headlong into a farm's long rectangular dam, where it sank to the bottom with the three terrified youngsters trapped inside.

Farquharson, a poor swimmer, miraculously managed to escape from the sinking vehicle and swim through the darkness to the edge of the dam, then clamber up the embankment and on to the highway to flag down an oncoming car.

His astonishing explanation and bizarre behaviour in the aftermath of the tragedy set the tone for the most widely debated court case since the infamous jailing of wrongly convicted Australian mother Lindy Chamberlain, who was sentenced to life imprisonment in 1982 and later cleared of murdering her baby daughter Azaria, who she'd insisted had been taken and killed by a dingo.

Farquharson's own eight-year legal battle, involving two controversial trials, two separate findings of guilt and three appeal hearings, centred on two crucial questions. Was the hapless dad really the innocent victim of a terrible freak accident sparked by a sudden coughing fit that had caused him to black out behind the wheel? Or was this, as the Crown contended, a deliberately planned and callously executed murder perpetrated by a vengeful father to inflict a lifelong punishment on his former wife for ending their marriage?

Farquharson's ex-wife refused to believe the tragedy was anything other than a terrible accident. In spite of his initial animosity towards her after their separation, the notion that a loving dad could consider harming his own flesh and blood in a malicious act of revenge was as inconceivable to Cindy Gambino as it was to the people of Winchelsea. Nobody wanted to believe that a 'top bloke' and devoted father like Robbie Farquharson could be guilty of such evil.

The Farquharsons' marriage had been an unfulfilling portrait of disappointment and resentment. The couple, who had both grown up in the close-knit community around Winchelsea, had already been together for more than six years and had two sons before they finally married in August 2000. Yet even on their wedding day, Cindy had had her doubts.

On the surface things seemed unexceptional. Farquharson was not a savvy man, but he was hardworking and friendly enough. After a couple of house moves around Winchelsea, the couple had moved to a rental property in Austin Street, close to both sets of in-laws, while they built a new house on the other side of town. But underneath the facade they were drifting apart.

By the time Bailey was born, two years into the marriage, Cindy felt nothing could plaster over the cracks. She was going nowhere with Rob, who behaved like a spoiled and demanding fourth child. Rob was a mummy's boy who'd remained at home with his parents until he finally moved in with Cindy, who'd lived independently for years. Born prematurely, Rob was the family baby. He had an older brother, but had been coddled by his mum and two older sisters. When he moved in with Cindy, he expected the same attention. She soon felt trapped and bored in a relationship where the responsibility for everything seemed to fall on her shoulders. Things deteriorated after 2000 when Farquharson's mother, Faye, was diagnosed with cancer and passed away before Bailey was born.

By then Farquharson was so moody and unpredictable that it had become miserable to live with a man in the grip of a depression he didn't want to know about. Behind closed doors he harassed and criticised Cindy, and relentlessly teased the older children. It left her feeling resentful and frustrated. There was something quietly angry, almost abusive, about his taunting behaviour.

After months of agonising, Cindy finally told Farquharson their marriage was over. In November 2004, she left the house while he packed his bags. Within days of the split, she'd filed for divorce and reverted back to her maiden name, Gambino.

Having Farquharson living around the corner wasn't ideal, though it meant he could still see his kids regularly. When he discovered his ex-wife had a new man, he started stalking her, sitting in his car outside his former home at all hours and monitoring her growing friendship with single dad of three, Stephen Moules.

Initially Farquharson had blamed the 38-year-old Moules for the breakdown of his marriage, accusing him of having an affair with his wife. Cindy had met Moules, a concreter and local scout leader, when he poured the slab for their new house. But Moules was recovering from his own relationship breakdown and had no interest in becoming involved with anyone else's marital woes while he built a new life for himself and his children, who were a similar age to Cindy's older boys.

After the separation, the pair's blossoming friendship infuriated Farquharson, who complained about the split to anyone who'd listen. A particular bone of contention was Cindy's insistence on keeping the newer family car, while he got landed with the old 'shit one'. Farquharson complained that he had seen Cindy and her new man swanning around town in it, and fumed that if he ever saw Moules driving the car, he'd drag him out of it. He even inquired about getting someone to have Stephen 'done over'. Farquharson grizzled endlessly about being broke because the new house Cindy no longer wanted wouldn't sell. When he started turning up uninvited at his former home on the pretext of seeing the kids, Cindy said they needed some ground rules. It was agreed he'd have access to the kids every other weekend.

Despite the initial acrimony, Cindy believed her ex-husband was finally moving on. She was wrong. What she hadn't realised was that

Farquharson's love for his kids was horribly overshadowed by his festering hatred towards her.

But there had been no hint of this bubbling rage on Father's Day when Cindy kissed her children goodbye for the last time and instructed her estranged husband to have them home by 7.30 p.m. in time for bed.

Farquharson spent that afternoon with his kids at a loose end. He called in at his good mate Mick Hart's home to ask if the single dad wanted to join him on a trip to the Geelong suburb of Belmont for a meal at KFC. But Mick had been unwell and wasn't up to it. Farquharson then headed to Kmart in Waurn Ponds where his sister Kerrie worked. There, her two younger nephews showed her the DVDs their dad had bought them, while Jai produced his new cricket ball.

Afterwards, Farquharson and the children sat in the car listening to the radio while Bailey took a nap. Then they piled into KFC for the feast he'd promised.

On the drive home, Farquharson took a detour to Kerrie's house in nearby Mount Moriac to collect the football Jai had left there on a previous visit. At just after 7 p.m. Farquharson headed for home, his two youngest children in their child restraints in the back seat, and Jai beside him in the front passenger seat.

At Austin Street, Cindy lit the log burner and warmed the house for her children's return. It was after 7.30 p.m. and Rob was running later than usual. The unsuspecting mum prepared school uniforms and lunches, unaware of the hideous drama unfolding three kilometres up the highway, where the railway overpass descends towards the outskirts of Winchelsea.

Ten minutes earlier, local lads Shane Atkinson and Tony McClelland had been driving along the Princes Highway from Winchelsea towards Geelong when they noticed a car ahead of them swerve to avoid something on the road. Twenty-two-year-old Shane's partner had just come out of hospital that day with their new baby, and he'd celebrated his first Father's Day as a dad at a family barbecue. The friends were on their way to Geelong when they noticed a short, stocky figure leap into the oncoming traffic, wildly waving his arms in the headlights.

At first glance, Atkinson wondered if they had stumbled across a suicide attempt. His own brother had committed suicide a few months earlier, so he immediately pulled his car over on the hard shoulder to find out what was going on.

'Are you trying to kill yourself, mate?' Shane asked the shivering man. Breathlessly, Farquharson replied, 'No, no, no! I just killed me kids!'

Stunned, Shane asked him what he meant. 'No, no, no! Fuck, fuck, fuck, what have I done?' Farquharson babbled. The bewildered Shane tried to calm the soaking-wet father down.

'Give me a lift back to Winch,' Farquharson demanded. 'I've got to tell Cindy that I've just killed the kids.' Then he suddenly asked: 'Can I grab a smoke off you?'

Astounded, Shane handed him several, asking in disbelief, 'What do you mean, you just killed your kids? Where are they?'

Farquharson was vague. 'I just put my car in the dam.'

Shane, who had lived in Winchelsea all his life, asked, 'Which dam?' He knew there was a farm dam in the nearby paddock and another on the opposite side of the highway, towards Geelong. The dams were innocuous features the locals passed each day without ever paying attention. By the time the night was over, one dam in particular would be etched in the town's consciousness forever.

Farquharson went on to say he thought he'd 'done a wheel bearing' and had suffered a coughing fit which had caused him to black out behind the wheel. He said that when he'd come to, his car was in the water and he hadn't been able to get to the kids. Again he asked them for a lift.

'I've got to tell the missus that I've killed the kids,' he gasped.

The men were incredulous. 'I'm not going anywhere if you've just killed your kids,' Shane replied, pulling out his mobile phone and asking Farquharson if he wanted to call an ambulance or the police.

Bizarrely, Farquharson turned it down. He just wanted a lift so he could tell Cindy about the accident before she heard it from anyone else.

Atkinson and McClelland offered to go down to the dam to search for the car and the kids.

'No, don't go down there,' Farquharson replied, dismissively. 'It's too late — they've already gone. I'll just have to go back and tell Cindy.'

The two friends couldn't believe that a father who had just driven his children into a dam would ask for a lift instead of wanting help. Atkinson was convinced the man was 'not the full dollar' and later told the police he thought he might have Down syndrome. Cautiously, he gestured Farquharson towards his front passenger's seat, telling McClelland, out of his earshot, to sit behind them and watch his back in case the guy turned out to be a nutcase. Turning his car around, Atkinson again offered Farquharson his mobile, and suggested he call an ambulance. 'No, I've just got to go to Cindy's,' the answer came.

On the ride into Winchelsea, Farquharson repeatedly blubbered, 'What have I done?' and rambled on about the coughing fit, and doing a wheel bearing. But now he claimed that when he'd 'come to', he discovered his car was full of water. He gestured towards his chest, to illustrate how high it had been.

When Atkinson turned on his interior light he recognised Farquharson as the guy who'd once mowed lawns around Winchelsea, and realised he knew who 'Cindy' was. He guessed they had separated because he'd seen her around with Stephen Moules, whose parents lived in his street.

'Cindy's going to kill me,' Farquharson told McClelland as they pulled onto the driveway of his former marital home.

Shane Atkinson raced up the dive and thumped on the security door, calling Cindy's name. Tony stood behind him with Rob, listening uneasily as the mother rushed through the house.

'What the fuck's happening?' she shouted, the unfamiliar faces on her doorstep stopping her in her tracks. 'Where's the kids?'

Farquharson shivered. 'I don't know ... I don't know what happened,' he said vaguely.

'What do you mean?' said Cindy, suddenly aware that Rob was soaking wet.

'I've had an accident,' he spluttered. 'I couldn't get the kids ... They're in the water ... It's too late.'

Shane Atkinson stepped forward and Cindy recognised him as a local. 'We picked him up,' he explained.

Farquharson continued hysterically, 'I must have had a coughing fit and passed out. I woke up in the water. I couldn't get them out.' Atkinson's heart sank. He knew he shouldn't have left that dam and would later say, 'I done the stupidest thing of my whole life.'

In shock, Cindy began to thump her ex-husband's chest.

'Where are they?' she howled.

'Near the overpass,' replied Farquharson blankly. 'In the dam.'

'Why didn't you stay with them?' Cindy wept.

'They've already died.'

Atkinson and McClelland rushed off to the local police station to get help.

'I'll wait here for you,' the dripping father said lamely.

If the sodden dad saw no point in searching for his children, the distraught mother could think of nothing else. Ordering Farquharson into her front passenger seat, and Stephen Moules' seven-year-old son Zach into the back, she screeched up the Princes Highway. Holding the steering wheel with one hand, she telephoned Moules, screaming something about an accident involving the kids and a dam. The entire time Farquharson sat in silence, observing her panic.

When Cindy asked where the dam was, he was sketchy. He watched her drive past it then pointed. 'It's back there.'

She pulled over and raced back towards the embankment, scanning the darkness for signs of water and the car. Behind her, Farquharson hovered by the fence, watching as his trembling wife dialled Triple O. 'My husband's had an accident ... We can't find the car,' Cindy screamed. The operator tried to calm her down.

The Princes Highway was very long; they needed a landmark.

Delirious, Cindy described the railway overpass. 'I don't know where the car has gone. Someone picked my husband up and he doesn't remember where the car is ... He blacked out,' she sobbed.

'We can't see a thing ... it's dark ... I wasn't in the car with him.'

Cindy explained about the access visit, and the accident. The operator sounded confused.

'Your husband's had a car accident and some people picked him up from the highway?' she queried.

'And bought him back to my house,' Cindy added.

'And what... sorry... is anyone in the car?'

'My three kids... They're in the water and we... they can't find the car... Oh my God! Oh my God!'

On the other end of the phone, the operator asked the question that would soon be on everybody's lips. 'So how did your husband get out?'

Cindy relayed Farquharson's answers about waking in the water and trying to get the kids out. 'They sunk down,' she wept, the gravity of the situation slowly becoming clearer. 'The car's submerged ... my children are gone ... My God! My children are gone. There's three children trapped in the car. Oh my God! Oh my God!'

'Don't hang up,' the operator instructed. In the dark, Farquharson approached as if to comfort his former wife. Inconsolable, she warded him off.

When Moules arrived on the scene with his cousin Ahren, he was stunned to hear Farquharson ask, 'Where's your smokes?' Unlike the hysterical mother calling for her babies in the dark, Farquharson appeared eerily calm and Moules was outraged that anyone would think about smokes at time like this.

'Where are your kids?' he snapped. Rob said they were in the water.

'What water?' asked Stephen, peering into the darkness.

Farquharson pointed. 'Down there.'

Stephen asked how the car had got there and again, Rob told the strange story about the coughing fit and the blackout. Moules was incredulous.

'What do you mean a coughing fit? Have you been drinking? Have you taken something?'

Rob said he hadn't.

'Are you sick?' Stephen asked.

'Yeah, I've got the flu.'

'What about your children? Why didn't you get them out?'

Rob said he'd tried. 'I'm soaking wet — look at me!'

His response made Stephen furious.

'Get out of my fucking face before I fucking kill you,' he snarled, rushing off towards Cindy who was still sobbing on the phone in the dark.

If Farquharson was content to wait for help, Moules was not. He told Ahren to point his car towards the paddock and turn his headlights on high beam. Glimpsing water, he pulled off his boots and jacket and raced towards it, wading gently into the icy dam. From beside the fence, Farquharson watched this other dad frantically searching for signs of life. He made no comment when his estranged wife told the operator she'd found the broken fence where the car had ploughed through.

When Atkinson and McClelland returned with a few local men to help with the search, Farquharson asked again: 'Have you got any smokes?' In disbelief, McClelland piffed the whole packet over his shoulder and carried on racing down the embankment towards the dam. Behind him, the crash's sole survivor continued to observe the unfolding drama. If he was distressed or panicked, his blank expression didn't betray it.

'Where the fuck are your kids?' Moules yelled, emerging from the water, hypothermic. 'What's going on here? Where did the car go in?'

Farquharson shivered. 'I dunno,' he replied unhelpfully.

At 8.07 p.m. flashing sirens and emergency vehicles converged on the embankment and a police chopper beamed a spotlight from the air onto the chaotic scene below. Cindy was helped into the front seat of a car, sobbing for her babies. Her estranged husband stood close by, blankly observing, his arms folded across his chest. Moules would later say he looked like a boss supervising some mundane work project.

While investigators from Victoria's Major Collision Investigation Unit (MCIU) scoured the scene for evidence, Farquharson was stripped of his wet clothes and placed in the back of an ambulance with a cellular blanket around him.

When Senior Constable Ted Harmon asked him for simple details, like his name and his children's ages, he answered easily. But when he asked specifically about the accident, Farquharson's story began to change. Now he claimed he'd had a chest pain before blacking out over the bridge, failing to mention the wheel bearing or coughing fit he'd described earlier. When paramedic David Watson asked him what had happened, Farquharson reverted to his original story about the coughing fit and the blackout behind the wheel.

The medic listened carefully to his chest with a stethoscope but found no evidence of wheezing or crackling. He only coughed once, when requested, and it was a dry, unproductive cough, rather than the chesty sort he claimed had caused his blackout. His oxygen levels were surprisingly normal for someone who had lost consciousness.

In the ambulance his strange story changed again. Earlier, he'd claimed he'd woken in his car, up to his chest in water. Now he said the water poured in after his eldest son opened the passenger door. Later he told a doctor that when he'd woken, his car was floating and he could see water all around.

His bizarre behaviour at Geelong Hospital continued to raise eyebrows. When a police officer arrived to request a blood sample, Farquharson did not even inquire about his children's fate. Instead he asked, 'What's going to happen to me?' He asked the officer the same thing again before he left.

When Senior Sergeant Jeff Smith and Senior Constable Rohan Courtis from the MCIU arrived to conduct a tape-recorded interview, Farquharson's responses were disturbing.

'How are you going?' asked Courtis politely.

Farquharson removed his oxygen mask and replied, 'Good.'

The officers were amazed. How could a father feel 'good' when his three sons had just drowned?

Holding the microphone to the patient's mouth, they asked Farquharson to recount the accident again. 'I just started coughing and then ... um ... don't remember anything, and then all of a sudden I was in this water and my son screamed out and he opened the door and we nosedived. I ... I shut the door and I tried to unbuckle them because they were screaming... It's just a nightmare.' This was the first time Farquharson had mentioned trying to rescue his children, contradicting his earlier account that he hadn't been able to get to them. And this time he made no mention of chest pains.

Farquharson said he'd climbed out of the car thinking the water was only about a foot deep. He planned to run to the other side, drag Jai out and then rescue the younger two boys. He remembered he had dived 'three or four times' but then changed his mind and headed back to the highway to get help.

'It's just a big blur,' he said vaguely.

Farquharson spoke of his depression following his mum's death and mentioned his separation from Cindy. He also told the officers he'd been sick and on antibiotics for a throat infection. He said it had been cold in the car, so he turned the heater on. The warm air triggered the coughing fit and blackout.

The police found Farquharson's answers as troubling as his demeanour. As he'd done at the scene, he answered routine questions easily but remained sketchy about the accident itself. His answers were almost clinical and throughout the interview he seemed oddly calm. Despite his terrifying ordeal, Farquharson had taken the trouble to comb his hair and laughed aloud when Smith asked him if he'd been smoking dope. He'd coughed, on cue, when describing his coughing fit.

Most significantly, at no time during the interview did Farquharson mention his children by name or inquire if they'd been found. He did, however, ask repeatedly what was going to happen to him. In the end, Smith raised the subject of the children.

'Do you realise that the children have not made it out of the car?'
he said.

Showing no emotion, Farquharson replied, 'Ah, I gathered that.'
Then he asked again, 'What's the likely scenario for me?'

The seasoned policeman, convinced he was not getting the whole
story, asked if there was anything else he wanted to tell them.

Farquharson shook his head vigorously. 'No, well that's exactly
what happened,' he insisted. 'I've got no reason to lie or anything
of that nature.'

The officers left the hospital feeling distinctly uneasy. Blood
tests had showed no signs of alcohol or drugs, the patient's X-rays
were clear and revealed no chest infection, and his oxygen levels
were completely normal. What wasn't normal was Farquharson's
calm behaviour and his lack of concern for his missing children. By
contrast, in Winchelsea's community hospital, the children's heavily
sedated mother asked repeatedly if they'd found her babies yet.

When daylight broke over the tiny town, news of the terrible
Father's Day tragedy was making headline news everywhere. A trickle
of locals made their way out to the dam to place flowers in the mud
and on the water to honour the three little lives lost and the shattered
community rallied around the grief-stricken parents.

But Farquharson's bizarre story was not stacking up. Police experts
examining the scene had found no evidence to support his claims of a
blackout. There were no skid marks and the flattened grass leading to
the dam was more consistent with the vehicle simply rolling into the
water. Later, an examination of Farquharson's recovered car would
reveal that the vehicle's headlights, ignition and heater had all been
turned off. If he'd really been unconscious when the car left the road
and plunged into the dam, who had done this? With the lights off, the
car had been harder to locate in the darkness. And if Farquharson
really had blacked out and come to in the water, wouldn't he have
instinctively turned the car's interior lights on to check if his kids
were OK? He'd already claimed his coughing fit had been triggered
by turning the heater on. So who turned it off?

The police also noticed that the child safety lock on the rear door behind the driver's seat had been engaged, and that the handle on the rear passenger door was broken. With the child lock activated, and the other door handle not working, it would have been impossible for either door to be opened from the inside.

Most poignantly, the children's bodies had been out of their seatbelts, leaving police to conclude that Tyler must have attempted to free his baby brother in the back, while little Jai almost made it out of the car after his father, his small head discovered protruding from the open passenger door.

Further crucial evidence later emerged to cast doubt on Farquharson's strange story. Investigators the following day determined that the car had 'bounced like a stone' when it hit the water, skimming almost 30 metres across the dam. It sat on the surface for a short time and nose-dived when the driver's door opened. This made the father's account about his oldest son opening the door, and the car filling with water, impossible. Later a police re-enactment of the accident, using an identical car, further contradicted Farquharson's account. In a car fitted with internal cameras, with a police diver behind the wheel attached to a rope, it took just 16 seconds for the submerged car to fill with water and sink once the driver's door was opened. If Farquharson had been unconscious, how had his car travelled so far across the paddock to land at the farthest edge of the dam? Crashing through a fence would have slowed the vehicle down, but the distance Farquharson's vehicle travelled suggested it had gathered speed. More disturbing, three different manoeuvres of the steering wheel had been required for the car to travel from the highway to the dam, narrowly missing a tree in its path. Only a conscious driver could have managed this.

When Sergeant Smith discovered that the account Farquharson had given in his taped interview was different to the story he'd told Atkinson and McClelland, and varied again from the version he'd given the police and paramedics at the scene, he contacted a colleague in the Homicide Squad. By 8.30 on Tuesday morning the triple fatality had become a murder investigation.

Detectives Gerard Clanchy and Andrew Stamper were dispatched to Winchelsea to pick the father up and drive him back to Victoria Police headquarters in Melbourne for further questioning.

During the journey from Winchelsea, Farquharson was at pains to point out the Holter monitor he was wearing under his t-shirt. He told them the ECG device, wired to patches on his chest, was measuring his heart rhythms to determine whether a cardiac problem had caused his blackout. According to him, he was still so confused he'd had to ask his sister what day it was.

When Stamper asked about his marriage breakup, Farquharson claimed he and Cindy had simply drifted apart. He failed to mention his previous accusations about an affair, simply telling police she might be seeing someone now. He denied being jealous of Cindy's new man, saying he wasn't the sort of guy to be pushed aside and that no matter what, the children would always be his.

'The boys are owed the truth ... the boys, the family, the mother, everybody's got questions,' said Clanchy.

'Mmmmmm,' Rob replied.

The detectives said they'd understand if he'd made 'a horrible mistake'. If there was a different version to the account he'd given, he would still be treated with respect.

'No I'm telling you the truth ... I've got nothing to hide,' Farquharson protested. He said Cindy wasn't blaming him for this terrible accident because she knew how much he loved his children.

Again, when they asked specifically about the accident Farquharson couldn't remember much. He'd tried to get his kids out, even diving down a few times. But it was all a blur and the 'shock and all that set in'. He couldn't recall if he'd seen water, or if the headlights were on or off when he came to. He'd glimpsed headlights on the highway and decided to get help. He didn't remember being offered a phone, or being offered help to find the children, or asking for smokes. He just didn't know.

'A lot of don't know, isn't it?' remarked Stamper.

After being formally cautioned, Farquharson stuck to the story about the coughing fit. Twice in his video-taped interview he gave the detectives the same account, failing to mention anything about repeatedly diving into the dam to find his children. When pressed he said: 'I'm pretty certain I tried ... I think I went ... Yeah I did go down, cos I remember, I think I was swallowing a bit of water.' Contradicting himself, he then claimed the water pressure had stopped him 'going down'.

He no longer mentioned trying to get around to the far side of the car to get the boys out. Now he stated he'd got out of the car and swum straight back to the bank to get to the highway and get help.

But he hadn't got help, pointed out the detectives. He'd gone straight to his ex-wife's house instead. Why?

'I don't know ... I can't answer that,' Farquharson replied, squirming.

When they repeated the question later, he said, 'I had no phone, nothing to ring anyone or anything ... I don't know ... I said, "I need to see her to tell her, 'Look we've had an accident,' or 'take me to the police'" ... I don't know. She was probably the first thing — the first person I thought of. I don't know ... I can't answer that.'

'Did you drive off the highway deliberately into the dam?' Clanchy asked, eyeballing him.

Farquharson fidgeted and looked away. 'No, I did not.'

He said he felt 'pretty shithouse' knowing his children were dead. They were his world. He wouldn't even take a holiday because he'd miss them. That's why he'd never bothered with other women. If he was guilty of anything, it was being an overprotective father.

So why hadn't he unbuckled any of the boys' seatbelts?

'I've got two arms, two legs. I can't save three. How was I supposed to do it?' he said, his bottom lip quivering. 'I tried and tried.' His explanation was beyond belief and the detectives both thought the trembling lip was an act. He hadn't saved even one child, and had shown no genuine distress throughout the entire interview. Curiously, Farquharson avoided referring to his children by their names, referring to them instead as his 'family' or his 'kids'. But he was telling the truth, he protested. This was a terrible accident.

If the police didn't believe a word he said, Cindy Gambino clung desperately to his outlandish explanation. Paralysed by the trauma of losing her children, she believed her ex-husband loved their boys as much as she did. It was unthinkable to contemplate that the man she'd spent all those years with could be capable of such a heinous act. If he was, then what did that say about her own judgement? Cindy's denial became a subconscious survival mechanism that kept her upright for the next five years until she finally saw the truth.

When news leaked out that Farquharson had been interviewed by Homicide detectives, Cindy and her family were outraged. In a show of support her family wrote Rob a card and she signed it from her hospital bed. As Farquharson was released without charge, her father, Bob Gambino, stood on the steps of Winchelsea Hospital holding up the framed photograph his daughter had given the children's father. Her brother Scott read a statement saying this was a terrible tragedy and a difficult time for both families. By the next day, Cindy's photo of her three boys had found its way into the news and would return to haunt her throughout the legal marathon.

While the community's heart bled for the grieving parents, damning new evidence began to emerge that revealed a more chilling story behind the triple drowning.

Since hearing about the accident, Farquharson's closest friend, Gregory King, had been in hiding. Unable to sleep or eat, he'd been agonising over a disturbing conversation he'd had with his mate three or four months earlier. The conversation was now giving him nightmares and he'd been unable to work because he was plagued with waking visions of the drowning children. When he returned to work he kept bursting into tears and his boss, a former policeman, rang Geelong police and suggested it might be worthwhile speaking to King about his friend Robert Farquharson.

In a statement on 9 September, King recalled some of the conversation, which had taken place on a Friday night as he sat outside Winchelsea's fish-and-chip shop waiting for his children, who were inside picking up chips.

Farquharson was inside and came out to talk to his friend. While they chatted, Cindy turned up in the new Commodore, greeting King and her ex-husband, who ignored her. When she disappeared into the chip shop King chided Farquharson, telling him he needed to move on.

'Move on, how?' Farquharson snapped. 'I've got nothing. Nobody does that to me and gets away with it. It's all her fault.'

Surprised, King asked, 'What is?'

'Take that Sports Pack car Cindy pulled up in. I paid $30 000 for it, she wanted it and they are fucking driving it. Look what I'm driving — the fucking shit one.'

Farquharson then complained about the new house they'd been building, saying Cindy always wanted the best of everything, even when they couldn't afford it. The conversation turned to her new man, Moules.

'Now it looks like she wants to marry that fucking dickhead,' Farquharson seethed. 'There's no way I am going to let him and her and the kids fucking live in my house together and I have to fucking pay for it and I also have to pay fucking maintenance for the kids. No way.'

By now he was fuming. 'She's going to pay big time! I'll take away the most important thing that means to her.'

'What do you mean?' King asked, shocked.

Farquharson muttered something about a dream where he went into a dam. Greg started to ask what he meant, but his children came out of the shop with their chips and the conversation halted.

Since the accident, King had been distraught about the conversation, blaming himself for failing to act on it.

King and Farquharson had been friends for over 20 years and had met when they both worked for the local council. They'd played sport together, drank together at the local pub and spent time at each other's homes. King had been a guest at Robert and Cindy's wedding, though contact had dwindled when they both became fathers.

While Cindy Gambino had believed her ex-husband had been moving on after the break up, King told a very different story. The Farquharsons' relationship had always been troubled, he recalled. The couple were always niggling at each other and arguing about money. Having children and building a new house put even more pressure on them. He said Farquharson was never happy and 'always had something to bitch about' — mostly his wife's spending. His complaining got worse after the separation. He hated his job and called Cindy a bitch when he found out about her new man.

After the separation, Farquharson had been so depressed that he'd been contemplating suicide. In late 2004 he'd told King he'd been thinking of driving into a tree, or driving his car off a cliff. A few months later, King spied his mate sitting in his car beside the highway. Later Farquharson confessed he'd been considering 'lining up a truck'.

Concerned, King mentioned it to his wife, but they'd dismissed it as 'just Robbie being Robbie again'.

At the time he made that first statement, King was highly distressed and struggling to recall the whole conversation, though more details slowly began to return in bits and pieces. A few days later King added to his statement. He remembered that when Farquharson mentioned the dream, it was about an accident where he survived but his kids didn't. And when he'd made the threat to pay Cindy back 'big time' by taking away the thing that mattered most to her, he'd gestured his head towards the chip shop window where his three children were standing at the time.

'What ... the kids?' Greg had replied, stunned. 'You don't even dream of that stuff, Robbie.'

At the time, King hadn't taken the threats seriously. After all, Farquharson hadn't acted on his earlier suicide threats. He believed Robbie was just talking 'bullshit'.

King agreed to help police elicit a confession. The day after the town closed down for the children's funeral, he visited Farquharson at his father's wearing a hidden wire, and covertly recorded their conversation. In it Farquharson grizzled about money. He complained that his employer was only paying 80 per cent of his wages while he was off sick after the accident, even though he'd lost three children, and said he still had the mortgage to pay on the new home Cindy didn't want. The shit car, which had been hauled from the dam, was still on his mind. Farquharson said blackly: 'At least it will save me on petrol!'

King nervously raised the payback threat Farquharson had made outside the chip shop. He said he hoped this had nothing to do with the accident.

'No, no, no, no, no . . . You know I would never . . . No,' the suspect protested.

When King revealed that the police wanted to speak to him, Farquharson warned him not to mention that he'd been angry with Cindy, and insisted his payback talk was 'just a figure of speech' said in anger.

'No way would I do anything like that. What, I'm not a mongrel, and I'm not a bastard, and I'm not an arsehole — I'm not a cunt. I would never, ever, ever. That has never, ever entered my mind.'

Farquharson instructed his mate to tell the police that he was a great dad and top bloke.

'Always say all the positive things that you know,' Farquharson cajoled.

But handing the tape over to police, King felt anything but positive. He felt even less positive after secretly taping a second conversation with Farquharson when he raised the payback threat again.

'That was all bullshit talk of being upset,' snapped Farquharson. 'I was just pissed off that I had this really good car, and that cunt was driving it. That's what I was angry about — and I was angry with her — with him,' he elaborated.

But what about the dream, where Rob survived and the kids didn't?

'No, no, no, no, no,' Rob protested. 'I never, never said that. You're getting it all wrong. You're getting it all twisted. I mean one day she's going to wake up that I'm not as weak as piss as what she thought, in the sense of I'm going to accomplish something.'

This didn't make sense to King. But Farquharson was playing the sympathy card, saying he was 'gutted' and 'cut deep' that his own mate could think he'd harm his own children. He reminded King he'd been sick at the time of the accident, 'coughing his guts up . . .

fainting and all that stuff.' Farquharson claimed he'd had an earlier dizzy turn while talking on the phone to Cindy. Yet at the hospital after the accident he'd told paramedics and doctors that he had no history of blackouts.

'If you think that I could look in the mother of my kids' eyes and tell her a lie and walk away, I'm not an animal,' Farquharson protested. Even his psychologist had told police he didn't fit the profile.

'When people do these things it's a very planned thing,' he told King. But that was exactly what was eating at Greg. This stuff about a dream where his mate's kids died in an accident and he survived had been mentioned a whole three months earlier.

'You've got to get that out of your head,' Farquharson snapped.

When King mentioned he was going to see a counsellor, his mate became very rattled.

'Don't go mentioning that,' he said, panicking. 'It would start something up that's not there ... it's only going to stir up bloody crap. But I'm not trying to justify myself or trying to convince you — I'm just telling you. I think if you just clear that out of your head you are going to feel a little better.'

But King said the waking visions were sending him 'stupid'. Why? Farquharson asked, puzzled. Was King worrying something like this might happen to him too?

Farquharson's inability to understand this is significant. His mate was describing classic flashback symptoms of post-traumatic stress, which many would have expected the only survivor of this terrible ordeal to have been experiencing himself. Yet it's clear from Farquharson's response that he had no understanding of what his troubled mate was describing.

Two other secret tape recordings were added to the growing evidence from secretly bugged conversations between the suspect and the children's shattered mother.

The police were listening in when Farquharson telephoned his ex-wife on 20 September. Asked again what he remembered about the accident, he stuck to the story about the coughing blackout. But the account was changing. Now when he came to, he said he thought he was on the side of the road and made no mention of floating on the water, or having water in his car. He claimed the water only poured in after Jai opened his door.

Farquharson complained that some people were blaming him but insisted he'd never hurt his children. Cindy believed him, but asked why he hadn't stayed at the car and tried to save the kids. 'That might have saved time,' she reasoned. Her question upset Farquharson, who cut the conversation short.

The police were listening in again on 1 October when Cindy told Farquharson that detectives wanted to interview her. Sounding worried, Farquharson warned her to be careful, saying the police were 'full of shit'. They were already trying to 'twist things around' and intimidate people, including Greg King.

Cindy's curiosity was piqued. Why did they want to speak with Greg King?

They probably wanted background, he said. They'd already spoken to his psychologist.

'It's just so hard for me,' he whined.

Cindy returned to the accident, asking if he knew how the headlights had been turned off.

'I may have turned them off or something, I don't know ... You know what I mean?' Farquharson replied. 'I could have done anything. I don't know. Probably when it first happened ... I thought I was in a ditch.'

Cindy made no reply and Farquharson added, 'So I stopped the car, thinking, you know, just in case ... if it was a fire. I don't know.'

Cindy reminded him about his earlier account when he said he'd woken up to find water in the car.

Farquharson hesitated. 'I can't remember everything, you know what I mean.'

The police zoomed in on Farquharson's admission that he'd stopped his car in case it was on fire. This was new and contradicted his previous claims of waking from the blackout to find his car had come to a halt on its own. He'd also admitted turning the headlights off, something he'd earlier denied.

By 19 December Gregory King had fully remembered the entire fish-and-chip-shop conversation. What he told police was startling. Not only did he reaffirm the information he'd already given them, he'd remembered additional chilling details about Farquharson's threat to pay Cindy back. When Farquharson had threatened to take away the thing that mattered the most to Cindy, King had asked if he meant he was going to take the children off her.

But Farquharson had looked him straight in the eye and said, 'No, kill them!'

Shocked, King had responded, 'That's bullshit. That's your own flesh and blood, Robbie.'

Farquharson replied, 'So, I hate them.'

'You'd go to jail,' King warned.

'No I won't. I'd kill myself before it gets to that.'

King asked, 'What would you do?'

That's when Farquharson mentioned the accident in the dam, which he'd survive but his kids wouldn't. The accident would happen 'somewhere close by' and on a special day like Father's Day, when he would be the one to have the children for the last time.

'Then every Father's Day she would suffer for the rest of her life,' Farquharson said.

King had said, 'You don't even dream of that, Robbie.' As his own kids bounded out of the shop, King told his mate, 'You deserve to get caught.'

At home, King told his wife, Mary, what Farquharson had said. They agreed this was Robbie 'bullshitting again'.

This third statement was referred to as the 'extreme' version of the fish-and-chip-shop conversation, and became the crux of the police evidence against Farquharson. In a largely circumstantial case, it not only demonstrated his intent to kill his children, but provided his motive for murder — to pay Cindy back for ending their marriage.

Farquharson had taken away the most important thing in Cindy Gambino's life in an accident where he survived and the kids didn't. More disturbing, he'd stuck around to deliver the news himself so he could see the pain his crime had caused, and watch her suffer for the rest of her life.

Robert Farquharson was arrested and charged with three counts of murder. He spent Christmas in custody and was bailed in time for what should have been Bailey's third birthday on 31 December.

'Nobody believes it — nobody in this family,' Cindy's Uncle Tillio Gambino told reporters. The family were sticking by him, including his former wife. They all believed he was innocent.

*

Farquharson's later trials would ultimately turn on two conflicting arguments: the Crown's claim that this was a deliberately planned murder of three innocent children by their vengeful father; and the defence's counterclaim that Farquharson was a loving dad, 'down-trodden by planet earth' and the victim of a dreadful freak accident.

If Gregory King was the prosecution's star witness with his recollections of the damning conversation that provided a motive for the murders, the children's mother, crippled by denial, would be the trump card for the defence.

When Farquharson's first trial finally opened in the Victorian Supreme Court in Melbourne in August 2007, the Crown relied on three main strands of evidence. First was the medical evidence, which they said proved that Farquharson's tale about a coughing blackout was a lie. Second was the reconstruction and mechanical evidence, which would show that the car had been deliberately driven off the road and into the dam. And third was the damning evidence of King. This evidence, combined with Farquharson's bizarre behaviour and ever-evolving story after the tragedy, would prove beyond a doubt that he had callously killed his children to punish their mother for ending the marriage.

Paralysed by denial and clinging to the belief that Farquharson was innocent, Cindy Gambino told the trial only the positive things about their failed marriage. She did not mention Farquharson's relentless sexual harassment of her — how he grabbed her breasts while she juggled hot vegetables, or groped her private parts so roughly while she bathed her children that it hurt. Cindy failed to mention the constant put-downs, how Farquharson called her 'fat mumma', how he teased Jai until he burst into tears, prompting outrage from her family. Neither did she mention Farquharson pinning her up against a wall, or threatening her after the breakup that she shouldn't underestimate him. Like King, she'd thought Rob was 'bullshitting'.

Instead, the jury heard all about the devoted dad who would never have harmed a hair on his children's heads. Still, her description of her ex-husband's behaviour at the dam was a worry.

'There was no movement ... nothing,' said Cindy. 'He wasn't doing anything — he was just like in a trance.' Her graphic account of the scene on her doorstep, and later at the dam, reduced some jurors to tears.

Exactly how the car had wound up in the dam was the most hotly contested subject with a procession of witnesses for the Crown and the defence giving conflicting technical and mechanical evidence.

Police experts told how the car could only have gone off the road and into the dam as it had if it was being steered by a conscious driver. That driver had to have performed three separate manoeuvres of the steering wheel: the first directed the car off the road, the second to straighten it up, the third to miss a tree in its path. This contradicted Farquharson's claim of being unconscious behind the wheel. An expert for the defence said a fault with the steering could have caused the car to veer to the right.

The medical evidence was at odds too. A thoracic specialist for the Crown said it was unlikely that Farquharson had ever suffered from cough syncope, which was mostly diagnosed in middle-aged men suffering from obstructive airways disease. Another doctor said the rare condition was unlikely in someone with normal heart, lung and neurological functions and doubted Farquharson had ever suffered a coughing blackout before the accident. Doctors for the defence believed he did have the rare condition, though they couldn't explain how a window cleaner from Winchelsea would be familiar with the medical term 'grey out', which he used when describing his blackout later to a doctor. Only thoracic specialists would be familiar with that expression. This suggested strongly that Farquharson had researched the rare condition, laying the ground for his 'accident' by faking a couple of coughing fits and dizzy spells before and after the tragedy to bolster his story.

What the jury never heard was that Farquharson had been seen by a psychologist in Geelong on 11 November 2004, just after his separation from Cindy, and he had expressed suicidal thoughts. Dr David Sullivan had been so alarmed that he'd immediately written to Farquharson's GP expressing concern that Farquharson was planning suicide, just as King had told the police.

'I'm concerned about the potential for Mr Farquharson to behave impulsively, and accordingly I have asked him to consider making a commitment to seek out and speak with somebody he trusts when he feels vulnerable,' Sullivan wrote.

Farquharson's GP responded by making an immediate appointment for him to be assessed by a psychiatric service and arranged for him to come into the surgery a few days later. The doctor recommended ongoing psychological treatment with Dr Sullivan, but Farquharson claimed he couldn't afford it. Still, the issue of Farquharson's suicidal ideation influenced the GP's subsequent management of his depression. He ensured the patient attended psychiatric counselling and monitored him through regular follow-up appointments.

Though Dr Sullivan was ultimately never called to give evidence, his report shed new light on a case where the police had always considered the possibility that this was a murder–suicide gone wrong.

After hearing legal argument about this report in the jury's absence, Justice Philip Cummins said, 'It's always seemed to me that although the prosecution case is that he intended to murder the children, there are two ways that it can be looked at. One way is that he intended to murder the children, full stop; the motive being to get back at Cindy. The second is that he intended to kill himself and murder the children, and he opted out at the last minute, either just for himself or perhaps the four of them — but failed to rescue them.'

But it supported King's testimony that Farquharson had been contemplating suicide, and had threatened to harm the children. And though the witness was never called, it was clear Farquharson had taken Sullivan's advice and confided in someone he trusted when he felt vulnerable. He just hadn't expected his good mate to blab.

Throughout his first trial, Robert Farquharson remained as silent as he'd been at the dam, opting not to give evidence on oath.

Speaking for him, his defence barrister, Peter Morrissey SC, said the loving dad was a 'chubby smoker' with a respiratory ailment that made him a likely candidate for cough syncope. Such a blackout had caused him to black out and lose control of his car, resulting in the tragic accident that killed his children. The case was circumstantial. Why would a father about to murder his children invite his close friend to join them for dinner and buy his children presents?

But prosecutor Jeremy Rapke QC said there were two possible views of the Crown's case, both involving murder. One view was that on a sudden impulse, the accused father had decided to kill his children by driving his car into a dam. The other possibility was that he'd been contemplating it over time as an act 'of profound vindictiveness' towards his estranged wife. Either way it was murder.

The jury agreed. In October 2007 Robert Farquharson was found guilty of the three murders and subsequently sentenced to life without parole.

'You wiped out your entire family in one act,' Justice Cummins said, sentencing him in November. 'Only two parents remained; you, because you had always intended to save yourself; and their mother, because you intended her to have a life of suffering.'

The judge said Farquharson's 'burning resentment' about financing his estranged wife's new life led to a 'dark contemplation'.

Cindy Gambino refused to accept this, telling *Woman's Day* magazine that an innocent father was behind bars for a crime he had not committed. But though she didn't blame him for her children's deaths, he was still accountable for the tragedy, because he shouldn't have driven that night. That made him guilty of negligence, not murder. She told Channel Nine's *Sixty Minutes* show the same thing. These comments resulted in her being vilified. Among the many kindly letters she received, there was also anonymous hate mail. One angry writer told her she must be stupid to believe such a pathetic story, or to consider supporting a man who overwhelming evidence showed had murdered her children in cold blood. Even the interviewer on *Sixty Minutes* asked Cindy if she considered herself naive for still believing in her ex-husband's innocence when everyone around her was convinced this was a revenge murder.

The personal attacks continued after the TV show. A woman recognising her in a Geelong shop bailed her up and told her she was a stupid mother. Cindy went home in tears and hid herself away. Her children weren't dead because of anything she'd done wrong. Their deaths had ripped her life apart and now complete strangers felt entitled to tear what was left of her to pieces.

In the two years that followed, Cindy Gambino continued to support her estranged husband's fight to clear his name. But despite her constant letters begging to visit him in prison, she never received a reply. It made no sense to Farquharson's biggest supporter that she hadn't received a single card or a phone call, not even on Mother's Day, or on the anniversary of their children's deaths. As the months passed, Cindy's grief and disappointment turned to outrage and anger. Perhaps Farquharson had something to hide after all? Was this why he hadn't given evidence at his trial?

In late 2008 she wrote to Farquharson again, asking, 'Is this all my fault because we separated? My existence is hell — I hate myself and what this has done to me. I live on so many drugs to keep me going and get me out of bed. I don't have many OK days.' Cindy, battling an addiction to painkillers and struggling to bond with a new toddler son, asked again, 'Did I cause all this, or was it just a plain and simple accident?'

Stephen Moules, now her partner and father of their son Hezekiah, had always believed Farquharson was as guilty as sin and hoped Cindy, who had been blind to the truth, might soon see it too.

After penning another, angrier, letter, she was contacted by a grief counsellor who had been supporting Farquharson in prison. At a meeting with Cindy, he explained that Farquharson was struggling to deal with his loss behind bars, and that a meeting would be too damaging for him. He said Farquharson was also suffering from post-traumatic stress, experiencing flashbacks in prison where he heard himself screaming above the water in the darkness.

But why hadn't Rob taken the stand at the trial and told the jury: 'I'm innocent ... I did not do this!' The counsellor said this had been his lawyer's advice.

Cindy was troubled. She needed to look him in the eye to know if he was innocent or not. The damaged mother now had her doubts. It was just a matter of time.

But from behind bars Farquharson continued to protest his innocence and lodged an appeal against his three murder convictions and his life sentence.

The appeal was heard in June 2009 at the Victorian Court of Appeal, where the defence argued that the Crown had withheld crucial information at Farquharson's trial in relation to its star witness Gregory King. King had been facing charges arising from an assault at the time of the trial, and the defence contended he'd struck a deal with the police to testify in exchange for a letter of support when he faced the Geelong Magistrates Court in December 2007.

The defence argued they'd been denied the chance at trial to question King about his own character, after the Crown posed the question to the jury, 'Why would this witness lie?'

'There is a very easy answer to that question,' contended Mr Morrissey. He'd lied because it was in his interests.

The defence also launched a stinging attack on the original trial judge, Justice Philip Cummins, and several expert witnesses. They contended that Justice Cummins had failed to properly instruct the jury on key evidence, including the police reconstruction of how the car had ploughed into the dam.

On 17 December 2009, as Cindy nursed another new baby son, Isaiah, Farquharson's appeal was upheld by the Victorian Court of Appeal, which overturned all three murder convictions and quashed his sentence. Farquharson was later bailed, pending a new trial, and was free in time for Christmas.

The court upheld five of his 24 grounds of appeal, all of them relating in one way or another to Gregory King's evidence. Chief Justice Marilyn Warren said part of the difficulty in the case was that King had given three statements to police, each progressively more damning than the last about what he claimed to have been told outside the fish-and-chip-shop. By King's final statement, what had begun as a general threat to pay Cindy back 'big time' had become a direct threat by Farquharson to kill his children in an accident involving a dam on Father's Day. This 'extreme' allegation was the version the Crown had relied upon when King gave his evidence at the trial.

But in the taped conversations before he made his final statement, the appeal justices ruled that King hadn't raised the specific threat he later mentioned in the extreme allegation. The trial judge had failed to point this out to the jury, or to instruct them fully on the differences between the statements. The Crown had also failed to disclose the fact that King faced criminal charges of his own. The prosecution had not considered it an issue because King hadn't been charged at the time he made his statements to police. The appeal court agreed that the information was 'rationally probative' but should have been disclosed to the jury even if it had been of limited value.

The news came as a blow to Cindy, who was now questioning Farquharson's innocence. She studied the new baby boy asleep in her arms and felt as though her children had just died all over again.

By the time Farquharson's new trial began in May 2010, his former wife had done a complete turnaround. At the first hearing she'd only spoken for her ex-husband, firmly believing he was innocent. This time, convinced of his guilt, she would be a voice for her children.

Cindy had not glimpsed Farquharson since he'd been jailed in 2007. Seeing him squirming in the dock as she gave evidence at his new trial made her so furious that when she was asked to describe their failing marriage, her lip instinctively curled into the snarl of a wounded animal. When the defence confronted her with a photograph of her ex-husband propping her up at her children's funeral, Farquharson crying crocodile tears as three small white coffins were lifted into the hearse, Cindy erupted.

That photo, capturing the entire charade, made her physically sick now she could see the truth. Farquharson had robbed her of her children, delivering the news himself so he could witness her distress first hand. Then he'd stuck around to watch her suffering at the dam and through the funeral, where he'd played the grieving father. He had watched her relive her suffering through one trial and was using the system to punish her again. In a sick joke, Cindy later learned he intended the punishment to follow her beyond the grave, booking a burial plot for himself beside her and the children he'd murdered.

While the killer dad had been awaiting trial, someone had chiselled his name off the children's headstone at Winchelsea Cemetery. His defence lawyer now asked Cindy if she was the culprit.

'Oh you disgust me,' she spat. 'That's my children's final resting place. That was my children's headstone ... I can't help it if my children's father's name was Robert Farquharson. I would never, ever do anything like that to my children. How dare you.'

The defence confronted her with cuttings from her magazine interview and grabs from her TV interviews when she'd supported Farquharson's innocence. Five years had changed many things, she said. She'd been in denial then.

At the second trial, startling new evidence emerged from a motorist who had been following Farquharson's car along the Princes Highway that fateful night. Warrnambool dairy farmer Mrs Dawn Waite remembered following an old white Commodore along an open stretch of road towards Winchelsea at around 7.15 p.m., and being concerned about the erratic driving of the motorist ahead. When the car began to veer back and forth across the white line, braking and slowing down, Mrs Waite flashed her lights to indicate her intention to overtake.

As she passed, she gestured to the male driver, who appeared not to see her. She had a clear view into the car, and noticed he appeared to be gazing, transfixed, to his right as if he was studying something in his side-view mirror. He was fully conscious when she overtook and was certainly not coughing. She observed three small boys squashed in the back seat, which is in conflict with Farquharson's evidence that Jai was in the front passenger seat. Seconds after overtaking, Mrs Waite looked in her rear-vision mirror, and observed the car headlights descending down the overpass and suddenly veering right.

She assumed the driver must have turned onto a side road, and thought no more about it until she saw the same white car being hauled from the dam on the next day's TV news.

Despite a police appeal for witnesses, Mrs Waite did not come forward, explaining that she'd been ill at the time and was later diagnosed with cancer, requiring chemotherapy. But when she'd learned Farquharson had been freed pending a retrial, she immediately contacted the police and made a statement. This damning new evidence would ultimately seal Farquharson's fate.

Other damning evidence came from the accused himself. In his first trial, Robert Farquharson had not given evidence. This was an effective defence strategy that denied an aggressive Crown prosecutor the opportunity to pick his story to pieces. It had been a wise move. At the second trial Farquharson took the stand, and he made a terrible witness. Even in his evidence in chief there was much he could not remember or explain.

Perhaps his mechanic had accidentally activated the child safety lock. Maybe Bailey had reached from the opposite side of the back seat and done it. Maybe Jai had turned the headlights off and fiddled with the heater and car ignition.

He didn't recall Atkinson offering to help find the children, or handing him his mobile and suggesting he call for help, though he did remember saying he thought his kids were dead.

'In me [sic] heart I was hoping that wasn't happening,' he said. Farquharson couldn't remember asking anyone for smokes, or recall why he hadn't jumped into the dam to help find his children.

'I have been sitting in here listening to all different evidence and I am getting a bit confused with a lot of stuff,' he complained. 'I'm trying to fill in the gaps meself [sic] to find out why this accident happened.'

His confusion extended to his conversations with the paramedics and the police. It was all one big blur, though he remembered he had *not* told King he hated his kids and was planning to kill them. That conversation had been misinterpreted. Despite saying the car had sunk after Jai opened his door, he now remembered it had been too dark to see a thing. The car only sank after he got out.

The holes in his story widened with every probing question. He couldn't remember why he'd asked for a lift to Cindy's place, and denied lying to a respiratory doctor who saw him after the accident by claiming he'd lost consciousness twice before the tragedy. And he denied that he'd collapsed in prison and again at his sister's while on bail awaiting his second trial, in a bid to bolster his lie.

In closing for the prosecution, Mr Tinney said that Robert Farquharson had not been able to let go of his resentment, anger and sadness after his separation. He nurtured those negative feelings towards his former wife.

'In the end, these feelings overwhelmed him and led him to take an unspeakable revenge.' His 'delicious reward' was delivering the shattering news to the true target of his rage — the mother of his children.

Despite the defence's attempts to portray Farquharson as a down-trodden simple country bloke who was not sophisticated enough or Machiavellian enough to have concocted such an elaborate murder plot, the jury did not agree.

After 11 weeks of evidence, Farquharson was found guilty for the second time. In November 2010, he was jailed for life for the second time. This time, however, the judge ordered him to serve a minimum of 33 years on each of the revenge murders, before being eligible for parole. This time Cindy agreed justice had been done.

Justice Lex Lasry, sentencing Farquharson, said in his 38 years of practising law, the tragedy of this crime defied imagination. 'Appreciable thought' had gone into the murders, and when he delivered the news to the children's mother, he'd plunged her into 'the most horrible odyssey' of her life.

'You were devoid of any interest or concern for your children or even upon the recovery of their bodies,' said Justice Lasry, noting that Farquharson's lack of remorse was implicit in his ongoing protests of innocence.

Some wondered if it was more strategic than that. By continuing the lie, he could prolong his true target's suffering. Dragging Cindy back to court and having her relive the anguish allowed him to observe her torment over and over again. Cindy's nightmare was not over yet and he appealed again, stating his convictions and sentence were 'unsafe and unsatisfactory'.

In December 2012 the Victorian Court of Appeal rejected Farquharson's appeal. His lawyers had contended that the police traffic expert's evidence was unreliable as was King's recollection of the fish-and-chip-shop conversation. They said the Crown hadn't proved beyond reasonable doubt that Farquharson's account of the accident was not credible. Getting behind the wheel when he was sick had compromised his driving and put his children and other road users at risk. This was negligence, the lawyers contended, and the jury should have been given the option of considering the lesser charge of manslaughter.

The Victorian Court of Appeal rejected the appeal. The evidence of the police expert had to be taken in context with the unchallenged evidence of Dawn Waite and other significant strands of evidence. The accused's explanation about the payback threat had been implausible and strengthened the prosecution's case argument that King had been telling the truth. More significantly, Farquharson's unusual behaviour after the tragedy made it difficult to reconcile his claims that his children's deaths were accidental. As for manslaughter, it had never been raised in the two earlier trials or previous appeal and was not an issue in this case. This ground was dismissed and the appeal thrown out.

Still Farquharson kept the legal marathon going, wasting taxpayers' money and milking the system for all it was worth. In a last ditch bid for freedom in August 2013, Robert Farquharson asked the High Court of Australia for special leave to take his appeal to Canberra. A tribunal of justices rejected the plea.

Today the lifelong suffering Robert Farquharson intended to inflict upon his former wife continues.

Now married to Stephen Moules, the birth of their children was devoid of the same carefree joy she'd experienced at the arrival of Jai, Tyler and Bailey. Her grief made it difficult to bond with her babies, who have grown up in a house where her depression and post traumatic stress resulted in her absence during repeated spells of hospitalisation. In the lead-up to the second trial, an accidental overdose of painkillers almost killed her. When the second appeal was pending, Cindy drove her car into a tree in a failed suicide attempt. Moules' own two sons have also grown up with the spectre of three little boys who would never grow old. Ironically, Zach and Luke have never officially been acknowledged to have been victims of Farquharson's crime.

Cindy's new partner believes the events of that night have caused him to grow old before his time. Like Cindy, he battles constant ailments that he believes are the physical symptoms of years of emotional trauma. They both suffer post traumatic stress. He hasn't been able to dive in the water since.

Today, as the road-widening works along the Princes Highway outside Winchelsea near completion, three small white crosses are a haunting reminder of the terrible tragedy that drove a wedge through the tiny town's big heart, a heart that remains broken. It is a painful landmark that Cindy glimpses each time she drives along the highway in and out of town.

'Rob meant this pain to last a lifetime — and it will,' the mother reflects.

But she won't be letting that suffering follow her into the afterlife, staking her claim on the burial plot that was among the assets frozen after Farquharson's conviction. Almost ten years after the murders, the issue of the frozen assets has been resolved, though the argument over the burial plot continues.

'He won't be buried anywhere near me or our children,' she said. 'He can rot in hell.'

CHAPTER 4

'Say goodbye to your children — you'll never see them again.'

The story of Peta Barnes and Darcey Freeman

The first day of the new Victorian school term in late January 2009, opened to hot northerly winds and searing temperatures. Youngsters across the state sweltered in their new uniforms as they headed off to school, many for the first time.

In the small coastal township of Aireys Inlet, a stone's throw from the popular surf town of Lorne (where killer father Robert Farquharson had once worked as a window cleaner), another father of three was in a panic as he dashed around his parents' beach house scrambling to get his kids into the car in time for the most important day in the Australian school calendar.

Two days earlier, on 27 January, Arthur Philip Freeman had lost a bitter and protracted custody battle for his three children — a six-year-old son, his four-year-old daughter Darcey, and his youngest son aged 23 months.

Freeman's separation from his ex-wife, Peta Barnes, two years earlier had been anything but amicable, and his growing animosity towards his ex-wife, and towards a justice system he considered to be weighted in favour of mothers, had been noted by the professionals involved during the negotiation process.

Since their divorce in June 2007, the parents had shared custody of the three youngsters, with each parent having the children for three days every other week and four days on alternate weeks. They met in McDonald's in Kew for the twice-weekly handover like scores of other separated parents.

But the new arrangements reached on 27 January meant the divorced father would now only have custody of his children on alternate weekends, plus a few hours every other Thursday evening.

Freeman's determination to share the care of his children had bordered on obsession as the couple's lawyers attempted to negotiate a mutually agreeable arrangement between the parents. By the time the final arrangement was agreed upon in January, there was no obvious sign of his previous bitterness towards the children's mother. Peta Barnes certainly saw no outward signs that her ex-husband was angry or resentful about his reduced access. She would later tell police that she thought Freeman seemed 'happy' with the new care arrangements.

But Peta was wrong. While she returned to her home in the leafy Melbourne suburb of Hawthorn, Arthur Freeman was making his way back to his chaotic flat, where he spent hours on the phone to friends angrily venting about the decision over access. Later, he headed across the city in his white Land Cruiser towards the Great Ocean Road. There, in the pretty fishing town of Aireys Inlet, his children were spending the last couple of days of the long summer holiday with their paternal grandparents, Peter and Norma Freeman. It had been decided that the children would escape the sultry temperatures in the city, to enjoy a few days at his parents' beach house on the coast, where it would be cooler and he would join them once the new access arrangements were sorted out.

The traffic was light at 10 p.m. on that sticky Tuesday evening when the 35-year-old computer expert drove over Melbourne's landmark West Gate Bridge towards the Princes Freeway, knowing that he would only have another two days with his children before handing them over to their mother for two weeks.

But Freeman was still ruminating on his reduced access when he made another call, this time to an old friend, Aussie expat Elizabeth Lam, who lived in the UK. Between 10 p.m. and 1.54 a.m. the following morning, Arthur Freeman phoned his friend nine times, but only managed to get through to her answering machine.

When he finally arrived in Aireys Inlet it was midnight and he was still complaining. He appeared particularly upset about the psychological assessment of him, which had been prepared during the custody process, and which he believed portrayed him in an unfair and unreasonable light. Freeman told his parents that he had been 'ambushed' by the system. Peter and Norma would later recall him arriving in 'a bit of a trance'.

It had been agreed that Freeman would return the children to the gates of St Joseph's Primary School in Hawthorn early on Thursday 29 January in time for the new school term. The day was particularly important because it was their daughter Darcey's first day of school. The four-year-old, described by her family as a determined little girl with a passion for music and dancing, was thrilled to be joining her older brother at 'big school'.

On the Wednesday evening Peta, aware of her daughter's mounting excitement, telephoned her former husband and asked to speak to her children. Freeman curtly told her the youngsters were not with him and were not around to chat to her. He promised he would get them to give her a call the following morning before they left for the return drive to the city. The call was never made.

While Arthur Freeman was up bright and early on the Thursday morning, in plenty of time for his little girl's big day, Darcey's first day at school was apparently not foremost in his mind. At 6 a.m. he was back on the phone again, desperately wanting to speak with his friend Elizabeth Lam about the access agreement even though it had been mutually accepted after negotiation by both parties. By 8.08 he had made seven phone calls but had still not managed to speak to her.

By 7.30 a.m., while Peta Barnes and her mother, Iris, were getting ready for Darcey's milestone, tensions down at the holiday house in Aireys Inlet were rising. Arthur Freeman was now running late, and his elderly parents, observing their son's stress, thought he seemed tired and agitated as he herded the three youngsters towards the car for their trip back to the city. Despite the significance of her big day, Darcey was not ready when Freeman left his parents' house. While his oldest son had appeared for breakfast, already dressed in his school uniform, Darcey's new uniform and school shoes had been left behind when her father left his cluttered flat in Hawthorn. He had not even found the time to prepare the older children's school lunches and his parents observed their son was anxious and distracted as he piled his children and their school bags into the back seat of the car.

Peter Freeman, a school principal, was so concerned about his son's demeanour that he offered to accompany him on the trip to the city. When Freeman rejected his offer, the worried grandfather suggested it might be better if the children missed the first day of school altogether and they all remained at home instead. This was not an option, argued Freeman; the children's mother would be waiting for them.

Freeman's mother, Norma, would later tell the police that she recalled her son being 'short' with her when he left the house and obviously stressed. But despite her concerns for Arthur, she had no cause to feel worried about her three grandchildren.

If Arthur Freeman was weary and distracted when he left Aireys Inlet, by the time he reached the Princes Freeway his stress levels were building further. In the back seat of the Toyota, the two older children played games, completely unaware of their father's soaring anxiety. Beside them, their little brother sipped quietly on his drink bottle and looked out of the window at the scorched fields.

There were no outward indications that Freeman was harbouring any sinister intentions or was mentally unravelling when he called his sister, Megan Toet, from his mobile phone for a chat as he drove. Freeman's sister would later tell police that throughout their phone conversation, Arthur had seemed more worried about having nothing to give his older children for their school lunches. The traffic was already building by then, she would recall, because her brother told her that he did not think he would make it to school on time.

During the drive from Aireys Inlet, Freeman made another call to his English friend. It was now 8.09 a.m. — after 10 p.m. in Britain — when Elizabeth Lam finally picked up the phone. But in this conversation he was no longer concerned about school lunches or traffic; he was back on his soapbox, complaining again about his reduced access. His children had been taken away from him. Elizabeth Lam listened sympathetically as the divorced dad sobbed down the phone. Elizabeth had known the Freemans during the six years they'd spent working and living in England. A former colleague of Peta's, she remembered each of their three children being born and was aware of the problems within the family over their decision to return to Australia in 2006.

She would later tell Australian police that the conversation revolved around the recent custody settlement and his disenchantment with a legal process he was convinced was stacked against men.

The distraught call came to an abrupt halt when the battery in Elizabeth Lam's phone suddenly went flat. She would later tell police she had not bothered to call Freeman back, hoping instead that his outpouring may have helped him offload some of his angst and helped him come to terms with the reality of his situation. There was nothing in his call to ring any alarm bells, she said, or anything to suggest he was poised to hurt someone.

Thirty minutes later, on the western approaches of the city, the traffic continued to build, and so did Arthur Freeman's stress. By now he wasn't the only one worrying. His former wife and her mother had arrived at the gates of St Joseph's Primary School at 8.30 a.m. They wanted to be there in plenty of time to welcome Darcey when she arrived in her new school uniform and to photograph the little girl taking her first steps through the school gate with her big brother.

The two women had waited patiently for almost 15 minutes in the scorching sunshine, anxiously scanning the leafy suburban street for signs of Freeman's car. But the clock was ticking, and at 8.45 a.m., as the other parents began to usher nervous youngsters into their classrooms, Peta called Freeman's mobile to ask where he was. Nothing could have prepared her for her ex-husband's chilling response.

'Say goodbye to your children,' Freeman said evenly. Peta Barnes was so shocked, she would later struggle to recall her response, though she would never forget his words.

'Just say goodbye,' he said again, and hung up.

Panicking, Peta Barnes tried to call Freeman back. She made several calls to his mobile before he finally picked up.

'Who is it?' he asked vaguely.

'It's me,' she replied, consumed with anxiety.

'You'll never see your children again,' he snapped, cutting her off again. The stricken mother immediately telephoned the solicitor who had represented her in the recent custody negotiations, and related the disturbing conversation to him. Then she called the police to report her children missing, explaining hurriedly that their father had just threatened their lives. Afterwards she rushed into the school and spoke briefly with the principal before dashing home to find some recent photographs of the children to drop off with the police.

At around 9.10 a.m. Freeman pulled his vehicle over into the emergency lane at the highest point of the West Gate Bridge. When he parked, he had the presence of mind to turn on his hazard lights to alert other motorists that he was stopping. Then he climbed out of the car and walked around to the front passenger door. Other drivers cruising by observed him leaning into the front passenger seat. His oldest son would later tell police he remembered his dad leaning into the back seat and asking his little sister to climb into the front. He even said 'please', the boy would remember. Then 'everything happened'.

Arthur Freeman lifted Darcey from the passenger seat and carried her across to the railing overlooking Port Phillip Bay. Motorist Barry Nelson, who was driving to work with his wife Michelle that morning, watched in utter disbelief as the fair-haired man hung the child over the edge of the bridge.

'Oh my God, I think that guy's going to throw his child off the bridge,' a stunned Mr Nelson said, turning to his wife. The couple wondered if this was some misguided attempt by a frustrated father to try to frighten an errant child. They continued to watch, half-expecting to see the man pull the child to safety at any moment. To their horror, the guy calmly dropped the child over the edge, peering down after her before making his way casually back to his vehicle.

'It was like he was holding a bag and tipped it over,' the stunned husband would later tell police.

Certain he had just glimpsed a falling child, Mr Nelson jumped out of his car and approached the man.

'Hey, what are you doing?' he asked. Freeman stared blankly through him, making no reply. The witness would later tell the Victorian Supreme Court that Freeman did not look angry, or even panicked. His expression was 'neutral', as if he'd just completed some ordinary mundane chore like posting a letter. Mr Nelson looked over the railing but could see nothing; his wife, however, who had also rushed over, observed a tiny lifeless figure floating face-down in the water below. Until then Mrs Nelson had been in denial, wondering if in fact this guy had tossed some sort of toy over the side.

Now she followed her husband back to the car, still trying to comprehend what they had just seen. Her husband was already on his mobile, speaking to the police.

'It was definitely a child,' she gasped.

On the bridge, another woman got out of her car and asked a male witness: 'Did I just see what I thought I saw?' The man's hands shook as he also tried to dial Triple O.

In stark contrast to the shock and confusion around him, Freeman calmly started his car and pulled off in the direction of the CBD. His shocked older son climbed from the back seat into the front passenger seat, just as his sister had done a few moments earlier. The little boy now begged his dad to turn around and go back.

'Darce can't swim, Dad,' the child reminded his father. But Freeman just kept driving.

While Arthur Freeman negotiated his way through the rush-hour traffic into the CBD, police phone lines were ringing hot with reports from drivers who had just witnessed the horror. Footscray officers Constable Colleen Spiteri and Senior Constable Tamara Wright were on morning shift at the nearby Highpoint Shopping Centre. They had already been on duty for two hours, and with temperatures already peaking at 40 degrees by 9 a.m., the pair were glad that their mundane patrol duties had led them into the air-conditioned shopping mall, out of the heat.

It was all quiet on the shopping front that morning as parents who had just dropped children off at school sat in cafes admiring first-day-of-school photographs on their mobile phones. A few early-bird shoppers were already browsing the shops, which had only just opened for business.

The rest of Melbourne remained safely at home under their air conditioners, hoping to escape the oppressive heat that had kept people awake for days. The policewomen anticipated a quiet, uneventful shift. But a police radio alert at 9.14 a.m. changed everything.

The two officers looked at one another in amazement as their crackling radios conveyed the first reports that someone had just been sighted throwing a female child from the top of the West Gate Bridge.

'Did you hear that?' Spiteri asked her colleague. Surely someone had got it wrong? Perhaps someone had tossed something resembling a child, they pondered. Who on earth would dream of throwing a child off the West Gate Bridge?

The policewomen headed off to the Bridge to investigate the reports, not knowing what to think. Spiteri would later tell the Supreme Court in her victim impact statement tendered at Freeman's 2011 sentencing hearing that during the short ride to the West Gate Bridge the evolving reports on her radio left her with such a sense of dread that she found herself gripping the dashboard, afraid of what they were about to find.

When the two policewomen arrived on the shore beneath the West Gate Bridge at Yarraville, close to the Spotswood Pumping Station, the water police were already out on Port Phillip Bay.

Leading Constable Andrew Bell had swum across the water towards the body that his colleague, Sergeant Alistair Nisbet, at first glance thought resembled a limp little doll floating on the surface. From her position on the shore, Spiteri estimated the child was no more than four years old. She watched helplessly as the water police attempted to revive the unconscious child, their efforts seemingly in vain.

Constable Spiteri, a mother of two grown-up children, would later admit in her victim impact statement that she felt her legs begin to buckle as she observed the harrowing scene. She covered her face with her hands and told herself she could not fall apart.

At 9.30 a.m. the water police ferried the little girl to the shore, where Spiteri, now on autopilot, began to perform chest compressions on the child. Her colleague, Senior Constable Wright, began mouth-to-mouth resuscitation. They worked on the little girl for almost 20 minutes, Spiteri feeling 'zoned out' by the horror, and praying for a miracle.

When a medical helicopter arrived, paramedic Kristine Gough took over the CPR from Wright. Spiteri continued with the chest compressions while other paramedics intubated the tiny patient. Spiteri felt for the little girl's pulse, convinced she detected signs of life. Later she would wonder if she'd simply imagined it.

Gough had attended call-outs to hundreds of dead or dying children, and had performed the technique countless times. But she would later say it was the first and only time she had ever spoken to her patient, urging the little girl between breaths to keep on fighting.

'As if my words of "don't give up on me" would make any difference,' the paramedic would later state in her victim impact statement. She also revealed in her statement that before the call-out, 29 January had been a special day for her. It was her birthday. But that day changed everything.

'It's no longer my birthday,' she wrote. 'It's the day I was sent to the worst case I have ever been to since I joined Ambulance Victoria in August 1998.'

While the unconscious little girl was being airlifted to Melbourne's Royal Children's Hospital, her distraught mother was at home waiting for news. Peta Barnes had earlier handed photographs of her children to police who advised her to wait at home while officers scoured the city for them. She was still at home when she received the call that would change her life.

Her lawyer, having heard news reports about a child being thrown from the West Gate Bridge, immediately called his client. Struggling to find the right words, he gently explained that a female child had been thrown from the bridge and was now being airlifted to hospital. Peta immediately raced back to the local police station and was escorted to the Royal Children's Hospital.

What should have been one of the proudest days of Peta Barnes' life was descending into an unimaginable nightmare. At the hospital, the two policewomen who had fought to revive Darcey watched on as the doctors attempted to breathe life into their patient. When the girl appeared to respond, Spiteri burst into tears.

'I cried so hard. I kept thinking, 'What were this child's last thoughts?' she revealed later. Spiteri and Wright were still at the hospital when Peta Barnes rushed in. Spiteri tried to comfort the distressed mother, telling her that her little girl had 'fought hard' and that everyone had given her the best care they could.

Doctors led the shattered mother into a private room to allow her time alone with her critically injured daughter. When Spiteri and Wright left, the tiny patient was on her way for brain scans. The two officers learned later that the little girl they had fought so hard to save had died in her mother's arms at around 1.35 p.m. The injuries Darcey Freeman received in the fall had been so extensive that doctors pronounced her brain dead. Her distraught mother was forced to make the agonising decision to turn off her daughter's life support machine, cradling her baby in her arms as her life ebbed away. Darcey Freeman was just two weeks shy of her fifth birthday.

*

While emergency workers had been attempting to revive the little girl, Victoria Police had launched a manhunt for the man responsible for the atrocity. With one child clinging to life, and two little boys still in the suspect's care, police feared they might soon be faced with a second crime scene unless the children were found quickly. An alert

Above left: Devoted mother Michelle Steck with her daughter, Kelly, in 1991. By then her abusive marriage to Kevin East was already floundering
Courtesy Michelle Steck

Above right: The last-ever photo of Kevin East with his two young children, Wesley and Kelly, taken in late 1993, two weeks before he abducted and murdered his three-year-old daughter
Courtesy Michelle Steck

Right: Michelle Steck's favourite photo of her daughter, Kelly, taken in 1993, two weeks before her murder
Courtesy Michelle Steck

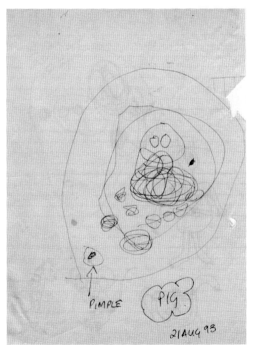

Left: Amongst Michelle Steck's most treasured possessions is this poignant drawing of a pig with a pimple on its face, which her daughter Kelly gave to her shortly before she was murdered

Right: Michelle made the news each time another child was murdered, demanding to know what the government was going to do about the epidemic of family violence
The Sunday Times *(Western Australia), 9 April 2006, p8*

Left: Former One Nation Candidate Jayson Dalton pictured with his new wife Dionne in 2000, four years before he murdered their children Jessie, 19 months, and Patrick, 13 weeks, and took his own life
Courtesy Dionne Dalton

Below: By 2004, Dionne Dalton had joined the campaign to give a voice to children like Jessie and Patrick, who were casualties of domestic violence
Jamie Hanson / Newspix

Bottom: On Anzac Day 2004, Dionne Dalton arrived at her former home in Kelvin Grove to discover that her children had been murdered by their father, who had also killed himself; her subsequent collapse was screened from waiting cameras by emergency workers
News Ltd / Newspix

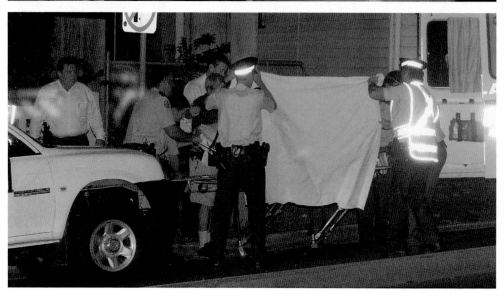

Left: Robert Farquharson with newly pregnant Cindy at their engagement party in March 1994
Courtesy Cindy Gambino

Right: An aerial shot of the dam in Winchelsea, Victoria, where Robert Farquharson's three sons, Jai, Tyler and Bailey, drowned inside their father's car on Father's Day; he was the sole survivor
Jay Town / Newspix

Left: The haunting shot that Cindy Gambino took of Jai, Bailey and Tyler on the day of Tyler's birthday party, July 2005, quickly found its way into the news after the tragedy
Courtesy Cindy Gambino

Right: Cindy clutching her Bible and clinging to Robert for support during the children's funeral, 14 September 2005
Newspix / Kelly Barnes

Left: The family photo of Darcey Freeman that was circulated to media in the wake of her murder on 29 January 2009

Centre: Darcey's mother Peta Barnes leaving Victorian Supreme Court after her ex-husband Arthur Freeman was found guilty of murdering their daughter, Darcey, by throwing her from the West Gate Bridge in January 2009
Newspix / Craig Borrow

Right: Mad, or bad? A dishevelled Arthur Freeman brandishes his handcuffs for waiting cameramen during his murder trial in 2011
Newspix / Trevor Pinder

Melbourne's West Gate Bridge at Spotswood in Melbourne, where Arthur Freeman threw his daughter to her death in January 2009
Ben Swinnerton / Newspix

Rachelle D'Argent at the funeral of her daughter, Yazmina Acar, on 25 November 2010

Ellen Smith / Newspix

Inset: Two-year-old 'Mimi' with her father Ramazan Kerem Acar; he murdered her a few days before her third birthday

Karen Bell and children Jack, Maddie and Bon. Soon after, in June 2008, her husband Gary killed them and took his own life
Courtesy Karen Gray

Karen Gray, née Bell, visits the grave of her three children Jack, Maddie and Bon, a short drive from their farmhouse in Bega, NSW
Courtesy Karen Gray

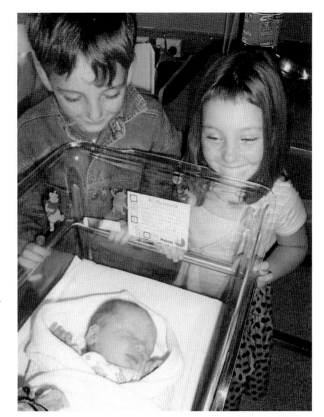

Right: Jack and Maddie welcome their baby brother Bon into the world on world on 5 March 2007.
Courtesy Karen Gray

Below: The entrance to the Bells' isolated farmhouse in Pericoe, near Eden in southern NSW, where Gary Poxon killed himself and his three children
Ray Strange / Newspix

Top left: Rebecca Poulson addresses the media in September 2003 following the murder of her father Peter and her niece and nephew Marilyn and Sebastian by the children's father, Phithak Kongsom
AAP Image / Mick Tsikas

Left: Marilyn and Sebastian Kongsom with their grandfather Peter Poulson, who tried in vain to save them from their father's knife attack at his home in rural Wilberforce, NSW
Courtesy: Rebecca Poulson

Below: Phithak Kongsom pictured with his children Marilyn and Sebastian shortly before he murdered them in September 2003
Courtesy: Rebecca Poulson

had gone out across the city, and officers everywhere were looking out for a fair-haired man with two little boys.

While the water police had been ferrying the injured girl to the shore, Arthur Freeman had been parking his car in the city's court precinct. Freeman shuffled with his baby son in his arms and his six-year-old son trailing beside him towards the Commonwealth Law Courts building on the corner of La Trobe and William Streets.

At around 9.30 that morning, Freeman was captured on CCTV, shaking uncontrollably as he limped into the lobby, now sobbing and staring wildly.

Security staff immediately noticed the dishevelled figure who approached them in a state of obvious distress, his nose dripping profusely and saliva dribbling from his mouth. His children continued to cling to their father, but Freeman appeared unaware of everyone and everything.

'Can you take my kids from me?' he asked, trying to hand over his toddler, who was dressed only in a nappy and t-shirt. When a security guard refused, Freeman began to sob. Then he slumped over and proceeded to rock backwards and forwards. His children sat at his feet, trying to gain his attention. But Freeman appeared disconnected as he stared out of the window.

A child psychologist, Ilana Katz, approached the distressed father, who she would later describe as in a 'frozen' and catatonic state. She immediately organised for the Crisis Assessment Team to be notified.

Family court counsellor Christine Bendall came down the staircase and approached the unravelling father.

'Everything will be all right,' she told him.

Freeman stared past her. 'No,' he replied. 'It will never be all right.'

Behind them, an alarmed security officer was already on the phone to police. A colleague would later say he thought the sobbing man looked like 'he'd had enough'.

Within minutes, two uniformed officers arrived at the courts. They found Freeman sobbing loudly, still rocking to and fro in a chair outside a private room where staff were changing his toddler's nappy. His six-year-old watched in silence as Senior Constable Shaun Hill attempted to question his unresponsive father.

Hill turned to the little boy and gently asked his name. Then he asked: 'Is this your dad?'

'Yeah,' the boy replied.

'Are you and your brother OK?'

'Yep.'

Hill asked the sobbing father what had happened.

'Take me away,' Freeman muttered. He was still sobbing when the officers led him away. At the time he arrived at the court nobody made the connection between this distressed man and the suspect the police were scouring the city for in connection with the atrocity on the West Gate Bridge. Shortly afterwards a call came through to arrest Freeman and take him directly to the Homicide Squad's headquarters in St Kilda.

At St Kilda Road police station, Arthur Phillip Freeman was taken to an interview room where he continued to cry. A forensic psychiatrist who examined him found him unresponsive and determined he was suffering from 'acute psychic distress with decompensation'. He deemed him unfit for interview.

While anguished family members dashed to the city's court complex to collect the children, Freeman's shocked parents were making their way into Victoria Police headquarters. They found their son curled up in a foetal position on the floor of a police cell, covered in snot, trembling and dribbling. Arthur was like a newborn baby, his father Peter would later tell the Supreme Court. He was mute and uncommunicative even with the people who loved him; Peter had never seen his son like this before.

By afternoon, the story had spread across the country. At 2.20 p.m. *Herald Sun* journalists Norrie Ross, Matt Johnston and Mark Dunn described the shocking events. Under the headline 'Little Girl Hurled from Melbourne's West Gate Bridge', the report described only the bare facts, aware that a man was now in custody.

The story revealed that a man, believed to be the girl's father, had been arrested in the city's law courts where he had been captured on camera 'shaking like a leaf' and 'staring around with wild eyes'. He had offered no resistance when detectives arrested him. The story then briefly described the child being thrown from the bridge in rush-hour traffic. Sadly, continued the story, the little girl had since died of massive internal injuries.

Victorian Paramedic Team Manager Trevor Weston told the newspaper that medics had worked on the little girl for close to 50 minutes. He said any tragedy involving children 'took its toll' on the treating paramedics. Meanwhile, Detective Inspector Steve Clark of the Homicide Squad said the tragedy, which was so distressing for the little girl's family, had also been very upsetting for the police officers attending the scene, and for the motorists who had witnessed the events.

'A number of police here who have young children themselves have had to deal with this and they are obviously upset,' he said.

Detective Inspector Clark said a number of witnesses had already come forward, but urged anyone with any further information to contact the police immediately.

Arthur Phillip Freeman was charged with murder that afternoon. The psychiatrist who assessed him determined him unfit to appear at his brief remand hearing before the Melbourne Magistrates' Court, saying he was in deep shock and suicidal. Presiding magistrate Lance Martin said he would ensure the staff at the Melbourne Custody Centre were advised of Freeman's condition. Freeman was remanded to appear in court again on 21 May.

That night, thousands of heat-fatigued children, their heads still buzzing with the excitement of their first day at school, were hugged a little tighter as their parents tucked them into bed. The news had shaken the entire country, the shockwaves travelling across the globe.

The following morning, traumatised paramedic Kristine Gough, whose birthday would never be the same again, kept her own young children at home. She would later explain in her victim impact statement that she wanted her youngsters at home 'safe with me'. She just wanted to hug them 'over and over again, and tell them I love them'. Across the city, the new school uniform that would never be worn lay in Freeman's flat.

An article in the Fairfax papers by journalists Andrea Petrie, John Sylvester and Karen Kissane appeared the following morning pondering the little girl's last moments and asking how a supposedly doting father could commit the horrific crime he was now accused of.

With the case before the courts, the article carried no details of the crime itself, except to say that the little girl had died of her injuries after allegedly being thrown from the top of the West Gate Bridge. The story went on to note that police were now compiling eyewitness accounts from motorists on the West Gate Bridge and witnesses at the Commonwealth Law Courts Building where the accused had subsequently been arrested.

The journalists quoted a spokesperson from the legal firm that had represented Arthur Freeman.

'It's devastating and unexpected,' said Zelma Rudstein of Rudstein Kron Lawyers. 'We are just trying to come to grips with it.' Ms Rudstein described the accused man as a 'devoted loving father' and said this was a tragedy nobody could have predicted. Those who knew Arthur Freeman were stunned. The Arthur Freeman everyone knew was a loving, stay-at-home father who read his children bedtime stories, played soccer with them, and adored them. Interestingly, of all his three children, it was the little girl who resembled him the most and showered him with affection, whom he was accused of murdering. Nobody could believe it.

*

With Arthur Phillip Freeman now in custody, Homicide detectives began to build a case against the man allegedly responsible for the crime that had shocked Australia. The eyewitness accounts told a harrowing story about what had allegedly taken place. But these callous actions were difficult to reconcile with the man considered by his friends and associates to be a harmless computer geek and adoring father, who had no previous criminal record.

Over the coming days, the statements police took from Freeman's shattered parents certainly painted a portrait of a loving but unravelling father struggling to come to terms with his broken marriage and to adapt to his changing role in his children's lives. Peter and Norma Freeman told police their son had been stressed on the morning of the crime, though this had not caused them to fear he might harm anyone, least of all his own children.

But if Arthur Phillip Freeman had been seen as harmless, an ordinary nobody living an unremarkable life, there was something else that people would later remember about him. Arthur Freeman had always been a little *different.*

At primary school Freeman had struggled to form meaningful relationships and grew up a solitary kid. His odd, disconnected behaviour during his formative primary-school years were rumoured to have resulted in a spell at an alternative school for children with behavioural problems. But by his teens he was back in mainstream education, attending Newcomb High School in Geelong, where his old-fashioned name and bizarre behaviour made him a target for playground bullies. His six years there, according to newspaper reports, were a misery.

The only 'Arthur' in his year, Freeman was nicknamed 'Ardie Dunger' or 'Ardie Monster' after a bogan TV character created by comedian Paul Hogan. He was mocked, taunted, told he smelled and hounded relentlessly. When his tormentors ordered him to stand on a rock in the yard for almost half an hour, he did as he was told. The acquiescent Ardie Freeman never fought back or even argued. He just simmered.

By the time he reached puberty, Freeman was a ghost in his own life. He remained marginalised among his peers, and his lack of social skills and inability to engage relegated him to being the sad school loner.

But what Arthur Freeman lacked in social graces, he certainly appeared to make up for academically. He went to university and gained an honours degree in computer science, and made a few friends. But even then he remained a solitary figure, preferring his own company and indulging his passion for computers and tinkering with cars. Friends would later remember him as a young guy who was more comfortable with spanners than people.

During his first job, as a computer programmer, Freeman would sit up all night playing games on his PlayStation. He commonly turned up for work at 8 a.m. after snatching a few hours sleep, only to repeat the exercise again the following night.

Unlike Robert Farquharson, whose flat feet and back problem prevented him from joining in at sport, Arthur Freeman played football. He also played tennis, rode his bike and, for a while, pumped iron. But he was not a team player, and he never fitted in.

It wasn't just Freeman's personality that made him different; he looked quirky too. By the time he started work he had already lost the hair on the crown of his head. He looked more peculiar because he insisted on growing the long and straggly tufts of hair either side, giving him the look of a caricature nutty professor.

But life looked up for Arthur Freeman when he met the gregarious Peta Barnes. The pair were work colleagues who were introduced by friends when they were working for Colonial Mutual in Melbourne. Friends thought the more adventurous Peta was a perfect foil for the introverted, quirky Freeman. She certainly seemed to bring the young loner out of his shell and soon the strange haircut made way for a more fashionable short hairstyle that gave him the air of a yuppie professional.

Soon Ardie Freeman the computer geek became Artie Freeman, an entirely new persona. With his new partner's encouragement and support, Freeman began to attempt challenges he may never have considered.

Like Cindy Gambino, Peta Barnes was a millennium bride. She and Freeman exchanged vows in Perth on New Year's Eve 1999, as the countdown to a new century began. Three weeks later, the newlyweds left on an adventure to the UK, where they embraced new lives and careers.

There, for perhaps the first time in his life, Artie Freeman was making his mark. He enjoyed his new job as a database administrator and cultivated a social life. After work Freeman played tennis, enjoyed bike rides and went on skiing holidays, even joining mates in the pub for an occasional beer or an upmarket lunch. The couple settled in the London suburb of Maida Vale, where they had a comfortable home. Ordinary, unremarkable Artie Freeman had finally arrived.

Among the couple's expanding friendship group was fellow expat Elizabeth Lam, who worked with Peta at a major British company. The Freeman babies followed in quick succession; first a son, born in February 2002, followed by daughter Darcey in February 2004 and another son in February 2006. But the bubble was about to burst in 2006 when the young mother indicated that she wanted to return home for the sake of the children's education.

According to friends, Freeman was not happy about the return home. He enjoyed his new lifestyle in England and was openly resentful that his wife now expected him to relinquish his job to return to Australia. Elizabeth Lam would later tell police that Freeman had loved his life in England and claimed his wife had 'dragged' him back to Australia just when he had found a job he enjoyed.

The subsequent move back to Melbourne became a source of growing bitterness on Freeman's part, and the anger that had no doubt been slowly simmering since his schooldays found a new focus. He was furious with his wife and told her so at every opportunity. Two days after her daughter's death, Peta Barnes told Homicide detectives that when they returned to Melbourne, things became 'very difficult'.

She said her husband did not cope well with change and was a rigid, inflexible man who was prone to angry outbursts and dark, brooding moods. The growing discord between the couple escalated after Peta secured fulltime work, leaving the now unemployed Freeman at home to care for their children. The stay-at-home father played soccer with his son, took his daughter to ballet, and read his kids stories at bedtime. But this was a far cry from the rewarding professional life he had enjoyed in England, and there were constant arguments.

After her granddaughter's murder, Freeman's mother, Norma, told police that while her son appeared to be coping well enough, with three children to care for and a wife working long hours, it was clear 'they sometimes didn't understand each other's positions'.

Behind closed doors, Freeman's extreme mood swings erupted without warning. Peta Barnes later told police his emotions swung from 'anger to vengefulness, to remorse and back again'. In her statement to police she wondered if her ex-husband had some sort of personality problem, or if he'd been suffering from a depressive illness.

By March 2007 the strain on the marriage ultimately proved too much. Peta Barnes left Arthur Freeman, taking their children with her, and filed for divorce. Freeman was not happy about the separation and remained in Hawthorn to be close to his children. He expressed fears to relatives and friends that he was losing his children and feared his ex-wife might take them back to her native Perth and he'd never see them.

But if his friends and family told the police that there was nothing about Freeman's behaviour to set alarm bells ringing or to indicate he might be capable of hurting his children, his former wife painted a darker, far more chilling picture.

In April 2007, one month after they separated, she told a doctor about Freeman's angry, irrational outbursts towards herself and the children. She described occasions when her former husband had shoved and pushed her around. At approximately the same time she told another doctor that she feared her ex-husband might be capable of hurting their children to pay her back for ending the marriage.

'I told the doctor that I believed Arthur would kill my children and that I believed he was vengeful enough to kill my children to get back at me,' she later told Homicide detectives. The worried mother's concerns were never passed on to Protective Services, in spite of the mandatory reporting obligations in Victoria that require GPs to report suspected child abuse to the authorities. Peta Barnes' GP would later state he had no reason to believe that the children were at risk of imminent harm and did not think Ms Barnes' concerns were enough to trigger a mandatory report to social services. The doctor was aware that the authorities and lawyers were already involved with the family, and believed they were better placed to raise concerns if there were any.

Yet, unknown to both doctors, not long after she had shared her concerns, a disturbing altercation erupted between the separated couple, which confirmed Peta's deepest fears. At Freeman's request, Peta had agreed to go around to his flat in Hawthorn to talk things through. Her mother, Iris, accompanied her. Peta told police later that speaking to Freeman proved 'a complete waste of time'.

'Arthur just wanted to berate me for all of the things that I had done wrong,' she said. 'This had been a consistent theme since I had arrived home from England. Arthur was incredibly resentful in the time since we had come home.'

When the two women got up to leave, Freeman snatched the baby from his mother's arms. Convinced he was about to throw the infant into the fireplace, a struggle followed in which Peta's mother slammed her former son-in-law in the back with the baby's metal pusher.

'Mum and I fought him and I bit him to get him to let the baby go, because he is incredibly strong and he wouldn't let go,' Peta Barnes told detectives.

The police were called and a shared custody arrangement was put in place. This was the arrangement that was ultimately changed two days before Darcey's murder.

The couple were officially divorced in June 2008, though Freeman refused to take his wedding ring off, or move on. In September that year he flew back to England to finalise a UK passport and his British citizenship. During the three months he was there, friends glimpsed his escalating paranoia and increasingly obsessive behaviour. He bitterly complained that his former wife was sabotaging his phone contact with his children and became paranoid when friends suggested that being overseas in the middle of a custody dispute might interfere with his bid for access.

Elizabeth Lam would later tell Victoria Police that Freeman seemed consumed by his marriage breakdown. In their conversations he appeared 'very bitter about his wife's behaviour towards him'.

What was increasingly clear to everyone was that Freeman, described by one relative as a 'calculating control freak', was slowly spiralling out of control.

In December, Arthur Freeman returned to Australia, where the wrangle over custody continued. After Freeman's trial, a former associate, who did not wish to be identified, would tell journalist Paul Anderson from the *Herald Sun* about a veiled threat Freeman had made at a Christmas party shortly after his return. The associate recalled that the disgruntled father had stated that if he lost custody of the children his ex-wife would 'regret it'.

The associate told the newspaper, 'That comment has gone through my head over and over. I thought he'd go after Peta, by that I mean making her life hell through legal channels.'

Yet despite his angry outburst and his threats towards his estranged wife, Freeman insisted he was the one being bullied as he grizzled about the division of the family finances. Like Farquharson, he complained he would not have enough money left after the divorce settlement to house his children. Friends said that while money had never 'meant that much' to Freeman, they recalled his frustration and anger when he discovered his newly separated wife had apparently transferred more than $300 000 from a joint account.

His own father, Peter Freeman, would later tell a Supreme Court jury that his son's mental health severely deteriorated after the collapse of his relationship. After the divorce he appeared paranoid, anxious, confused and highly emotional, though he was unwilling to seek professional help.

The more out of control he became, the more Freeman appeared to strive to instil order and routine into his life. Perhaps in response to his own inner turmoil, he began to obsess over his environment and daily routines.

'Strange things were happening,' his father told the Supreme Court. Just as an unravelling Jayson Dalton had scribbled copious notes about conversations with his ex-wife Dionne and hoarded receipts about the money he spent on the children, Freeman also began obsessively collecting receipts relating to his expenditure on his kids. His home became a chaotic jumble of toys and children's clothes, and he continued to add to the clutter. His father described the stockpile of washing-machine parts and other unnecessary items his son hoarded that added to the chaos in his Hawthorn flat. Freeman also became miserly, making DIY beds and storage drawers for his children in order to save money for his ongoing custody battle.

It appears Freeman's personality was slowly splintering, perhaps in an attempt to distance himself from his out-of-control life and the disintegrating Artie. The *Herald Sun* reported later that detectives searching his messy flat after the crime found a handwritten note stuck to Freeman's television screen. It was not clear who had actually penned it, but the officers assumed it was probably Freeman. The note was a reminder to keep 'keep a clear head' because of the 'big fight on his hands'. Curiously, Freeman was referring to himself in the third person, which strongly supports the possibility that he was already disconnecting from the confused, distracted divorced father he had become.

After Darcey's murder, Freeman's stunned friends and associates clung to this belief. Those who knew him became convinced that his escalating confusion had led him to disconnect from reality and it was in this state that he had committed a single, unthinkable, uncharacteristic act of violence.

There had been no sign he had been plotting to harm his children when he told friends on 27 January that he planned to join them for a drink when his access was finally settled. Nobody had glimpsed any hint of the festering anger that was poised to culminate in a revenge killing.

After Freeman's arrest, his lawyer said nobody could reconcile the heinous act with the loving, 'excessively caring father' who wanted to play a significant part in his children's lives. What on earth had caused him to suddenly snap?

As Constable Spiteri asked herself that morning after hearing the report on her radio, who on earth would even think about throwing a child off the top of the West Gate Bridge? You'd have to be out of your mind!

Ultimately, this was the question the jury had to ask themselves when the case finally reached the Victorian Supreme Court in 2011. Was Arthur Phillip Freeman mad or bad when he hurled his little daughter to her death on 29 January 2009? It was the question at the very heart of Freeman's trial when the accused entered his controversial plea of not guilty by reason of mental impairment or disease.

If Freeman's family and friends believed he was mad, the police and the Barnes family were not convinced. One of his in-laws would later describe Freeman as a 'control freak' who had lost his control over his family in the wake of the divorce. But one thing the detectives knew for sure, as they added revealing new statements to the mounting bundle of evidence, was that this supposedly harmless computer geek had been a ticking time bomb.

*

Against the backdrop of the evolving police investigation, the shattered family asked the public and the media to respect their privacy as they made plans to say private goodbyes to a bubbly four year old with a mind of her own and a passion for music and dancing.

While community groups and outraged parents called for a public memorial service to honour the little girl lost, Darcey Freeman's maternal uncle, Tim Barnes, made a formal statement to the press. He began by thanking the many emergency workers and doctors for the 'wonderful' efforts they'd made as they valiantly battled to save his niece.

Reading from a prepared statement, Mr Barnes revealed that the family felt an 'an extreme sense of loss and emptiness'.

'Darcey had a very determined nature,' he said. 'She displayed a very strong will and stood up for everything she believed in. She loved both of her brothers, and particularly adored her older brother.' Mr Barnes went on to describe the four-year-old's passion for music, in particular her favourite song, 'Tie Me Kangaroo Down Sport'. Her family would always remember the little girl who enjoyed playing with her brothers and cousins, and who especially loved bouncing with everyone on the trampoline.

Mr Barnes said the family had been 'overwhelmed' by the out-pouring of support and love from strangers who had reached out to them in their grief. But there were 'still many issues to be resolved', he said, referring to the ongoing police investigation. He was aware that the public had called for a national memorial day in Darcey's honour. It would be a day when Darcey and other innocent young casualties of violent crimes would be remembered. While the grieving family commended the Australian public for the initiative and had no objections, in the meantime they wished to hold their own private funeral for the little girl they knew and loved.

Tim Barnes poignantly reminded Australia that two other children were also casualties of this terrible tragedy. Darcey's brothers, who had witnessed the horror, now required ongoing support and care. He asked the media to respect the family's privacy as they mourned and helped one another heal.

While the media kept a respectful distance from the private funeral, Constable Spiteri, who had attended the call-out, and paramedic Kristine Gough, who had battled so hard to breathe life into the little girl, felt compelled to attend and pay their respects.

Spiteri said in her victim impact statement, 'I am a police officer and I am supposed to deal with these situations. It's part of our job. You need to be unemotional and move on and be strong.' Sadly, Spiteri would find this impossible. 'Other police officers say it was the worst day of their career, and they weren't even there,' she revealed. But the horror she witnessed that day would later prompt the seasoned officer to change police stations, unable to cope with the flashbacks and emotions triggered by the very sight of the West Gate Bridge.

Similarly, the paramedic who had attended many child fatalities, from SIDS to accidental death, would later admit in her own victim impact statement that nothing had affected her more than this tragedy.

In a similar statement another witness, who had been on the West

Gate Bridge that morning, would tell the court about the 'black hole' of depression that had followed the crime and left her incapable of driving over the bridge ever since.

'I cannot see myself ever forming a relationship with a male as the trust would not be there,' she stated sadly.

While parents everywhere pondered the forces that had driven this supposedly devoted father to murder his own child, the Crown and the defence began building their respective cases.

Freeman looked dishevelled when he next appeared before the Melbourne Magistrates Court in May 2009 via video link from prison. Darcey's grandparents and her uncle, Tim, attended the hearing. Freeman was remanded in custody again until his committal hearing in October. The magistrate, Peter Reardon, asked Chief Crown Prosecutor Gavin Silbert SC how the victim's brothers were coping. Mr Silbert said the boys were with their mother and the family did not want to say anything further at this point in the proceedings.

If Freeman had looked windswept during his earlier video link appearance, he looked positively unkempt when he appeared in person at his committal hearing on 8 October 2009. The short, neat hair he had sported upon his arrest nine months earlier was gone. He looked unrecognisable, with long, wild hair and an untamed beard.

But Mr Silbert contended that Freeman's new 'Rasputin-like appearance of a mad monk' was just a ploy to bolster his defence that he was insane and therefore not responsible for what the Crown believed to be a cold-blooded murder.

Freeman sat expressionless as Mr Silbert described the painful final moments of his daughter's brief life. His face remained blank when traumatised witnesses gave their graphic accounts of watching the child being tipped over the side of the bridge by a father who walked away as casually as if he'd been posting a letter.

'I wouldn't say he was robotic at all, he appeared like nothing was wrong — that was the overriding impression,' motorist Barry Nelson explained. Freeman had been in no particular hurry to get back into his car or to rush away into the city-bound traffic.

Staff from the Commonwealth Law Courts Building gave evidence about the dishevelled father who arrived dripping saliva and snot shortly after they opened for business on 29 January 2009. Now that same father stared right through them, carefully avoiding all eye contact with his former in-laws in the court's public gallery.

The revealing statement Peta Barnes had given police expressing the dark prediction she'd made to her GP almost two years before Darcey's murder was tendered into evidence. The statement also described the frightening incident at Freeman's flat in which she feared he was about to throw their baby against the fireplace. But most damning was the evidence about the harrowing telephone conversations between Freeman and his ex-wife on the morning of the murder when he'd told her to say goodbye to her children and that she would never see them again.

Arthur Phillip Freeman was remanded in custody after pleading not guilty to murdering his daughter. He was committed to stand trial at the Victorian Supreme Court.

*

The high-profile trial began in March 2011. Freeman pleaded not guilty to murder by reason of mental impairment.

Mr Silbert told the jury they would have to consider two questions: was this father in the dock really mad when he hurled his little girl to her death, or was this the vengeful deliberate act of an enraged, bitter husband intent on paying back the real target of his rage, his children's mother?

He explained that the defence case, in a nutshell, would be that Freeman had committed the crime but had been suffering from a mental illness at the time and was therefore not culpable for his actions, which had been involuntary. But the Crown would argue that this was a retaliatory killing, a clear act of spousal revenge intended to inflict suffering on his former wife for ending their marriage. Mr Silbert warned the jury that the Rasputin-like mad-monk caricature in the dock was indulging in theatrics to convince them he was not sane when he committed the unthinkable.

But the evidence would reveal that there were too many other things about Freeman's actions on the day of the murder to quash the contention that he was in the grip of a psychotic mental breakdown at the time.

That day he had driven his children, without incident, through heavy morning traffic to the West Gate Bridge. During the journey he had made, and returned, telephone calls. He'd held discussions about issues that mattered to him, and was both lucid and coherent during those discussions. These conversations, in which he'd fretted over school lunches and running late, or complained about his custody arrangements, illustrated that he was neither disorientated or confused, but fully aware of where he was and what he was doing. More significantly, his chilling telephone threats to Peta Barnes, instructing her to say goodbye to her children because she would not see them again, made his intentions very clear.

The Crown said what was most disturbing was Freeman saying she would not see 'them' again. He had used the plural, suggesting he was about to hurt all three children. Ultimately it was only the little girl, the child who resembled him most, who was hurled from the bridge. It was left to the jury to ponder whether Darcey had simply been the first child he chose to kill that day, rather than the sole target. Either way, said the Crown, this was a clear-cut case of spousal revenge.

'Freeman was upset. He was angry. The threat to Peta Barnes in the two phone conversations related by her indicate that his anger-management problems were about to bubble over,' Mr Silbert told the jury. 'What it amounts to ... is that in a paroxysm of anger with Peta Barnes, he stopped on the bridge and threw Darcey over the rail.' Mr Silbert said the threats to the children's mother just minutes before the murder demonstrated 'he knew the nature and quality of what he was about to do. We are perhaps indeed fortunate that he didn't throw all three children over the bridge.'

The Crown argued that the menacing threats had been consciously and deliberately made by a furious man who felt he was losing control. It was telling that Peta Barnes had already been worried enough about her ex-husband's explosive mood swings that she had reported her concerns to her doctor after they separated in 2007. Even then she believed her husband was vengeful enough to consider hurting their children to pay her back.

Far from experiencing a psychotic breakdown or acting on 'insane automatism', as the defence was suggesting, the evidence showed that Arthur Freeman had known exactly what he was doing when he called his little girl into the front passenger seat of his car, then carried her to the railing of the West Gate Bridge and thrown her to her death. He'd even had the foresight to turn on his car's hazard lights to alert other road users to his intention to stop.

Afterwards he had calmly walked away and started his car, negotiating heavy rush-hour traffic as he drove into the city. There he parked his car in a familiar location, again without incident, before making his way to the Commonwealth Law Courts. All this showed that he was acting consciously and voluntarily at the time of the crime and dispelled the argument that Freeman was out of touch with reality and behaving in some disconnected fashion as if he were in a trance.

He knew exactly what he was doing when he asked court staff to take his children. More significantly, he understood the gravity of what he had just done. When the counsellor Christine Bendall had tried to reassure him that everything would be all right, he replied, 'No, it won't.' Far from supporting the defence's claims that he had been acting in a daze, this answer showed he'd known what he had done was wrong. He was guilty of murder.

The counter-argument put by Freeman's defence lawyer, Mr David Brustman SC, contended that the accused father had been mentally ill at the time of the crime and was therefore not culpable. He argued that his client had been in a dissociative state and acting unconsciously when he threw his daughter to her death. He had committed the atrocity, but had been unable to distinguish right from wrong at the time.

Only one of the six medical experts who had assessed Freeman in custody agreed. Professor Graeme Burrows, a psychiatrist with 40 years experience who was called as a witness for the defence, said

Freeman had been at the severe end of the dissociation scale and 'really didn't know what was going on' when he threw his daughter off the bridge. He described Freeman's state as one of 'fluctuating dissociation, as if sleepwalking or hypnotised at the time'. Burrows believed Freeman had been suffering a major depressive disorder and possibly psychosis at the time of the crime.

This diagnosis was rejected by two other experts for the Crown. Dr Douglas Bell said Freeman's behaviour on the morning of the crime showed an 'awareness' of his environment and demonstrated 'a purposeful execution of behaviour'. There was no basis for concluding that he was in a profound state of dissociation at all.

Consultant psychiatrist Yvonne Skinner told the court, 'There's no evidence to suggest that Mr Freeman was incapable of forming intentions.' Dr Skinner had been involved in more than 80 murder cases where parents had been charged with killing their children, and said this was a clear case of spousal revenge in which children were the collateral damage rather than the true targets of the offending parent's rage.

In retaliatory filicides like these, she explained, the child becomes a weapon of mass destruction, used by the vengeful parent to inflict the worst possible injury imaginable on the real object of their anger — their former spouse.

The majority of the expert doctors who examined Freeman agreed that while he was anxious and stressed during his drive into the city, this did not mean he was suffering from a mental illness or impairment. He had known what he was doing, but was so angry he did it anyway.

Freeman's father, Peter, gave evidence about his son's disintegrating mental state and firm belief that he had been 'set up'.

'It was a very strange thing that was happening,' Peter Freeman told the jury. 'He had a system going with his dishes and his food and dishwasher. All that stuff was super-efficient yet the rest of his life was in confusion. He was starting to collect hard rubbish and he would collect every receipt. He had a box full of them in the kitchen ... every receipt relating to the children.'

In her evidence, Elizabeth Lam testified that Freeman had been distressed about his reduced access. His biggest bone of contention had been the assessment prepared by clinical psychologist Jennifer Neoh, for the custody hearing. He was upset because the psychologist had described him as a man who 'tended to be irrational and contradictory'. She stated that he had demonstrated 'passive aggressive traits' and 'seemed to cause chaos around him'. Neoh's assessment of Freeman had reflected interviews with him two weeks before the murder.

Neoh noted that he had turned up late for one of their sessions. She had rescheduled their appointment, and on the next occasion he turned up too early. She observed that this erratic behaviour was a cause of distress to at least one of his children, though Freeman was clearly oblivious to it. As far as Freeman was concerned, the report was unfair. He told Lam in his distressing phone call on 29 January that he intended to seek a review of the psychologist's report. A day earlier, he'd told another friend that he intended to pursue a personal development course in order to obtain more time with his children and overturn the psychologist's report.

It is possible this damning report may have fuelled Freeman's warped perception that the system was stacked against separated fathers, prompting his paranoid remark that the courts were filled with angry women who offered no support to men like him. Ultimately his comments prompted Professor Burrows to observe that the damning report by Jennifer Neoh may have tipped Freeman over the edge. During his interview with Burrows, Freeman alluded bitterly to the psychologist's report.

In her report, Jennifer Neoh determined that Freeman had chronic personality and interpersonal problems. These included issues with rationality. She speculated that his personality might create a harmful environment of conflict, which could pose psychological harm to his children.

If Arthur Freeman was putting on an act for the jury, it was a spectacular one. And it worked, for the media at least, who noted his every move in the dock. During crucial evidence, reporters zoomed in on Freeman's responses, or lack of them. When he showed nothing, they described him as 'expressionless' or 'zoned out' or 'lacking in any emotion'. When he sobbed loudly into his hanky, they reported that, too. When he gazed around, reporters described him 'staring wildly'.

In their coverage of the trial for Melbourne's *Herald Sun*, journalists Patrick Carlyon and Paul Anderson colourfully described the accused killer 'shuffling' into court each day, 'shackles clanking, shoulders hunched, his body resembling a block of concrete wide and thick'.

'Sometimes Freeman bared his teeth in expressions of pain. He whimpered and wept and guzzled water during evidence about the autopsy of his daughter … mostly he stared with wide eyes like a zoo exhibit who could not grasp how he arrived where he was,' they wrote.

In other reports, Freeman was likened to a cartoon character, a sci-fi alien and a mad monk with his long, wild hair, bald patch and quizzical expression. Journalist Stuart Rintoul, in an article headed 'Time Won't Heal the Grief', which appeared in *The Australian* on 12 April 2011, described the accused father's 'permanently furrowed brow'. To most of the media, it seemed that the man in the dock still had no idea how he had got here.

But if these theatrics inside the court supported the defence's argument that the father in the dock was mad, outside the court Freeman demonstrated the simmering anger that the Crown claimed had erupted into cold-blooded murder. And it painted a more disturbing picture. As he entered the Supreme Court one day, flanked by his guards, Freeman paused for the cameramen and aggressively held his arms aloft, rattling his cuffed wrists in an angry show of defiance. Far from showing a dazed, confused, disconnected prisoner, his actions highlighted the same focused rage the Crown had argued resulted in his little girl's murder.

The trial of Arthur Phillip Freeman was complex and heartbreaking. It highlighted the anguish of so many friends and witnesses who, two years later, were still tormenting themselves over whether there had been signs they had missed or something they could have done to prevent the tragedy.

After Freeman's phone call on the morning of 29 January, his close friend Elizabeth Lam had not been concerned enough to call him back, assuming that his tears may have helped him to finally accept the reality of his situation. There had been nothing about his call to suggest he was about to hurt his children. Similarly, Freeman's parents, observing his stress that day, had not been concerned that he posed any threat to his children. Even the associate who recalled Freeman's menacing threat when he claimed his ex-wife would 'regret it' if he lost custody of his children, never imagined he might have been considering harming his kids when he made that remark.

Yet Freeman's former wife had certainly entertained the ugly possibility when she reported her concerns to her GP. If the trial of Arthur Freeman highlighted anything at all, it was the many casualties of his crime who lost something that day.

'I've lost my granddaughter,' Peter Freeman told the court during his testimony.

Justice Coghlan nodded sympathetically. He was a grandfather too, he told the witness. 'I understand,' he said.

Throughout the entire trial, Freeman sat observing proceedings in silence. His only sign of emotion was during the evidence of consultant pathologist Dr Matthew Lynch. When Dr Lynch testified about the extensive injuries Darcey Freeman had suffered after being thrown from the bridge, the defendant began to sob.

Darcey Freeman, who was only 119 centimetres tall and weighed 29 kilograms, had sustained serious injuries consistent with falling from 'a great height', the pathologist said. These included a ruptured spleen and torn small intestine, bruising to her neck, cheek, stomach, arms and legs, as well as a bruised heart and collapsed lung. Her 15 minutes in the water before being rescued by the water police left the pathologist pondering whether her brain damage had been caused by a lack of oxygen or from falling 58 metres.

The uncharacteristic show of emotion, which left Freeman

weeping into his handkerchief, prompted the judge to ask if he would like a glass of water. But Freeman's tears had dried up by the time his former wife took the stand. All the while his former father-in-law, Wayne Barnes, a former old-school policeman, scowled at the ragged-looking man in the dock.

Peta Barnes remained composed as she described the collapse of their marriage, her former husband's mood swings and explosive temper, and the chilling prediction she'd made to her GP. A hush fell on the court as she described Freeman's telephone conversation when he told her to say goodbye to her children and threatened that she'd never see them again.

But the most poignant testimony of all came from the mouth of a six-year-old boy. In his earlier videotaped interview with police, which was replayed to the jury, Darcey's older brother related what had happened in those final fateful seconds in the back of his dad's car before his little sister was thrown from the bridge.

He said Darcey 'didn't even scream in her fall … I said, go back and get her, Darce can't swim. But he kept on driving. He didn't go back and get her.' His father listened and gaped. If Arthur Freeman was sorry, there was no sign of it.

As the trial came to a close, Freeman announced that he wanted to dismiss his defence lawyers and make a statement on his own behalf. The request was denied.

In closing, his defence lawyer, David Brustman, asked the court to consider why a father would commit such a 'truly horrible crime'.

'Very few cases could induce more prejudice,' he said. 'There in the dock sits a man who flung a four-year-old girl, his own daughter, to her death. Now how bad does that get? Is this simply the face of pure evil?'

The defence said the crime had been committed by a mentally impaired man, not a father intent on punishing his wife in the worst possible way, as the Crown contended.

At the end of the trial, in which Freeman's mental health was carefully scrutinised, the jury retired to consider their verdict. Was he bad, or was he mad? The jury was divided. After four days of deliberations they returned to ask for further clarification about the testimony of the medical experts. The foreman told the court that it was unlikely they would be able to reach a unanimous verdict.

But Justice Paul Coghlan stated that while he had the power to discharge them, he was not yet satisfied that an impasse had been reached and instructed them to consider deliberating further. The following day they reached their final verdict.

Arthur Phillip Freeman was guilty of murdering his daughter. It was a unanimous verdict. They concurred he had been bad, not mad, when he killed his little girl to punish her mother for ending their marriage.

*

The composure that Peta Barnes maintained throughout the trial finally collapsed at the pre-sentence hearing on 1 April 2011, just three days after Freeman was found guilty of murdering their daughter. She broke down in tears as she attempted to read her victim impact statement to the court, describing the personal nightmare she had lived since her ex-husband's crime.

Crown Prosecutor Diana Piekusis took over, reading the statement for the distressed mother, who described herself as an 'intensely private individual' who found it difficult sharing her emotions about the 'most painful incident' of her life.

'Since the loss of Darcey I grieve on a daily basis and realistically do not see how that can ever change,' she wrote. 'The saying "time heals all wounds" is not true for myself and I don't ever expect it to be. Not a day goes by where I do not constantly think of Darcey; where I don't miss her and wish with all my heart that she was with me. I can feel her little hand holding mine when I walk down the street or drive in the car. I lie in bed at night and hold her in my arms. I talk to her and think of her daily.'

Peta Barnes said no words could ever truly describe the loss of a child. 'The emptiness that sits within you, the piece of you that no longer exists, the fact that you no longer go on in life as a complete person.' It took great restraint when she glimpsed little girls who resembled her daughter, because of the overwhelming urge to hug them.

Not a single day passed when she didn't suffer flashbacks of the emotions she felt when Freeman told her she would never see her children again.

'The panic and fear these words set off inside me resonates with me, even today.' Such feelings now caused her anxiety in everyday situations that would not have affected her before. She said the strength of character and resilience which helped her survive each day did not lessen the impact of losing her child.

'Darcey lives with me daily and can never be quantified by a statement I make in court. Nothing can change the loss of my daughter and nothing can bring her back. I have now and forever only memories of her when I intended to have a lifetime of love and laughter. I will never get to live the life I dreamed and hoped of with Darcey, and nor will she with me. The loss of her is indescribable.'

She would never 'erase' the thoughts of her 'beautiful girl, so willingly and trustingly going to her father at his request at the top of the West Gate Bridge; of falling to her death and what her last thoughts must have been.' The horror of her daughter's last thoughts still gave her nightmares and caused sleep deprivation 'too horrific' to describe. And nothing could erase the pain of giving her permission to the doctors to turn off Darcey's life support machine. 'Or of holding Darcey in my arms as she passed away and knowing that this decision would take her from me and knowing that there was no other option available to me.' Now suffering from post traumatic stress and undergoing intensive counselling, she said she doubted her anxiety would improve significantly in the future.

In another victim impact statement Iris, Darcey's maternal grandmother, revealed her own agony.

'I lie in bed at night and agonise at the terror and fear that Darcey was going through as she fell to her death. I have had many sleepless nights trying to comprehend how some human being could do this to an innocent child,' she said. 'Not a single day goes by that I don't think about my granddaughter Darcey and wonder what might have been.'

The Chief Crown Prosecutor said the great betrayal of trust that led to a father murdering his own child, and the very public nature of the murder, meant that only a life sentence without parole was appropriate in this case.

But the defence argued that a while life imprisonment was appropriate, it was not the only sentencing option available to the court.

On 11 April 2011 Justice Paul Coghlan sentenced Freeman to life in jail, ordering he serve a minimum of 32 years before being eligible for parole. Passing sentence, the judge said that the crime could 'not be more horrible' and that the image of the falling little girl haunted the case from beginning to end. The child's last thoughts did not bear thinking about.

Justice Coghlan said while he understood the argument that Freeman needed to be locked away forever, he was obliged to consider other factors.

'You have yet to say sorry for what you have done,' observed Justice Coghlan. 'Your attitude to these matters remains self-centred.' Yet while he regarded Freeman's rehabilitation prospects as 'bleak', he did not believe he was 'beyond redemption'. And though there was little evidence that Freeman had been suffering from a mental illness at the time of the murder, the judge accepted it had not been premeditated.

In the end, the motive for the murder had 'nothing to do with the innocent victim', Justice Coghlan said. 'It can only be concluded that you used your daughter in an attempt to hurt your former wife as profoundly as possible. You chose a place for the commission of your crime which was remarkably public and which would have the most dramatic impact. It follows that you brought the broader community into this case in a way that has been rarely, if ever, seen before. It offends our collective conscience.'

The public nature of the murder was so keenly felt that the judge departed from court protocol by allowing the victim impact statements of police, emergency workers and court staff to be tendered alongside those of actual witnesses and immediate family ahead of sentencing. It was a case that had impacted on so many lives, he observed.

The judge said one of the 'most unfortunate features' of the case was that so many others continued to blame themselves for what he alone had done.

'They should not,' he told the killer in the dock. 'You did what you did, you are responsible for it, and nobody else.'

Throughout the 40-minute sentencing, Freeman sat unflinching, his face betraying nothing. But as the judge rose to leave the bench, the convicted killer stood and bowed to the court.

'I just want to make a statement,' he announced.

The court fell silent as lawyers, court staff, media and family turned towards the dock. Was this an apology? Some last-minute expression of contrition?

But Freeman had other, more pressing things on his mind than the tiny girl he had thrown to her death. He launched into a bizarre rant, accusing one of his ex-wife's relatives of threatening his life. He went on to claim this relative had been involved in an Argyle diamond robbery in Western Australia and rambled on about Federal Police taps. Amid the commotion, he was restrained by three burly security guards, who handcuffed him, still yelling, and led him away.

As Arthur Freeman began a sentence that would keep him behind bars for years to come, many unanswered questions lingered about his horrific crime. The officer in charge of the investigation, Senior Sergeant Damian Jackson, would later tell an inquest into the little girl's death that her father had never provided an account of what had taken place on that sweltering January morning. And as Justice Coghlan observed during sentencing, in the absence of any explanation, nobody would ever really know what was in Freeman's mind when he murdered his only daughter on what was to have been her first day of school.

Freeman himself claimed to have no memory of the crime, telling at least one psychiatrist after his arrest that he didn't even remember the chilling phone conversation with his ex-wife. Curiously, what he did recall with some clarity was feeling 'trapped' as he drove onto the bridge and feeling like a failure when he realised he would not make it to his children's primary school on time. Freeman admitted it was plausible that he imagined his ex-wife would berate him for his lateness. But apart from these recollections, the rest remained a blur.

Perhaps the only real insight into Darcey's murder is contained in one of the reports by the psychologist Freeman so disliked. Clinical psychologist Jennifer Neoh revealed that when Darcey was asked which parent she preferred to be with, the little girl chose her mum.

Neoh noted that Darcey had become very close to her mother during Freeman's absence after the divorce. One of the factors that had to be considered was the little girl's educational and social needs and it was agreed they were best met by her mother.

Sadly, the whole truth may never be known, lost somewhere in the colourful distraction of Arthur Freeman's claims of insanity.

Days before the second anniversary of his crime, *Herald Sun* journalist Paul Anderson revisited the crime that had shaken Melbourne. In his article, Anderson revealed that Freeman's bizarre antics had not been reserved for the spotlight of the courtroom. He cited an occasion when Freeman supposedly refused to appear in court, stripping off his clothes in the back of the prison van in a show of protest on his way to his trial. On another occasion Anderson claimed Freeman was rumoured to have refused to leave his holding cell to attend court.

He said that after the trial, Freeman's friends continued to struggle to reconcile the deranged mad monk character in the headlines with the 'excessively caring father' who, after his arrest, had fretted that there would be nobody to read his children their bedtime stories.

Months after being sentenced to life imprisonment, Arthur Freeman appealed against his sentence, arguing it was manifestly harsh and should be reduced. His appeal was rejected by Supreme Court Justice Chris Maxwell. Before the year was out, Freeman made another bid for a reduced sentence, asking Supreme Court Chief Justice Marilyn Warren and her colleagues Justices Geoffrey Nettle and David Beach for leave to appeal again. Again the Victorian Court of Appeal rejected his request, and once again there was no sign of emotion — or any reaction at all — from the appellant, who took part in the proceedings by video link from prison.

Freeman wasn't the only one to launch legal proceedings. One year after Arthur Freeman was jailed for life, his former wife launched a civil action against VicRoads, the authority responsible for the West Gate Bridge, alleging it had ignored warnings about the need for safety barriers on the bridge. In her writ, Peta Barnes claimed her daughter's life might have been saved if VicRoads had followed the recommendations of a former state coroner who called for the installation of safety barriers on the bridge as far back as 2005. The coroner's urgings came in response to the average eight suicides a year then occurring on the landmark bridge. But his recommendations were ignored after VicRoads advised the State Government that the estimated cost of the works would be $10 million.

After the murder, temporary safety barriers were installed on the West Gate Bridge and a project to erect permanent fencing was fast-tracked by the Victorian Government. It was finally installed at a cost of $20 million. Suicides since then have reportedly fallen by 85 per cent.

In her Supreme Court action against VicRoads Peta Barnes claimed her daughter's death had been due to their negligence and had caused her nervous shock. The case reached a confidential settlement in 2015.

In July that same year, an inquest opened into Darcey Freeman's death as the Victorian Coroner's Court investigated the exact cause of death and whether improvements could be made to better protect children in the wake of the little girl's murder. At the family's request, Darcey was referred to throughout the proceedings by her name, rather than as the 'deceased'.

State Coroner Ian Gray heard that two different doctors had been told that Arthur Freeman was violent in the months before his daughter's murder. In a statement tendered into evidence one of the doctors agreed Peta Barnes had told him in April 2007 that her former husband was angry and irrational, had shoved and pushed her, and been angry towards his children. Peta Barnes' GP also conceded in his statement that the worried mother had expressed fears that Freeman might harm her children. But the doctors said they had observed nothing about his behaviour to suggest he was being violent to his children, or might harm them.

Professor Kelsey Hegarty from the Royal Australasian College of General Practitioners told the inquest that the doctors had not acted inappropriately, despite the mandatory reporting obligations on Victorian doctors when informed about suspected child abuse. She said reporting requirements for GPs were subjective and that both doctors knew the separated mother was already dealing with police and lawyers, whom they assumed were better placed to take care of safety issues relating to the children.

Later, outside court, Professor Hegarty called for mandatory family-violence training for GPs and called for a Medicare-funded 'family safety plan' to be implemented along similar lines to a mental health plan.

At the inquest Darcey's mother praised the water police for their efforts to save her little girl, describing them as unsung heroes. She also praised the work of the medical staff at the Royal Children's Hospital and other emergency workers involved in the case. Peta Barnes also said she believed the lead investigator on the case, Senior Sergeant Damian Jackson, should receive an award from Victoria Police for his exemplary conduct.

In October 2015, the Victorian coroner issued a report of his findings into the death of Darcey Iris Freeman, saying no one was to blame for her death except her father, who had murdered her. He said nobody could have predicted that Arthur Freeman was going to throw his daughter to her death that day.

'The evidence before me leads me to conclude that Freeman's actions, and Darcey's death, were unable to be predicted with any great certainty,' he stated. The responsibility for the little girl's death lay solely with her father. The coroner ruled that the little girl had died from brain injury after falling to her death from a great height.

While the coroner made no criticism of the professionals involved with the family, he found there was room for better training about the risks of family violence.

Today, the barriers on the West Gate Bridge that might have saved Darcey Freeman's life are a haunting reminder of the tragedy. For the families, the emergency workers, the court staff, and other witnesses whose lives were forever changed on the morning of 29 January 2009, it is impossible to drive across the West Gate Bridge without remembering the little girl whose life was cut so cruelly short.

A short drive away, in protective custody behind the bars of a high-security prison, the father responsible spends his days alone, busying himself with his tomato plants in the prison's gardens.

In December 2014, shortly before the fifth anniversary of the murder, the *Herald Sun* reviewed the horrific crime yet again. Journalist Paul Anderson spoke to friends and former classmates who had known Freeman well. One former close mate compared Freeman with another notorious Australian killer, Martin Bryant, who had killed 35 people and injured 23 more at Port Arthur in 1996. Bryant remains Australia's worst mass murderer.

Like Freeman, Martin Bryant had also been a misfit, a loner who had been tormented at school, where classmates nicknamed him 'silly Martin'. Like Freeman, Bryant struggled with interpersonal relationships and found it a challenge to express himself emotionally or verbally. At Bryant's trial it was suggested he suffered from Asperger's syndrome, which is on the autism spectrum. It has been speculated that Arthur Freeman may also have Asperger's.

Comparing the two killers, Freeman's friend, who refused to be identified, said that like Bryant, Artie Freeman was harmless until he got 'that look'.

'He would get that stare,' the friend told the newspaper. 'Bloody oath, it was scary. It was when he got bullied a bit and had had too much … they picked on him [Freeman] because he was harmless. But everyone knew he had that ability; that something inside him that could explode at any time.'

CHAPTER 5
'Look what you made me do!'
The story of Rachelle D'Argent and Yazmina Micheline Acar

A trail of pink balloons disappeared high above the clouds, casting a rose-tinged shadow over the crowd of 200 relatives and close friends who had gathered for a birthday party whose little star was absent.

Yazmina Micheline Acar's third birthday on 23 November 2010 was a far cry from the joy-filled celebrations her 24-year-old mother, Rachelle D'Argent, had envisaged when she promised her only child a day to remember. The tot was just old enough to grasp the notion of a milestone when people who loved her would shower her with cards and gifts. Her face had lit up as her mother described the balloons, the Dora the Explorer cake, the face-painting and the clown who would add a sparkle to her biggest day yet.

Yazmina — affectionately known as Mimi — would never get the chance to open her presents or experience the thrill of hearing her tiny guests sing happy birthday. There would be no more birthdays for the precocious little girl who loved singing and dancing and being the centre of attention. Her milestone was extinguished by the one man she trusted above all others to love and protect her.

Six days earlier, on 17 November, a drunk and drug-affected Ramazan Kerem Acar, aged 23, had turned up outside his estranged partner's home in suburban Melbourne demanding to see his daughter. It was the twenty-eighth time Acar had breached an intervention order taken out by Rachelle D'Argent to protect herself and Mimi from her ex-partner's explosive temper. His appearance meant he was in breach of a suspended prison sentence imposed on him for an earlier act of violence towards his former fiancée. But after three days on a drink-and-drugs bender, Ramazan Acar didn't care.

After a brief discussion with his ex, Acar tricked Rachelle into letting him drive his daughter to a nearby milk bar on the pretext of buying Yazmina a chocolate Kinder Surprise. Instead, he kidnapped the child, sparking a police manhunt across Melbourne. During the manhunt he cruelly taunted her mother with a barrage of bizarre, menacing phone calls and texts, and posted death threats on his Facebook page.

After six hours of torment, the snivelling father led detectives to a deserted reserve where he had dumped the lifeless body of the tiny girl who adored him. There was no doubting his motivation for the brutal murder. Before he attacked his daughter with a large ornamental knife, he posted his motivation on Facebook for the world to see: 'Paybk u slut.'

Six days later, in an incredible show of strength, the stricken young mother who had been the real target of Ramazan Acar's violent rage made one last stand against the brutal ex who had murdered their only child.

'We're going to celebrate ... it's not a sad day,' Rachelle D'Argent told reporters who gathered at Lysterfield Lake Park, where party guests dressed in Yazmina's favourite colour released matching pink balloons in honour of a little girl who would never grow up.

Hiding her pain behind giant sunglasses, Mimi's mother said, 'She would have wanted us to be smiling and dancing, because that is what she would have been doing ... She was the most beautiful girl in the world ... She is still with us. Her smile is still here, with everyone.'

Sadly, there were no smiles two days later when 400 people packed into Our Lady Help of Christians Catholic Church in Narre Warren to pay their last respects to the tiny girl who loved to ride her pink Barbie bike and sing French folk songs with her grandma, a member of Melbourne's Mauritian community. Sobbing into tissues, Rachelle repeatedly kissed the framed photo of Mimi and clutched her favourite teddy bear as relatives paid tribute to the little 'angel' who had been cruelly taken from them. As the tiny pink coffin covered in white flowers was lowered into the ground, the latest young casualty of family violence made news around Australia.

Father John Allen, the priest who conducted the service, told the congregation that Mimi's premature death was 'a tragedy beyond comprehension'. Nothing was said about the dreadful circumstances surrounding the toddler's murder, although the priest noted the anger and bewilderment of those who had loved her. He urged everyone to remember the joy the little girl had generated in her short life. A family friend addressing the service said that Mimi was now singing and dancing in heaven 'and probably bossing people around too'.

In the *Herald Sun* the following day, journalist Patrick Carlyon described the touching slide show capturing the highlights of a life so cruelly cut short. Mourners sobbed as Mimi's bright little face beamed for the camera, showing off on her bike and playing the drums for a proud mum who believed a lifetime of memories and dreams lay waiting.

Mimi's death was not God's will, said Father Allen. But God's will was at work in this shared sadness. And he said God's will demanded that people should never take anyone for granted, or ignore the struggles of others. 'They were fitting words for a send-off where no words would ever do,' Carlyon observed.

Ironically, words had never been in short supply during Ramazan Acar and Rachelle D'Argent's turbulent six-year relationship. The pair had been teenage sweethearts but, within months of dating, a dark side of Acar's personality had emerged. He became angry, jealous and possessive of his pretty new girlfriend.

Frequent arguments erupted over nothing, leaving Acar spitting furious threats at the stunned teenager. Eight months after the relationship began, his words gave way to fists and his hair-trigger temper became more frightening and unpredictable. He regularly bashed his partner and threatened her life. While Rachelle never understood what started these blazing arguments, she quickly learned how they would end.

In an exclusive interview with Channel Nine's *Sixty Minutes*, aired after Acar had been jailed for murder, Rachelle gave viewers a worrying insight into his dark explosive rages when she recalled an incident one night not long after they met.

'He seemed to have a problem with me for something or other,' she told viewers. 'He hit me pretty much like a man, and I fell straight to the floor and he spat on me. His temper just came out and he showed me the real him. He, in his exact words, said: "This is the real me. Now you know who the man is."'

By the time Rachelle D'Argent understood who the man really was, it was already too late.

One of five children, Ramazan Acar was born to hard-working Turkish parents who lived in Melbourne's northern suburbs. At high school Acar was an athletic student whose sporting achievements were never matched by his academic performance. By 13 he was regularly using cannabis and by 15 he had dropped out of school altogether. For a couple of years he drifted from job to job, trying his hand at various trades from panel beating and house painting, to roof tiling. His teenage years were marked by a string of petty offences, including a $750 fine for possessing a general-category handgun on a train, which he later argued was a cigarette lighter in the shape of a gun.

At 18 he met Rachelle D'Argent, but shortly afterwards his family sold their home and moved to Griffith in New South Wales. Acar and another brother moved with them, the siblings briefly working as farm labourers. While living in the rural community, Acar began using amphetamines and soon developed a taste for heavy drugs including speed and ice.

In 2005 Rachelle and her mother visited him in New South Wales. When they returned to Melbourne, Acar decided to leave with them. Back in Melbourne, the couple moved in with Rachelle's father, who lived at Hampton Park. But Acar's amphetamine use was growing, igniting his simmering anger and his violence towards his frightened partner.

In January 2006, after he'd been drinking with Rachelle and other family members, an argument erupted during which Acar attacked his terrified partner and held a knife to her throat. When the police were alerted, Acar became histrionic and stabbed himself in the stomach with two steak knives. The police later found him bleeding profusely and hiding in the house with the knives. He was subdued with capsicum spray and taken to hospital. Later he was arrested and charged with the assault on Rachelle. After spending two months in custody, he was bailed and returned to his family in New South Wales.

By the time the case reached the courts, his family had returned to Melbourne and bought a house in Meadow Heights. But despite the chilling nature of the assault on Rachelle and the threat to her life, their relationship was far from over. The couple began seeing each other again, though each remained living at their respective parents' homes.

In February 2007, Acar appeared before the Dandenong Magistrates' Court. He admitted the attack on Rachelle and received a three-month prison sentence, suspended for two years. He was convicted of three counts of unlawful assault, threats to kill and threatening serious injury.

But the suspended prison sentence did nothing to change the relationship's dynamic and the violence continued. Rachelle soon found herself trapped in a cycle of violent angry attacks, profuse apologies and promises that things would change. Nothing did.

In March 2007 Rachelle announced she was pregnant and the couple began living together again. Acar, who had found work as a panel beater, moved into Rachelle's mother's home in Hallam. He asked his pregnant partner to marry him and she said yes. By the time their daughter Yazmina Micheline Acar was born on 23 November 2007, the pressure was mounting.

In June 2008, when Mimi was seven months old, Acar fronted court again, this time for drink-driving matters. The new offences put him in breach of his earlier suspended sentence, which meant he had to be sentenced for the driving offences and the original assault on Rachelle. Acar ended up serving three months behind bars for the original crime, and received another suspended prison sentence for the driving offences. His time in jail cost him his panel-beating apprenticeship.

When Acar was eventually released from prison with yet another suspended sentence hanging over him, his difficulties in securing new employment added to the struggling young parents' burden. His heavy amphetamine use and his increasing dependence on cannabis and alcohol meant that his employment was sporadic and his moods became more unpredictable than ever. In another violent attack in November 2008, Acar hit Rachelle and again stabbed himself in the stomach. He was charged with this latest assault, which again put him in breach of his suspended sentence and spelled an end to the dysfunctional relationship. In January 2009, at Rachelle's request, he packed his things and moved back in with his family.

Acar's employer had become so concerned about his lifestyle and poor attitude to his work, that he suspended him for two weeks without pay and insisted he attend counselling. Despite their separation, the couple attended three joint counselling sessions at Positive Lifestyle Counselling Services in Dandenong. They abandoned the sessions after Acar assaulted Michelle again in April.

By this time Acar's continued threats left his estranged partner fearing for her life. Rachelle knew only too well what he was capable of. She took out a number of intervention orders, but let them all lapse.

At some stage during 2009, no doubt prompted by his looming court case and the possibility of another stint in prison, Acar enrolled in a program directed at tackling male violence. During his sessions, run by Kildonian Uniting Care, counsellors observed that Acar was 'a young man with very strong ideas that will require ongoing work in the area of change'. On a more positive note, the course counsellors noted that he finally appeared to be displaying empathy for the impact of his actions on others.

Amid the turmoil and the pending court appearance, the couple resumed their stormy on-off relationship. In June 2009 they moved into a rental property in Meadow Heights and Acar found new employment as a bricklayer. In November that year Acar again fronted court, where he was convicted of recklessly causing injury to Rachelle in his attack the previous November. He was given a two-month prison sentence, suspended for one year.

Sadly, neither the threat of another prison sentence nor the family-violence course did anything to address Acar's aggression or his growing drug problem. By the time the 12-month lease on their rental property was due to expire, the abusive relationship was on the rocks again. In May 2010, unable to cope with her partner's drug-fuelled mood swings and violence, the young mother told Acar it was over. He grudgingly returned home to his parents' and Rachelle moved to a new rental home in Hallam, determined to escape the cycle of abuse and make a fresh start for herself and her daughter.

But if Rachelle D'Argent was ready to move on, her former fiancé was not. Unable to accept that the relationship was over, he continued harassing and tormenting her. He sent threatening text messages and made menacing calls, and sometimes he turned up outside her new address 'drug fried' and harangued her. Frightened, Rachelle responded by changing her telephone numbers. But he was incorrigible and the harassment and threats continued.

On 12 September 2010, Acar turned up outside her home again, slashing her tyres and carving the word 'slut' onto a wooden post. He was reported to the police who charged him with tampering with a motor vehicle and intentionally damaging property. The frightened woman was granted an interim intervention order by an after-hours magistrate that same day to protect herself and her daughter. This order prevented Acar from approaching or having contact with Rachelle or their daughter. A copy was immediately faxed to the Broadmeadows police station, close to Acar's parents' home where he was now living.

On 16 September 2010 Rachelle attended the Dandenong Magistrates' Court where she gave evidence about the harassment and threats. She told the court about her fears for her own safety and that of her child. A full intervention order was served on Acar the following day at the Broadmeadows police station where the conditions of the order were fully explained to him. Constable Alison

Heap warned Acar he was not to contact Michelle in any way, or engage a third party to contact her on his behalf. He had to stay away from her and their little girl.

But it seems the police's stern warnings fell on deaf ears. Nine days later Acar texted Rachelle, who promptly reported the breach to Narre Warren police. The police warned him again to stay away. He ignored them. On 15 October Acar was arrested and interviewed at the Broadmeadows police station in connection with further breaches of the intervention order. He openly admitted he'd been contacting his former partner but claimed he had been motivated by a desire to see his daughter. This time he was charged with breaching the intervention order.

As far as Rachelle was concerned, the police were powerless to protect her. In just two months, from the time Rachelle was granted the intervention order to 18 November when he murdered their daughter, Acar breached his order 28 times.

At some time in late September, no doubt prompted by his ex-partner's refusal to allow him access to his daughter, Ramazan Acar inquired about the Family Dispute Resolution Program being operated by the Family Relationship Centre in Broadmeadows. It appears his interest was only fleeting, since he took no action beyond the preliminary inquiries. By then it was clear to the agencies dealing with him that the separated father was struggling with his life. In late 2010 he was referred by Centrelink to psychologist Peter Stanislawski.

Mr Stanislawski would later recall in a report to the Victorian Supreme Court that during the four sessions he had with Acar, the angry young father spoke openly about his dependence on cannabis. Acar acknowledged that it was an issue and one he wanted to address. He also spoke about his violent behaviour towards his estranged partner, for which he appeared genuinely remorseful. During their sessions, Acar told the counsellor he wanted to address his problems so that he could be a good father to his little girl.

Despite being charged with repeatedly breaching his intervention order, and the constant warnings of the police that he would be jailed if he continued, Acar remained unstoppable. Court documents would later reveal that Acar had not only threatened to kill Rachelle, he had also made threats to kill her mother, her partner and the partner's daughter.

In early November, desperate to see his daughter, Acar again attempted to call his ex-partner in spite of the apprehended violence order. When he discovered Rachelle had changed her phone numbers to avoid his constant calls, he called her mother, Micheline, asking her to pass his message on. When Rachelle telephoned her ex-partner he turned on the charm. He told her he was due in court to face new driving charges and wanted to see his little girl before he got locked up again. Despite his longstanding history of violence towards her and the repeated threats on her life, Rachelle acknowledged that he had never abused or threatened to harm their little daughter, who loved her dad as much as he appeared to love her. Reluctantly, on 6 November 2010, Rachelle agreed that she and Mimi would meet him at the Fountain Gate Shopping Centre.

When Rachelle first noticed Acar walking through the shopping mall towards her that day, she found it hard to hide her shock. 'Ramzy' appeared to be a changed person, she would later tell police. He seemed very gentle and affectionate towards their daughter.

She watched the proud dad carrying Yazmina on his shoulders with a new optimism. Perhaps Acar was finally changing for the better, she thought in relief, noticing the broad smile on her daughter's face as she ran towards her dad. That same enduring belief that Acar really could change had kept her trapped in a cycle of violence for six years. When she left him that afternoon on 6 November she harboured the same hopes all over again.

A week later Acar rang Rachelle again, asking for permission to have his little girl for an overnight access visit at his parents' home. Convinced he had finally turned the corner, the young mother relented. During the Saturday evening, Rachelle received a number of texts from her former partner, telling her about their daughter's excited reaction when she saw his family again after such a long absence, even detailing the meals she'd eaten. Acar also made several posts on his Facebook page during the night, indicating his delight at being allowed to have his little girl for the sleepover.

But by the time Acar returned Yazmina to her mother's unit the following afternoon the gloom was descending again. After dropping the little girl off, he drove to a nearby park where he smoked cannabis and began to fester about his changed role in Mimi's life. In his dope-induced haze, the paranoid Acar became consumed by the belief that he was being squeezed out of his daughter's life. Her mother appeared to be moving on and was studying to become a real-estate agent. Rachelle appeared adamant this time that there would be no further reconciliations. He believed she might even be seeing someone else. His black mood darkened.

During the late afternoon Acar made a series of harassing phone calls, ringing Rachelle so many times that she had to remind him he was breaching the intervention order. She told him that it would be less intrusive if he called every few days and only then to inquire about Mimi or to speak to her. He seemed reasonable and accepted the request.

Ironically, while Acar hated the idea of Rachelle seeing another man, he was already seeing someone new himself. Recognising his efforts to reconcile with his estranged partner were futile, he had recently struck up a relationship with a young woman called Gul Rose Ocal. But Rose had become cautious about the intensity of the fledgling relationship, and felt it was moving too fast.

After work on Monday 15 November, Acar spent the night partying, turning up at work drunk and sleep deprived the following morning. At work he smoked some cannabis and then left early. He drove to see Rose Ocal, but became upset when she told him the new relationship was progressing too fast and suggested they slow things down. Acar later texted her in Turkish saying dramatically: 'You were my last breath but I'm not shit, you've burned my heart.'

Feeling overwhelmed, Acar purchased more alcohol and disappeared into a local park where he consumed the alcohol and smoked more marijuana. The combination of booze and dope left him more maudlin than ever and he pulled out a knife and began slashing at his arms and abdomen. Later in the evening he telephoned his family, informing them that he was going to drive to the Broadmeadows police station armed with a knife in an attempt to force the police to either arrest him or shoot him. He said he preferred these outcomes to another jail sentence for the driving offences and breaching his intervention order.

Armed with the knife, Acar did drive to Broadmeadows police station. But when he arrived in the car park, his worried father and his brother's father-in-law were waiting for him. They were not prepared to stand by while he generated a possible 'suicide by cop' scenario, and attempted to persuade the drunken young man to leave with them. But Acar became abusive towards his father, raging, 'Life is at an end for me.' After some discussion, the two older men finally persuaded him to leave with them and he spent the night sleeping off his drink-and-drugs binge at his brother's home.

On Wednesday 17 November he arrived at work early and quit his job. Then he drove to the nearest bottle shop to buy alcohol and headed off to a nearby park where he again got drunk and started slashing himself.

By lunchtime he had sunk into a drunken depression, and found his way to his grandmother's grave and the resting place of a close friend, where he continued drinking. At 1 p.m. he sent a disturbing text message to Rachelle D'Argent stating: 'RIP Ramazan Kerem Acar 1987–2010.' Then from his mobile he posted on his Facebook page, 'The truth iz im in love.'

About an hour later, Rachelle received another bizarre text from her drunken former fiancé.

> You wantd to convert ma kid, do it. U wanted to lock me up, I did it. You wanted 2b independent, do it. U wanta take full custody do it, u wana kill me, I'll do it. Wat eva makes u happy … tel me. [sic]

At around 3.27 p.m. that day Acar drove erratically along the Monash Freeway towards the Heatherton Road exit, which is around three to four kilometres from his former partner's unit in George Chudleigh

Drive, Hallam. Ten minutes later he sent Rachelle another text, asking: 'Can I talk 2 Mimi?'

She responded, 'Mimz at creche, bt can u plz cal me?' Then she texted him saying she would be home in 20 minutes. Acar texted her back, telling her to hurry up because he needed to talk to her. At 4.15 p.m. Rachelle arrived home with her friend Natalie Young to find Acar's vehicle parked outside her unit. While the women parked behind the property, Acar moved his own car further down the street and pulled over. Being so close to the house put him in breach of the intervention order for the twenty-eighth time since September.

Rachelle approached the car to speak with Acar and noticed through the open window that he had a large 30-centimetre ornamental fantasy knife on his lap. When she asked him about the knife, he told her he'd had enough of life. To illustrate his point he showed her the superficial slashes along his abdomen and arms. This was nothing new to Rachelle, who had witnessed Acar stabbing himself in the past. She suspected it was another attention-seeking exercise.

Acar asked to see their daughter, and Rachelle and her girlfriend drove to the Amberley Park Drive Childcare and Early Learning Centre to collect Mimi. On the way, Rachelle told her friend that Acar had a knife and had been slashing himself. She suspected he was drunk. At 4.40 p.m. Acar texted asking where she was and she texted back to say they had collected Yazmina and were on their way home.

But Acar was growing impatient and sent another SMS demanding to know where they were. But when the two women arrived at the house at 5.15 p.m. there was no sign of him. Rachelle rang to ask where he was, and within minutes he was back in the street, parking his car on the nature strip out the front.

Yazmina was thrilled to see her father and bounded towards the car, smiling with delight. Her mother would later say the little girl 'had stars in her eyes' that day. Acar lifted the tot onto his lap where she played and scribbled with a pen on some bits of paper. At some stage Acar placed the large knife on the car dashboard in full view of Rachelle, who stood beside the car keeping a watchful eye on her daughter.

Mimi was still sitting on her dad's knee at 6 p.m. when Rachelle's friend, Sonia-Rita Mardirossian, called around at see them. The friend was still there 15 minutes later when Rachelle told the estranged father that she had things she needed to do with Mimi, and suggested it was time for him to say goodbye. Acar asked if he could drive the child around the corner to the local milk bar before he went, so that he could buy her a chocolate Kinder Surprise. Rachelle hesitated.

'What, don't you trust me?' he wheedled. 'I haven't taken her away from you, like you took her away from me.' Rachelle reluctantly agreed. The milk bar was one minute's drive away, she reasoned. She told him to come straight back with Mimi and watched as he drove his car erratically around the corner with their little girl inside. Her nightmare had just begun.

Out of sight, Acar rang his girlfriend Rose Ocal, who overheard a child talking in the background.

At 6.23 p.m. Rachelle D'Argent called Acar asking where he was. She was amazed when he told her he had taken Mimi for a McDonald's meal in Fountain Gate. At 6.40 p.m. she phoned again. This time he said he was near a 'weird church'. In the volley of phone calls and text messages that followed Rachelle pleaded with Acar to return their daughter. At some stage, her friend Sonia-Rita Mardirossian took the phone and sternly warned Acar that unless he returned Mimi within 10 minutes, she would contact the police. At the mention of the police he became abusive and hung up. At 6.50 Rachelle telephoned him again, anxiously asking where he was. Acar replied menacingly:

'How does it feel not to have your child when I didn't have mine for months?'

Rachelle nervously asked him to stop 'joking around' and to bring their daughter straight home. But by 7 p.m. there was still no sign of Acar. When she called again he sounded angry and informed her he had taken Mimi to a park in Narre Warren. He demanded to know whether the police had been contacted and ordered Rachelle to drive to Narre Warren police station and withdraw her statement reporting the earlier breach of the intervention order. When she refused, he told her cryptically, 'Well, I can't do you any favours,' and hung up.

When Rachelle rang again 15 minutes later, he said: 'Payback's a bitch, how does it feel?' She felt sick, and pleaded with him to bring their daughter home.

'Guess what baby, you're not getting her back,' he threatened. 'I loved you Rachelle and look what you've made me do now.' He went on to taunt her. 'I just have to decide whether to go 120 kilometres an hour head on with another car and kill the both of us, or take the knife and just put it through her throat. I loved you more than her, and that's why I'm doing this.' The menacing nature of the threat prompted the women to call the police and report the little girl's kidnapping and the threat to her life.

At 7.23 p.m. on 17 November, in a chilling omen of things to come, Ramazan Acar posted an update on his Facebook page from his mobile phone. It said, 'bout to kill ma kid'. One minute later, he sent Rachelle a text saying he loved her. Nine minutes later, at exactly 7.32 p.m., in yet another chilling SMS he wrote, 'It's ova, I did it.' This was followed by the Facebook post two minutes later saying, 'Paybk u slut.'

A distraught Rachelle D'Argent continued to text Acar begging him to bring her daughter back.

'Ramzy please just bring Yazmina back, we can work things out, just bring our daughter back.' He didn't reply.

In the harrowing 40 minutes of silence that followed his last text, Victoria Police put out an alert to find the kidnapped child. An intensive manhunt was underway to find the out-of-control father armed with a knife and threatening to kill his own daughter. While the police searched the streets and nearby parks for signs of Acar's car, his own father and two of his brothers, who had been alerted to Yazmina's disappearance, were also out looking for him. While everyone searched, Acar fled across the city towards the northern suburbs. At some stage during the early evening his father and brothers spotted his car on the freeway. But when they drove up behind him, he put his foot down and quickly lost them in the traffic.

Rachelle's panic was rising. Acar had never threatened to harm their daughter before. He had always been an attention-seeker prone to dramatic histrionics but, apart from slashing himself and hurting her, he'd never injured anyone else. While she told herself this was just another of Acar's melodramas, the police were not so sure. They urged the young mother to keep the lines of communication open if Acar contacted her again.

The frightened mother's instincts that Acar had been bluffing when he made his cruel taunt at 7.32 p.m. saying 'It's ova, I did it' proved to be correct. His daughter was still alive when he sent that message. The sick cat-and-mouse game continued as he fled across Melbourne, convinced the police were out looking for him. Even in his drunken state, he realised if they apprehended him he would be charged with drink-driving and who knows what else. For a man already contemplating a likely prison sentence, new charges would seal his fate and he would never see his daughter again. As his anxiety built, Acar got lost and found himself at Melbourne Airport. He promptly turned the car and drove towards Campbelltown. At 8.21 p.m. Rachelle was with the police when Acar rang again. Senior Constable Flower heard the enraged father's menacing threat from the end of the line.

'I'm going to kill her,' he said. The officer listened as the young mother pleaded again with her estranged partner to return their child. And he heard Acar's chilling response:

'It's too late, I'm going to do it, I'm going to do it. Do you have any last words for her?'

Acar put Yazmina on the line.

'I love you,' the unsuspecting toddler said.

'I love you too,' her anxious mother replied. Then the phone went dead.

Two minutes later, Rachelle received another text.

'Too l8t, c ya.' it read.

At some stage after this ominous text, Acar parked his car and observed Mimi quietly playing outside on the grass. He climbed out, armed with the large ornate knife. He would later tell a psychiatrist who assessed him that he briefly glimpsed the fear in his little girl's eyes as she surveyed the knife in his hand. The tot must have sensed danger because she'd started to cry. But not even the tears of his own flesh and blood were enough to dissuade him from the action he'd decided to take. Wielding the knife, Acar stabbed his little girl multiple times in the chest and abdomen. Despite the vicious nature of his attack, the blade somehow missed all her major organs. An autopsy would later confirm that Mimi's death had been a prolonged and painful one.

After the murder, Acar dumped his daughter's body in vacant scrubland off a track on the Greenvale Reserve close to a new housing development. At Narre Warren the child's mother waited patiently for news, telling herself Acar was just sadistically 'stirring' her up as he often had. She was with police when Acar texted her again at 8.47 p.m., asking her to call back. When she did, he told her coldly:

'I've killed her. She's just lying there next to me in her leggings and her top covered in blood and her guts are hanging out.'

Refusing to believe it, Rachelle told him not to be 'stupid' and asked where they were. During the eight minutes and twenty seconds of conversation that followed Acar replied:

'It does not matter any more. All I need to know is should I dump the body somewhere and how much time do you think I'm going to get for this. I've killed my daughter, man, I've killed her. I've killed her to get back at you. I don't even care if I go behind bars, I know that you are suffering. I've killed her, I swear to God I've killed her. You know those shows on Foxtel that you watch on the crime channel with the psycho people. I feel like one of them now. Seriously, I'm sorry.'

While the police continued their search, Acar had driven to his parents' home in Meadow Heights. He sat in the driveway in his car where his mother begged him to tell her where her granddaughter was and to return the child to her mother immediately. But he refused to tell her anything. When his older brother emerged from the house and demanded to know where the child was, the conversation became heated and Acar sped off.

In a couple of texts to Rose Ocal, the pair agreed to meet at McDonald's in Campbellfield. As he drove to the rendezvous, Acar texted Rachelle. 'I'm sorry,' he wrote.

At McDonald's, Acar dropped the bombshell that his little girl was dead. Rose Ocal did not believe him and suspected this was just an attention-seeking ruse. She believed him even less when he changed his story, saying vaguely that he had done 'something' and could not leave his vehicle at McDonald's. Ms Ocal agreed to follow his car to the Merri Creek Concourse in Campbellfield, an area occupied by light industry. She watched in amazement as Acar set his vehicle alight, then climbed into her car and ordered her to drive away.

From her front passenger seat, at 10.24 p.m., Acar called his mother.

'It's all over,' he said ominously. 'It's finished.'

Again, his worried mother urged him to return Mimi to her mum.

'She's in safe hands,' he replied vaguely.

Then he texted the child's mother again telling her: 'I H8t u.'

Shortly after this, he sent Rachelle another SMS message stating he was going to the Broadmeadows police station to hand himself in.

'Yazmina's in heaven,' he wrote. 'I feel lyk shit.'

Then he updated his Facebook page: 'I lv u Mimi,' he wrote. At 11.21 p.m., after five long hours of torment, Rachelle D'Argent received one final SMS from her former partner. It stated simply: 'plz'.

Nine minutes later, the car was intercepted in Epping by officers from the Special Operations Group.

Both occupants were arrested and taken into police custody. On the other side of the city, Rachelle D'Argent waited anxiously for news of her daughter. She had no idea that shortly after midnight, her former partner was confessing to Mimi's murder.

Acar told Detective Sergeant David Butler he had stabbed Yazmina multiple times and had later dumped her body on vacant land near a new housing development in Greenvale. He confessed he had discarded the murder weapon elsewhere. Acar agreed to take Detective Sergeant Butler and his colleague, Constable Mark Franco, to the spot where he had left his daughter's body. The officers placed him in the back of a police car and headed out into the darkness. During the car ride, Acar told Franco that he had done something 'really bad'. Again he admitted stabbing his daughter. 'Now she's dead,' he said.

He estimated that the crime occurred at around 8 p.m., which did not marry with the conversation Mimi had with her mother at 8.21 p.m. Later, in his formal statement, Acar qualified the time of the murder, saying the crime took place as the sun was going down. He also admitted that he was so embarrassed by the size of the murder weapon in comparison to his tiny daughter that he had disposed of it at an entirely different location.

When he and the police arrived at the remote track where his child's body lay, Acar remained seated in the police car. But if the enormity of his crime now appeared to be sinking in, it was his own situation that appeared to be troubling him more.

'Am I going to be on the news?' he later asked Franco, looking worried. 'My face and all … like Hudson.' He was referring to gunman Christopher Hudson, who had shot a man to death in the CBD and was jailed for murder in 2008.

'Fucking cunts will kill me in jail for this.' Acar then asked the officer naively: 'Is this murder?'

'What do you think?' Franco replied curtly.

'Yes, but I was drunk when it happened. I can't believe it,' Acar answered.

Franco made no comment.

'How long do you think I will get?' continued Acar. 'Do you think it may be life?' He began to cry. 'Why did I do it?'

Yazmina's blood-soaked body was finally located at 1.37 a.m. on Thursday 18 November on grassland off the Somerton Track on the northern end of the Greenvale Reserve near the Greenvale Reservoir. The bright little girl who had been so excited about turning three, lay on her right side, fully clothed. Police observed multiple stab wounds across her chest and abdomen. Acar had been telling the truth in his graphic description of his daughter's body. Mimi's wounds were so significant that her major organs were exposed. Another sizeable stab wound was found on the little girl's tiny elbow. Paramedics called to the remote location on the corners of Somerton and Kirkham Roads confirmed the child was dead. Police dog handlers later joined SES workers in a line search. The murder weapon was subsequently recovered from scrubland at Campbellfield.

After leading police to where he'd dumped the body, the killer father urged the police officers to put him in a cell 'with the dog', referring to the police dog involved in the search of the crime scene. Acar also told police he deserved 'a belting' and claimed he wanted to 'rot' or 'die'. He revealed he'd spent the three days leading up to the crime on a drinking binge and had also taken drugs. At some stage before his formal interview, he told police he knew what the father 'on the West Gate Bridge' had felt like. He was referring to Arthur Freeman, who had also callously called his estranged partner and told her to say goodbye to her children.

While Acar was being transported to St Kilda police headquarters in the city, Rachelle sat at the Narre Warren police station waiting to be reunited with her little girl. But when a detective finally emerged to tell her that her ex-partner was under arrest, it wasn't the news she'd been expecting.

'Where's Mimi?' she asked, bewildered.

After what Rachelle would later describe as 'the longest pause I have ever heard in my life', the detective gently explained that her little girl was dead. Yazmina's body had just been recovered from a suburban park, he revealed. Later, in her gut-wrenching victim impact statement to the Victorian Supreme Court, Rachelle Olivia D'Argent would describe her paralysing reaction to the shocking news in graphic detail.

'My ears went blocked,' she said. 'I could barely see or breathe and my whole body went numb … She was my reason for getting up in the morning.' All she remembered was the long agonising scream as she registered the sound of her own voice echoing across the police station.

While the child's grief-stricken mother was being comforted by family and friends, the man behind the unthinkable crime was sleeping off his drink-and-drug stupor in a police cell at St Kilda Road. The prisoner had earlier been assessed by a forensic medical officer who had deemed him unfit for formal interview. But after a few hours' sleep, he was reassessed by two other doctors who determined he was now fit to be questioned.

At 6 a.m. on 18 November, detectives from the Homicide Squad cautioned Acar and conducted a videotaped interview in the presence of independent advocate Fred Kent. Despite his earlier confession at Epping, Acar became emotional when asked specifically about the stabbing of his daughter. He refused to answer the detectives' probing questions or to give them specifics about the actual murder, though he did admit he had hidden the murder weapon out of embarrassment and torched his car. Acar's explanation for setting his car alight was that it held evidence of his drug use with other associates. During the interview he told police he had wanted to kill himself but hadn't had 'the balls' to do it.

He claimed alcohol, tiredness and frustration had all played a part in his crime. But a more sinister picture began to emerge as Acar explained how his estranged partner had wanted full custody of their little girl, and he had wanted her to feel what he felt.

'She took that kid away from me and I went through hell,' he told police. 'She won't understand what I went through, like ... I wanted her to feel it.' He also claimed that the knife had been in his car for at least three or four weeks after a friend supposedly left it there.

After blaming drugs, alcohol and tiredness for his crime, he then pointed the finger of blame at the victim's mother. It was all Rachelle's fault, he sniffed. After all, she'd been the one who had allowed him to take the child to the shops in the first place, even though she knew he had a knife.

'I was pretty surprised too when she let me go, like, all she had to do was call the cops and like, nothing would have happened —

fucking idiot! And the night before this I was going to hand myself in to the cops cos I was cutting myself. I was just fed up, man, just fed up with everything. Nothing goes my way. I didn't know why she let me go, cos I was sitting there, just having a good time with my kid right next to me, and it was nice. It was all smiles and laughs.'

Acar went on to elaborate: 'She put her trust back in me too, like, she's my kid and everything was going fine and she went and got the kid and she came back to the property and then my kid ran up. She ran up to my car with a big smile — she was happy to see me.'

On a more sinister note, Acar finally admitted that his offer to drive his little girl to the milk bar for a chocolate treat was nothing more than a ruse.

'I asked her [Rachelle] do you want anything from the shops, just to make her believe me so she thinks I'm really going there, coz I'm not ... so she thinks I'm not lying,' he said.

His decision to flee along the Monash Freeway was no accident either. He chose that route because he knew it was poorly lit. He had assumed that once his former partner realised he was not returning their daughter, she would call the police. If they were already in pursuit, he'd be harder to spot on this dimly lit highway.

While Acar had been sleeping, police inquiries into the background of the driver of the car he'd been found in ruled out her involvement in the crime. In her statement to police, Gul Rose Ocal was cooperative. She explained that although Acar had confessed to murdering his daughter, she had not believed a word of it. Like Yazmina's shattered mother, she'd thought it was just another drama and that he'd been attention-seeking.

At 7 p.m. that night, Ramazan Kerem Acar was formally charged with one count of murder. He made a brief appearance at an out-of-sessions hearing at the Melbourne Custody Centre and was remanded to appear before the Melbourne Magistrates Court. When he appeared there the following day he was barefoot, unshaven and dressed in overalls. He was remanded in custody and ordered to undergo a psychiatric assessment.

The day after his arrest, Melbourne's *Age* newspaper reported the tragic events, revealing that a post-mortem had confirmed the little murder victim had died of multiple stab wounds. Detective Senior Sergeant David Snare from the Homicide Squad told the paper:

'These are difficult circumstances for everyone involved. The young child, just starting life off, doesn't have the opportunity to grow into an adult. It's harrowing.'

The paper revealed that State Emergency workers had carried out a line search and the little girl's body had been taken away in a coroner's van at around 9.30 a.m. on 18 November.

The days that followed were a living nightmare for the grief-stricken mother, who should have been helping her little girl unwrap her birthday presents. Instead, she watched the pink balloons disappearing into the skies along with her dreams for her daughter.

In its coverage of the funeral, Melbourne's *Herald Sun* ran comments from the little girl's shattered grandfather, George D'Argent, under the headline 'Tears Flow for Little Yazmina Acar'.

'She was very much into the Wiggles and dancing to Lady Gaga's music,' George D'Argent said. 'We're still coming to grips with what happened. We're still trying to make sense of exactly why it happened. There are lots of ifs and buts. It's going to be very, very difficult.'

A man who claimed to be Acar's father but asked not to be named said Yazmina was 'an angel'. He told the newspaper, 'She always was. She always will be.'

Later, in her victim impact statement tendered to the Victorian Supreme Court, Rachelle D'Argent would describe the horror and disbelief she felt in the days following the tragedy.

'After Mimi's death, the next five days were hell,' she said. 'Not only did I barely know the details of what had happened, but every time I switched on the news, horrific details would appear and the story would come on and I stared in disbelief that that was my child. The first few weeks I cried every day. I yelled, I screamed, begging everyone to please bring her back to me. Then it turned to frustration. I realised that all the crying and shouting in the world could never bring my Mimi back to me.'

Frustrated and angry with everything and everyone, it would be four months before the shattered mother could even contemplate seeing a psychologist to begin to talk about her daughter's murder. She was unable to sleep, and exhaustion made every day a struggle. She was forced to postpone her studies to become a real-estate agent: the career that was to have given her daughter a better life.

In another bitter blow, Centrelink cut Rachelle D'Argent's child-care benefits, causing her financial hardship. With rent arrears mounting, Rachelle revealed she had no choice but to relinquish the unit that had been Mimi's home. She had lost everything.

Amid the family's pain, the police began to compile a brief of evidence ahead of the killer father's court case. The shocking picture of longstanding family violence emerged, providing a harrowing backdrop to the ultimate act of violence. Acar was still subject to a suspended prison sentence for his violence towards Rachelle at the time he killed his daughter. To him, Yazmina Acar was nothing more than collateral damage in a crime whose the real target was her mother.

Acar's concerns for his personal safety in prison were well founded. Initially remanded to the Metropolitan Remand Centre, he was placed in protective custody, away from the general prison population where child killers and sex offenders are marked men. Later, the blaze of publicity surrounding his court case would prompt authorities to arrange his urgent transfer to Port Phillip Prison, where he was placed in special protection. Confined to a cell where he would spend the majority of each day in lockdown, the child killer was safe from the other inmates and had plenty of time to reflect on his crime.

In preparation for his coming court case, Ramazan Acar was assessed by two mental-health experts. The report consultant psychiatrist Dr Danny Sullivan prepared for the court stated that Acar was a very immature young man with serious anger issues. Acar told the specialist that when he made his initial threats to kill his daughter on 17 November, he had not meant them. After absconding with the child, he said he had driven around the city panicking because he was convinced the police would be looking for him.

He was aware that if he was apprehended he would inevitably be charged with drink-driving. Taking his child while serving a suspended prison sentence for an earlier violent assault on her mother, and poised to appear in court again for breaching the existing intervention order, it was inevitable he was going to be locked up. He doubted he would ever see his child again. He had been contemplating this scenario as he sat in his parked car while his child played outside when the dark genesis of the murder first took root.

Acar told Dr Sullivan that when he climbed out of his car with the knife in his hand, everything seemed to be moving in slow motion. He remembered being gripped by a feeling of great rage, and seeing his little girl's worried look as he approached her. But he remained unable to describe any details of the actual stabbing.

In another assessment by psychologist Mr Bob Ives, the fog appeared to be lifting. Acar now remembered his daughter crying when she glimpsed the knife. He described the fear in her eyes and said she looked at him 'as though he were the devil'.

Mr Ives conducted extensive testing and found the prisoner to have a high average IQ of 106. He then performed an analysis of Acar's personality type and the prisoner's history of self-harming behaviours. Acar claimed he had been cutting himself since the age of 13, which the psychologist felt was an attempt to express and control his high emotional stress. He said it was also likely Acar's way of managing and expressing conflict was through very extreme actions.

It was the psychologist's opinion that the prisoner suffered from particularly 'rigid thought patterns' and was unable to moderate, or compromise, between two opposing points of view. Given his rigid thinking, Acar met the criteria for borderline personality disorder or paranoid borderline personality disorder. The psychologist further observed that despite Acar's profound and genuine remorse, the prisoner did not appear 'to question the nature of his views of the world which underpinned this tragedy'.

Mr Ives noted that the prisoner attributed the murder to his long-term drug use and reliance on alcohol. Interestingly, he was still blaming others for his crime. During his examination, Acar still insisted it was his estranged partner's fault for letting him drive off with their little girl. He also blamed the police for failing to arrest him for the repeated breaches of the intervention order. He even blamed his father for preventing him from handing himself in at the Broadmeadows police station the night before the murder.

The specialist did, however, note Acar's heavy use of drugs, including amphetamines and ice. He observed that the prisoner had been drinking and using drugs on the day of the crime and in the days leading up to the murder. This was significant and could have contributed to his actions.

Dr Sullivan agreed that Acar's long-term drug use was of significance. He noted that Acar had been using cannabis from the age of 13, and had progressed to amphetamines, including ice, which he began using at the age of 18. In spite of the diagnosis of polysubstance abuse, Dr Sullivan believed that at the time of the crime, alcohol was the only drug associated with the murder.

Given Acar's extreme emotional volatility and longstanding difficulties in controlling his anger, Dr Sullivan concluded the prisoner suffered from a 'mixed personality disorder' with borderline anti-social and narcissistic traits. It was Dr Sullivan's opinion that Acar had resorted to substance abuse as a way of dealing with his problems. But despite his tendency to self-harm, he felt the accused killer's suicidal statements leading up to the crime were neither persistent or pervasive.

During his examination of the prisoner, the psychiatrist noted Acar's preoccupation with a 'thug life'. Witnesses who had observed the dysfunctional violent relationship between the prisoner and his former partner described a domineering, aggressive young man with a great sense of entitlement.

But he found no sign of any significant cognitive impairment, or any evidence of psychotic symptoms or a psychotic illness at the time he murdered his daughter, though it was possible he'd been depressed. It was the specialist's opinion that Acar's personality and substance intoxication had contributed to the crime because it had impeded his ability to think clearly, or to make rational choices. In his report, the doctor felt Acar had been disinhibited by alcohol intoxication, though he was unable to confidently determine whether the crime was down to intoxication, or his personality, or both.

More significantly, Dr Sullivan concluded that Acar was 'consumed with hatred' for his estranged partner and a desire to punish her for restricting his access to his little girl, in spite of his past history of extreme violence. The combination of hatred and a desire for revenge made him incapable of appreciating the wrongfulness of his conduct on the night of the crime. Dr Sullivan determined that the prisoner was an immature young man whose adult personality was yet to form, though he was optimistic this might occur in prison and that his disorder might diminish.

It would take some time for Acar to process the enormity of his actions, and the specialist remained cautious about his prospects of rehabilitation. It was possible that with the passage of time, and intensive counselling, he might learn techniques to control his emotions.

On 3 May 2011 at a committal hearing before the Melbourne Magistrates Court, Acar pleaded guilty to one count of murder and was remanded in custody to appear at the Victorian Supreme Court. The court heard how he'd kidnapped his daughter Yazmina after tricking her mother into thinking he was taking her to the milk bar. The court also heard how he'd driven across the city, taunting the girl's mother with chilling calls and bizarre texts and Facebook posts in which he threatened to kill the child. He later stabbed his daughter to death and dumped her body on grassland in Melbourne's northern suburbs before disposing of the murder weapon. The court heard about the violent history of the relationship, and that Acar had repeatedly breached intervention orders. He was serving a suspended prison sentence for violence against his former partner when he killed the child in an act of revenge to punish the little girl's mother.

The Age reported the hearing on 5 May 2011 and ran comments from the murdered girl's mother, who explained to reporters why she had remained in such a violent relationship.

'I have been asked why I stayed with him, and one reason is that I was absolutely scared but also the smile on my little girl's face when she saw her dad come home from work was priceless,' Rachelle D'Argent said. She told the *Herald Sun* she wanted to be in court for her daughter.

'A quick glimpse was enough for me to see he was guilty,' said Rachelle. She described her daughter as an active, intelligent child who loved riding her pink bike and adored Dora the Explorer.

On 18 May 2011, Rachelle and her supporters packed into the crowded public gallery of the Victorian Supreme Court in Melbourne where Acar formally pleaded guilty to the murder of his little girl. He admitted a chequered criminal history of 31 prior offences, many of them involving violence towards his estranged fiancée. Justice Paul Coghlan remanded him to appear again in June for a plea hearing.

After the hearing Rachelle D'Argent told waiting journalists that Acar's guilty plea 'meant the world to her'. When asked what she would say to her daughter, she said she would tell her, 'Mummy is always going to be there for you.'

On 16 June Acar was back in the dock at the Supreme Court where Crown prosecutor Peter Rose SC outlined the background to the couple's violent on-and-off relationship, detailing the abuse, threats and bashings that led to its final collapse.

Justice Elizabeth Curtain heard about the countless intervention orders and the constant breaches leading up to the events of 17 November 2010 that culminated in the murder of Ramazan Acar's only child, Yazmina Micheline Acar.

The Crown prosecutor gave a chilling account of the events following the child's abduction, as the prisoner threatened and tormented the child's mother.

'Rachelle begged the prisoner to return the child,' Mr Rose told the court. 'The prisoner stated: "It's too late, I'm going to do it, I'm going to do it,"' Mr Rose said. He went on to describe the child's poignant last words to her mother.

Throughout the Crown's outline of events, Acar sat silently in the dock with his head bowed. In the public gallery, the child's mother wept as Mr Rose described her daughter's final moments.

Defence lawyer Gavan Meredith drew the court's attention to the bizarre scarring around the prisoner's eyes. He explained that while in custody Acar had gouged the shapes around his eyes using the phosphorous end of some matchsticks to represent tears and his endless sorrow over his daughter's murder.

'At close quarters you can see the line, or lines, under both eyes represent those [tears],' said the defence.

Mr Meredith said Acar felt it was appropriate that he should carry these scars for the rest of his life as a sign of his deep remorse for what he had done. The prisoner had also engraved his daughter's initials on his stomach using the same primitive method, though the marks were now fading with the passage of time, explained the defence lawyer.

'He indicates that he was found with the blade of a pencil sharpener in his cell and told the relevant authorities he was keeping it because he wanted to end his life and was endeavouring, in effect, to work up the courage to use the blade on himself, to open his arteries,' Mr Meredith said.

The defence barrister told the court that Acar came from a family of 'hard work and endeavour'. He said the prisoner's parents and two of his brothers and their spouses had been visiting him in prison, and continued to support him. They would not abandon him, said Mr Meredith. Members of his family had provided letters to confirm the remorse he'd expressed to them. Mr Meredith said the long solitary nights the prisoner spent in lockdown were the hardest. This was when Acar's thoughts returned to what he had done.

Referring to the doomed relationship, Mr Meredith said Acar's decision to leave his family in New South Wales in 2005 to return to Melbourne with his new partner illustrated the 'enormous emotional investment' he had put into the fledgling relationship.

He went on to describe the positive efforts Acar had made to change his life after the collapse of his relationship. After the police spoke to him in September 2010 about the seriousness of breaching his intervention order he had sought to 'clean himself up' so that he could resume contact with his child. Acar showed a willingness to obtain professional help. He sought psychological counselling and on 21 September he had attended the Family Dispute Resolution Centre, but felt that his estranged partner was not willing to participate in the program. Organisers reported that he had presented as 'open and engaging' and noted his willingness to change.

This view was shared by his psychologist, Mr Peter Stanislawski, whose report was tendered into evidence. Mr Stanislawski noted that the separated father appeared to be motivated to change his life, but had 'limited internal resources' to draw upon. Despite living with his family, his continued exposure to a 'negative peer group' in which drugs were readily available left him feeling emotionally isolated. The psychologist noted three barriers to his employment prospects. They included his limited employment history, his social isolation and anger, and his criminal history.

Dr Sullivan explained to the court the nature of a personality disorder. He said the term refers to 'persistent, pervasive and maladaptive difficulties' which are not caused by a mental illness but which make up part of a person's temperament and character. But the expert admitted that he had not been able to distinguish whether Acar's actions on the night of the crime were down to his personality or related to his substance abuse and intoxication.

Dr Sullivan told Justice Curtain that people with a personality disorder were inclined to act impulsively and to have difficulties in managing and controlling their anger. In his view, Acar's anger was a significant part of his offending behaviour and his inability to deal with his emotions lay at the heart of the crime. As he'd observed in his report, Dr Sullivan said the tragic case showed an overwhelming portrait of a man so intent on punishing his ex-partner that it overshadowed everything else.

His defence barrister told the court that the prisoner's guilty plea at the soonest possible opportunity not only assisted the course of justice, but showed the genuine remorse he felt for his crime. He had made full and frank admissions to investigators after his arrest, and cooperated by leading police to his daughter's body, and to the area where he had disposed of the murder weapon. And he had scarred himself for life as a reminder of what he had done.

Rachelle D'Argent shook and struggled to control her tears as she held up a photograph of her daughter smiling in her pink jumper. Reading aloud from her victim impact statement, Rachelle D'Argent said she did not know how to begin to explain the horror of losing her only child, 'someone more precious to me than life itself'.

'I was horrified the night I found out my one and only daughter Mimi had been taken away from me. Neither for a few minutes or a few hours or days, but for life. Yaz, or Mimi as we used to call her, was and still is my everything.'

The shattered mother went on to describe the debilitating exhaustion she suffered from lack of sleep. Her tiredness and inability to concentrate had forced her to postpone her studies. She revealed how she had been forced to relinquish her home because she had fallen behind with the rent. And she described the anger and frustration she felt toward everyone about everything.

More poignantly, she described what she missed about her daughter — she missed everything.

'I miss her face, I miss her smile, I miss her voice; I miss her laugh, I miss her hair, I miss her cheekiness, I miss getting her ready for childcare. I miss her coming everywhere with me. I miss doing our hand-painting together. I miss her riding her Barbie bike and pink scooter. I miss seeing her play in her toy room.

'I miss giving her a bath, I miss singing and dancing with her, I miss lying next to her at night and her playing with my fingers for her to fall asleep, but most importantly I miss her running up to me and jumping into my arms and hugging me while she tells me that she loves me.'

All she had left to remind her of Mimi were the photographs, videos, toys and clothes.

'I will never be able to take her for a first haircut or her first day at school, or having her lose her first tooth. So many firsts that I have been robbed of.' Her daughter would always be her everything, she said. 'And even though I can't see her I know she's watching over me every day and giving me the strength and courage to get through everything. It will always be Mummy and Mimi for life.'

Rachelle's mother, Micheline, also described her grief. She said her life had changed forever. Now suffering from heightened anxiety in everyday situations, she struggled to sleep and had lost weight through stress.

'Some days I don't want to talk, refuse to answer the phone and will cry for hours because Yazmina was my life. I miss her so much; I can feel there's something missing in the house,' she said.

Mrs D'Argent said she had been very close to her granddaughter, who had lived with her for a while and continued to spend a lot of time at her home.

'Since birth, I used to sing a French song for her every day at night, and by the age of two she was singing the song by heart. Rachelle recorded it for me, and I always listen to it and that breaks my heart.'

Surrounded by photos and memories, she found even a trip to the shops was now too painful because she found it hard seeing other small children when her own granddaughter had gone. Her fears and insecurities had prompted her to seek counselling.

'My last dream of her [Mimi], she was crying and told me ... "Grandmere [grandmother] ... I'm so cold, come and get me." And I wanted to get in my car and drive till I can find her.' [sic]

Mr Rose told the court that the murder of Yazmina by her own father was chilling and horrific, and fell into the worst category of child murder. He compared the murder to other revenge killings in which children were used by angry fathers as weapons to punish their mothers. Mr Rose mentioned the case of Arthur Freeman, and he compared Acar to triple child killer Robert Farquharson, who had driven his children into a dam on Father's Day 2005 and left them to drown. All these cases were examples of spousal revenge and this case fell into that most serious category.

Mr Rose said it was the Crown's view that Acar was a violent, angry young man and the only appropriate sentence for his crime was life in prison without parole. He urged Justice Curtain to set a minimum sentence of between 29 and 33 years.

But Mr Meredith, for the defence, submitted that Acar was an immature young man with a personality disorder who had not intended to kill his daughter on the night. He argued that the murder was an escalation of the unfolding situation. He said the phone calls, texts and Facebook posts were part of the dynamics of the relationship with Rachelle D'Argent and illustrated his frustration over his limited access to his daughter. He was now profoundly remorseful for what he had done and his lifelong scarring was outward evidence of that.

Justice Curtain did not agree. She said the text and SMS messages, along with the phone calls and the fact that he had told the child's mother he had murdered Yazmina at a time when she was still alive, showed a degree of callousness. The tone of the later texts and in particular the Facebook post saying 'bout to kill ma kid' was evidence of what he intended to do, and later did. The judge said he was an angry young man with a longstanding history of violence towards his former partner. She adjourned the hearing for sentencing.

On 1 July 2011 Rachelle D'Argent and a huge group of supporters packed the public gallery wearing pink ribbons in memory of her daughter. She wanted to be there for her little girl when Justice Curtain passed sentence on the man who had taken her life.

Justice Curtain said despite the submissions of his defence barrister that Acar had not gone to his former partner's home on 17 November 2010 with the intention of murdering his child, she did not accept this was a situation that simply unfolded and evolved after he abducted the little girl.

'Mr Meredith submitted that your state of mind was that you assumed the police had become involved,' she said. 'You had now breached the intervention order in an unparalleled way, you had outstanding matters hanging over your head, and you thought, effectively, by your conduct, you had lost what slim chance you had to maintain access to your daughter. And as a result of all those things coming down on top of you, you did what you did.'

The judge said while she accepted that what was happening on the telephone and in the texts was occurring within the dynamic of the relationship — and that in the beginning at least, he was taunting Ms D'Argent to increase her stress and anxiety — his later admissions to police and the nature of his communications with the child's mother told a different story.

Certainly by the time Acar made his chilling Facebook post at 7.23 p.m. 'bout to kill ma kid' and the 'succinct statement as to motive also posted on Facebook at 7.34 p.m. saying "paybk u slut"', Justice Curtain said 'no other inference could be reasonably drawn', other than that he intended to murder the little girl to punish her mother.

Justice Curtain remarked that Acar had driven around the suburbs, taunting the child's mother, demanding that she withdraw the intervention order and threatening to kill their daughter. She further noted the cruel Facebook post in which he claimed to have killed his daughter when he had not.

She said the 'unmistakable chilling act of putting your daughter on the phone having told her mother "It's too late. I'm going to do it, I'm going to do it, do you have any last words for her?"' were further evidence that he intended to kill Yazmina.

The judge had read the doctors' reports and was aware that the prisoner was currently on antidepressants in prison where he spent hours in lockdown 'ruminating' on his conduct.

'You feel as if you are a marked man within the system, and you are concerned about what might happen to you,' she observed.

Justice Curtain noted Mr Ives' diagnosis of a borderline personality disorder or paranoid borderline personality disorder, and Dr Sullivan's clear diagnosis that Acar was suffering from polysubstance abuse and narcissistic borderline personality disorder. But she also felt it important to note that at the time of the offence, alcohol was the only drug 'demonstrably associated with the offending'.

But more significant, she said, were Dr Sullivan's observations of Acar's consuming hatred for his ex-partner at the time of the crime and his desire to punish her for restricting access to his daughter. She said while this impeded his appreciation of the wrongfulness of his behaviour, she noted the doctor felt that at some level Acar had known what he was doing was wrong, but was 'blinded' by hatred.

Despite his defence barrister's submission that it was appropriate to impose a sentence with a non-parole period because of Acar's age, his guilty plea and his prospects of rehabilitation, Justice Curtain accepted the Crown's contention that this was a horrific killing in which his hatred overshadowed any consideration for the welfare of his own child.

Justice Curtain said that while Acar had accepted responsibility for the crime after his arrest, he expressed 'very little if any remorse'. Instead, he sought to blame the crime on everyone else, from his partner to his father, to the police. He also blamed the murder on his protracted drug use and the fact that he'd been drunk at the time.

'I accept that you are remorseful for your conduct, but you have yet to express any remorse or contrition for the irreparable pain and loss you have caused to the mother of your daughter, and indeed your own family,' the judge said. The murder of this little girl by her own father was indeed a chilling horrific crime, she said. 'The victim was your infant daughter, and she was killed by the one man in the world whose duty it was to love, nurture and protect her. As such, your conduct was a fundamental breach of the trust that reposes between parent and child; a fundamental breach of parents' most fundamental obligation.

'Further, you committed this murder for the worst possible motives: revenge and spite. You killed your daughter to get back at her mother. You used your daughter, an innocent victim, as the instrument of your overarching desire to inflict pain on your former partner.'

Justice Curtain said any sentence she imposed had not only to deter Acar from further offending, but to deter other like-minded people in the community so they understood life is 'sacrosanct'. Anyone choosing to act as Acar had could expect 'a stern and salutary' punishment. In all the circumstances, said Justice Curtain, only a life sentence was fitting.

Acar stood in the dock, his face stony as the judge ordered him to serve a minimum of 33 years jail before being eligible for parole. Throughout the sentencing, the victim's mother wept silently in the public gallery.

Outside court, Rachelle D'Argent told journalists: 'Mimi, it's our day today. Mummy told you there would be justice for you. And even though I haven't accepted that you're not here, forever you will be in my heart ... I know you'll always be smiling down on us, my beautiful angel.'

*

In July 2011 Rachelle D'Argent appeared on Channel Nine's *Sixty Minutes* in a segment entitled 'A Mother's Heartache' and told viewers that the crime still made her feel 'sick, sick, sick to my stomach'. She said she agreed that the death penalty was appropriate for angry fathers like Acar who murdered their children out of pure revenge.

'I hate him and I will never forgive him, ever, ever, ever, ever,' she said, and expressed the hope that he would suffer every day of his prison sentence. 'I hope Yazmina haunts him every night.'

If Ramazan Acar's tattooed tears were an outward sign of his supposed remorse, after he was sentenced his behaviour showed no signs of any contrition. Rachelle revealed on *Sixty Minutes* that just one week after he was sentenced, her mother had been stunned to receive a telephone call from Acar, who was now incarcerated in Port Phillip Prison, a privately run maximum-security facility.

'He contacted my mum's house and my mum was outraged,' she said. 'She told him not to call again. She didn't want to hear that name in her house again,' Rachelle said.

It is an offence for an inmate to contact the victim of his crime. But Acar, who had shown no regard for the law in the past, continued to show his contempt from behind bars.

Renowned Australian forensic psychiatrist Professor Paul Mullen, who also appeared on the show, explained what drove men like Acar. There were two explanations for crimes of spousal revenge, he said; one was perhaps less generous than the other.

'The first is that you have done something so terrible that you can't ever really look at it clearly,' he explained. 'You can't even begin to think about what you have done. The less generous explanation is that this was a person who had so little concern for other human beings that he did not even consider his own child.' In a scenario such as this, where victory was everything, Acar was the most brutal and dangerous type of revenge killer. 'They lose sight of the child as anything other than the prize in some kind of ongoing battle with their ex-partner.'

Rachelle D'Argent's revelations on the show caused an outcry in the following days as journalists asked how a killer could continue to torment the victims of his crime from prison.

The Age newspaper ran an article by Anthony Dowsley which revealed that police and prison authorities were now investigating the matter. A spokeswoman from Corrections Victoria confirmed that a call had been made from the prison on 11 July, which had been diverted to a person Acar had not been approved to have contact with. He had been banned from making personal telephone calls, she said. It is prison protocol that corrections officers call the numbers on prisoners' contact lists to verify that the nominated recipients are willing to take inmates' calls.

The article went on to say that the jail phone system operated on codes, not direct numbers, but that the matter was under investigation. Even facing a life sentence, Ramazan Acar remained incorrigible.

An inquest into the death of Yazmina Acar opened in Melbourne in October 2015 amid headlines denouncing Ramazan Acar as 'The Facebook Killer'. The Victorian State Coroner, Judge Ian Gray, presided over the inquiry which was being held in the context of the Victorian Systemic Review of Family Violence Deaths (VSRFVD). The criteria for consideration under the review was that the death had to have been caused 'directly, or indirectly by an offender through the application of assaultive force or criminal negligence or that the relevant parties (the deceased and the offender) were, or had been at any point in time, in an intimate or familial relationship as defined by the *Family Violence Protection Act* of 2008 (Victoria)'.

Sadly, Yazmina Acar satisfied every one of these criteria.

The coroner released his findings the following month, ruling that nothing could have been done to prevent the toddler's murder. Judge Gray commented on the tense and volatile relationship of Yazmina's parents, who had first met as teenagers.

'It was a clear there was a background of family violence,' he said, but went on to note that despite police involvement and Acar's repeated breaches of the intervention order, there had been nothing to predict the little girl's murder. Judge Gray observed that even if Acar had been remanded in custody for the penultimate breach in October, there was nothing to suggest he would not have been a free man at the time he killed his daughter.

'It is a matter of speculation whether an earlier interview, even if combined with arrest and remand in custody, would have affected the tragic outcome,' he said.

The coroner found that Yazmina Acar died of blood loss following the stabbing perpetrated by her father. But he made no criticism of the police handling of the case, noting that after being interviewed on 15 October 2010 at the Broadmeadows police station for his breach of the order on 30 September, Acar was released pending further inquiries.

'Even if he had been remanded in custody it can't be inferred that he would not have been at liberty the day he killed his daughter.' But while he did not comment adversely on the actions of the authorities, the delay between the breach itself and the interview presented a 'lost opportunity' to bring him to account for flouting the court order. The coroner said he noted that the offender had been referred for intervention, though it was clear those programs 'had no ultimate impact on his behaviour'.

'The fact does not in any sense imply a criticism of those who conducted the programs and who sought to influence Mr Acar in a positive way,' Judge Gray said.

The coroner found that Ramazan Acar had caused the death of his daughter, and passed on his condolences to the child's family.

In the end Ramazan Acar, the man who blamed everyone else

for enabling him to murder his only child, blamed the system for being too hard on him. Shortly after being sentenced to a minimum term of 33 years for stabbing his daughter to death, lawyers for the man media dubbed the Facebook Killer lodged an appeal claiming the sentence was too harsh. While his application for permission to appeal the sentence was initially denied, after reconsideration it was given the go-ahead. But one month after being granted leave to argue his case in the Victorian Court of Appeal, Acar's lawyers notified the court that he no longer wished to proceed. The Facebook Killer remains in prison, his fading tattooed tears a daily reminder of his crime. He will be eligible for parole in 2044.

CHAPTER 6
'I can't live without my kids —
and they can't live without me!'
The story of Karen, Jack, Maddie and Bon Bell

Throughout her turbulent 15-year relationship, Karen Bell had endured so many vicious beatings at the hands of her violent, heavy-drinking, dope-addicted husband that in the end she lost count of them.

When the drinking and the brutality became too much to bear, the 33-year-old mother of three realised the only way she could survive Gary Bell's explosive temper was to flee from their isolated farmhouse on the far south coast of New South Wales, leaving her three children — Jack, aged eight, Maddie, aged seven, and 16-month-old Bon — behind.

But for all the violence that took place behind the closed doors of the family's farmhouse in rural Pericoe, 50 kilometres inland from the coastal town of Eden, it was Karen alone who bore the brunt of her husband's rage. Gary Mark Bell never laid a hand on any of his children, who, despite witnessing the frequent beatings that left their mother sporting bruises, split lips and chipped teeth, appeared to love their father as much as he adored them.

Throughout the years of countless injuries and hurried escapes, the broken mother clung to the forlorn hope that somewhere deep beneath the alcoholic haze there still existed the charismatic, good-looking 'fantastic guy' who had once swept her off her feet.

When the couple first met in 1993, Karen Bell was a pretty and impressionable 17-year-old and Gary was 29 years old, with a failed marriage already behind him. His real name was Gary Mark Poxon, though after his first marriage collapsed, he began using his mother's maiden name, 'Mills.' Later, after marrying Karen in 2004, he adopted his new wife's last name. To everyone's amazement, Karen's 'Mr Right' became known as Gary Bell. By then, the bride was well aware that her new husband was not the loving, considerate partner, she had fallen in love with. After being in the de facto relationship for two years, she had already glimpsed a menacing side to her husband's personality. Bell's heavy drinking fuelled a barrage of abuse and it wasn't long before his angry words gave way to pounding fists. Karen quickly found herself on the receiving end of his violent temper, which first turned physical when he hurled the trunk of an ornamental tree at her, fracturing her finger.

Over the years the violence escalated and an uneasy pattern emerged. When the arguments inevitably turned nasty, Karen learned to make a run for it, fleeing the property nestled amid thousands of hectares of wild terrain in the Towamba State Forest, 10 kilometres north of the Victorian border. Generally the intoxicated Bell would throw his wife out to shiver in the darkness. In later years when he bashed her, Karen fled to her family or to the nearest neighbour's house.

Gary Bell was so volatile and unpredictable that there had been occasions during the marriage when he had kicked Karen out of his white four-wheel drive as they travelled along one of the winding dirt roads in Pericoe late at night. He thought nothing of driving away and leaving his hapless wife to pick her way home in the pitch dark past the scattering of shacks, caravans and derelict buildings in the area, back to the isolated farm where he would be waiting with his fists.

By 2008, the home of Karen's close friend and neighbour Tracey Wilson had become a safe haven when Bell's drunken rages got out of hand. With little or no mobile-phone reception in the densely forested region 300 kilometres above sea level, Karen knew she was safe and could use her friend's landline to call for help.

Generally, she called her older brother Tom, who would make the 45-minute dash from their parents' home in Bega to rescue his younger sister. When Tom wasn't around, Karen would wander down the dirt road and hitch a lift to safety. On at least two occasions, Ms Wilson, a mother herself, had made the drive down to Bega to deliver Karen into the safe hands of her concerned parents, Harold and Rosalie Bell. Nursing bruises and injuries, Karen would lie low for a couple of days, waiting for the storm to subside.

When Gary Bell finally sobered up enough to miss his wife, he would call Karen in Bega, sometimes apologising and occasionally promising to change. But more commonly he would simply pile their children into the back of his car and drive to his in-laws' home where he indulged in the kind of emotional blackmail guaranteed to ensure a disenchanted wife's speedy return.

The kids were missing their mum, he'd wheedle. He was missing his wife. They all needed Karen to come home so they could be a family again. Her children's small worried faces in the back seat of the car, and their father's apparent contrition, were more than enough to convince a wife whose self-esteem had been beaten out of her to get in the car and go home again.

In spite of the regular beatings, Gary was still a 'great dad' who loved his kids. Karen told herself the children wanted their parents to stay together.

Throughout this time, Karen clung to the belief that there might be a biological explanation for Bell's violence and dark simmering moods. It stemmed from an unexpected diagnosis in 2000, after he was referred to a neurologist to determine the underlying cause of his repeated fainting spells. After extensive testing, the specialist diagnosed Bell with temporal lobe epilepsy. The doctor said Bell's MRI showed the epilepsy had been caused by a brain injury, probably resulting from an earlier blow to the head.

Bell had indeed suffered a serious head injury. At 17, he had driven his speeding motorcycle into a tree. He had not been wearing a helmet and was knocked unconscious in the impact, also breaking his arm. His head injury was so severe that he had spent days in a coma and months recovering. After the accident, Bell suffered dizzy spells and seizures. His battered wife, trying to make some sense of Bell's explosive temper, was relieved to know that her husband's violence was not her fault as he had always claimed. Still, she struggled to understand why Bell flatly refused to take the medication the specialist prescribed for his epilepsy, but was happy enough to self-medicate with copious amounts of alcohol and marijuana.

Karen's first two pregnancies had been marred by Bell's violence, when he had shown no regard for either his expectant wife's condition or his unborn babies' welfare. The beatings had become so frequent after Maddie's birth in May 2001 that Karen was constantly packing her bags and fleeing from the family home. While in later years Bell would flatly refuse to allow Karen to leave with her children, there had been occasions, when Maddie was an infant, where he had let her take her little girl.

Bell had struggled to bond with his second baby, whose constant crying drove him crazy. He told his wife he couldn't stand the child, and was considering having Maddie adopted. Bell did not oppose Karen leaving with the newborn, knowing that keeping Jack would soon bring her running back. Later, as Maddie grew into a delightful little tot, and the reflux that had sparked her constant tears improved, Bell refused to let either child leave with Karen. Despite the violence, when Bell got down on one knee and proposed on Valentine's Day 1998, she still said yes. By then, she had accepted there was no escape. She believed Bell's threats that if she ran away with the children, he would hunt them down. After Maddie's birth, Karen went ahead with the wedding, hoping desperately that things might improve. But those hopes quickly faded as her tormentor took charge of the big day, controlling everything down to the guest list. Like everything in her life, Gary Bell called the shots, and Karen was to battle-weary to argue.

Bell's violence had continued into Karen's third pregnancy. When she was eight months pregnant, Bell had hauled her out of bed at 3 a.m., and ordered her outside in the cold to collect wood for the fire. While Karen made up the fire, an argument flared and Bell struck her on the head with a heavy rubber torch. Karen's screams woke the two older children who were terrified when they saw their injured mother, and asked why Dad had hit her.

The blow had been so forceful that Karen suffered severe headaches and a concussion that lasted several days. A couple of days after the incident, Jack had told a schoolmate what had happened. His mother was mortified. What Dad had done was wrong, she told her bewildered son, feeling ashamed and embarrassed. But this wasn't the sort of thing she wanted other people to know about. 'I'm never going to hit my wife,' Jack said, sadly.

With two small children to care for, and another baby on the way, Karen was desperate to keep her family together. She hoped that things might improve when the new baby arrived. Her optimism was briefly rewarded. During her pregnancy, Gary's fainting spells had become so frequent that he finally agreed to take the medication the specialist had prescribed several years earlier. To Karen's relief, his medication appeared to be working and Gary appeared calmer. Since Bon's birth on 5 March 2007, Gary had kept his fists to himself and, despite his ongoing verbal abuse, Karen felt no need to leave. She just felt bewildered that a man who supposedly loved her could berate her the way he did.

To those who knew her, Karen Bell was a devoted mother who would do anything for her family. It was for the sake of the children that Karen always returned to the farm, where the cycle of violence would begin again. Gary never failed to remind her that if she ever walked out on him, he would keep the children. He said he couldn't live without his kids, and they couldn't live without him.

This threat became Bell's sick trump card in a dangerous cat-and-mouse game. He continually raised the stakes, knowing all along that he held the winning hand. As time passed, Jack, Maddie and Bon (named after AC/DC rocker Bon Scott) became no more to Bell than tools to control their battered mother. It not only reminded her who was in charge of the violent relationship, but it kept Karen trapped in the cycle of abuse.

All Karen Bell ever wanted was a happy family and a peaceful life. She clung desperately to Bell's promises that he would try harder, apparently blind to the fact that the charming, attentive man she had fallen in love with had long gone. The years of heavy drinking and drug abuse had only served to increase Bell's thirst for power over his wife. While he adopted the public persona of a friendly Aussie bloke around town, behind closed doors he was a tyrant and a sadistic, violent bully who made his young wife's life hell. It is ironic that the words on the letterbox at the entrance to their farm ominously read 'Hells Bells'.

On Saturday 21 June 2008 at around 8.30 p.m., all hell did break loose on the farm. Gary Bell had been drinking heavily and smoking dope again, and a violent argument had erupted. His wife had been talking on the telephone to her friend Tracey Wilson, who could hear the commotion down the phone line. Over Karen's screams, Tracey heard Bell's voice in the background yelling abuse. He sounded really drunk, she observed, listening helplessly to her friend's fearful screams as the intoxicated father snatched the handset from his wife's hand, ripping out clumps of her long hair. The line fell silent as Karen, defending herself from his blows, was forced to hang up.

The three children were asleep in bed, and with Bell now swearing and ranting, Karen tried to diffuse the escalating situation by disappearing outside with a cup of tea. She lit a cigarette, hoping that the drunken yelling from inside the house would subside if she refused to engage. She did not want Gary waking the children, who had witnessed enough of his violence in the past.

While Karen was finishing her cigarette, Bell locked her out. Karen briefly considered making a run for it, but she had never left her baby before, and knew the distress this would cause to her children. Pushing her hand past the makeshift board covering the smashed window in the front door, where Gary had recently punched his fist through the glass, she let herself in. She dashed to the phone where she dialled 000 and hurriedly urged the operator to send the police to the farm. The call came to an abrupt halt when Bell tore across the kitchen and ripped the phone off the wall.

Livid, he warned her that if the cops turned up she had better not say anything. The commotion woke Bon, and Karen warmed up a bottle hoping that Bell would calm down. But the prospect of the police's arrival sent the drunken father into a panic. He grabbed Bon from Karen's arms and woke the older children.

Bell bundled Jack, Maddie and Bon into the car in their pyjamas. He wasn't going to hang around and wait to be arrested, he fumed. And he wasn't going anywhere without his kids.

They shivered in the back of the car while their mother pleaded with their father. Bell finally relented and Karen took her kids back into the house and put them back into bed.

With no sign of the police, Karen decided she would be safer in bed, too. With any luck, her drunken husband might fall asleep. But Bell was just getting going. He burst into the bedroom where the baby lay sleeping in his cot, and hauled the covers off his wife, spitting in Karen's face and swearing at her. He threatened to shoot her, and started kicking her with his heavy boots. The attack was so brutal that he sent Karen sprawling from the bed to the floor.

Fending off blows, Karen threw a punch that caught Bell in the face. She knew then that unless she made a run for it, this next beating could be her last.

She fled from the bedroom and out of the door towards the car. The keys were still in the ignition, and Karen started the engine and put her foot down. She fled in the darkness towards a neighbouring property where her Uncle Ian and Aunt Dianne lived.

It had been months since Ian and Dianne Auld had spoken to their niece, though they frequently heard the heated exchanges and the commotion coming from her farmhouse next door.

The couple hurriedly ushered Karen into the house, keeping an eye on the door as she rang the police again. It was now almost midnight, at least an hour since her first frantic call. Karen urged the operator to tell the police to hurry. She was still on the phone when two police officers arrived on the Aulds' doorstep, apologising and explaining that they had lost their way in the wild terrain. One officer, Senior Constable Kate Whitton, said they had spent ages driving around in the darkness scouring the area known locally as Two Creeks, looking for her farm. Karen directed them next door and hovered anxiously on her uncle's doorstep in the cold, listening as Bell ranted at the police.

'What do you want us to do?' asked the police, returning again to the Aulds' house.

Karen considered this impossible question. She had hoped the decision might have been taken out of her hands. If they arrested Gary as he deserved and took him away, he would be even angrier when he returned. But if they left without arresting him, God knows what he would do to her. Whatever she decided, she was going to cop it.

Karen's thoughts turned to her three children, who would no doubt be awake by now, terrified by the sight of police.

'Take him away,' she said, nervously.

The police accompanied her back to the farmhouse where Jack and Maddie were indeed awake and sitting on the sofa in their pyjamas, wide-eyed with terror.

'Tell the police I never hit your mother,' Bell drunkenly instructed his children. Jack and Maddie looked at the police with frightened eyes and robotically repeated what their father told them to say.

The police officers arrested Gary Bell anyway. Karen watched them frogmarch him outside to the police car with a mixture of relief and trepidation.

Karen crept into the bedroom to check on Bon, who was thankfully still sleeping. She helped Jack and Maddie back to bed and kissed them goodnight.

In the early hours of Sunday 22 June, Karen slipped out of the bedroom and found a spare phone cord to plug the phone back into the wall. Her brother, Tom, would be sleeping at their parents' home in Bega, but she wanted to tell him what had happened in case something happened to her when Gary was released. Tom listened to his sister with a heavy heart. There had been so many phone calls like this over the years. He had lost count of the times Karen had turned up at their parents' house, battered and bruised after yet another bashing. There had been occasions when she'd called him late at night after fleeing Gary's violence. He had dashed up to Pericoe in his car to find her hiding out at a neighbour's place, or shivering beside the road in the dark.

It had broken his heart watching Karen repeatedly returning to this violent, controlling man, who beat her black and blue and called her vile names she did not deserve. The family had never understood it, he would later tell reporters. The Bells felt so helpless; all they could do was stand by Karen and support her.

While Karen was on the phone to Tom, the police had been making the 85-minute drive to Merimbula, a pretty coastal town on what is commonly called New South Wales' holiday Riviera, with their drunken charge. Bell was less belligerent by the time they placed him in the sombre surroundings of a holding cell to sober up. He was even more subdued when he was finally charged with assaulting his wife shortly after 2.30am. Bell was also served with an AVO, which the police had taken out on his victim's behalf. The order strictly prohibited him from further threats or violence towards Karen.

It was the third time an AVO had been granted to protect Karen, and the second time since 1999 that Gary Bell had faced charges for assaulting her. In 2005, he had received a 12-month suspended prison sentence, and a good behaviour bond, after pleading guilty to a particularly vicious attack on his wife. The magistrates presiding over the case at Bega Magistrates' Court in 2005 had told Bell that he had only escaped a jail sentence because he had reconciled with his victim, who had taken the trouble to come to court to support him. Later, Bell told Karen that the only reason he got back with her was to avoid a prison sentence. Gary had served a stint in prison in his younger days, and never wanted to go back.

At 3 a.m. on Sunday 22 June, Gary Bell was released on bail with another court case and a likely jail sentence hanging over him. The police reminded him about this when they dropped him off on the unmade road leading back to Pericoe.

In the darkness, Gary Bell began the long walk back to Pericoe with his AVO in his pocket. Tragically for Karen, her children's names had not been included in the order of protection.

After a sleepless night, Karen surveyed the evidence of Bell's latest drunken rage. Apart from her bruised, sore body, the house was a mess. The door of the bedroom cupboard had been ripped off its hinges, furniture was askew and things lay strewn across the floor. The house was freezing cold, and the fire that fuelled the generator to provide power, heating and hot water had fizzled out. Cold, exhausted and afraid, Karen tried not to think about what would happen when Gary arrived home.

Winter had already set in and she had no idea how to use the chainsaw to chop the wood for the generator. Unless she could get it going, she could not imagine how the family could stay on the farm without Gary. More troubling, she could not imagine how she would remain there with him.

Karen studied the children's worn-out faces when they emerged from their bedrooms that morning. Everyone looked drained. She cuddled Bon and made him up a bottle.

'I miss my daddy,' Maddie said tearfully.

'I know,' replied her mum. It broke Karen's heart to see her children hurting.

Karen was contemplating her predicament when the phone rang.

'I need a lift home,' Bell snapped.

'No,' Karen replied.

But Bell warned he was coming home with or without her help. 'I've been walking since 3 a.m.,' he said, sounding sorry for himself. He went on to say that he had suffered a fit in the road after the cops threw him out of the police car.

'They stomped on my head and bashed me as I lay in the dirt,' he sniffed.

Karen did not believe a word of it. He had phoned on a previous occasion, when she'd left him after a beating, begging her to come back, claiming his doctors believed he might have a brain tumour. That turned out to be a lie. Karen suspected this outrageous story was just another of Gary's tales.

If Bell was sorry, it wasn't about his violence, it was for himself. He was playing the victim as he always did, manipulating Karen into believing that it was all her fault so she would feel sorry for him. The children watched their mum on the phone, Maddie's eyes silently pleading with her to go and get her dad.

Jack was silent. After Gary's arrest he had told his mother he was glad the police had taken him away. The little boy had imagined Dad had gone for good. But here he was, wheedling and playing the guilt card again. And it worked.

Shortly after breakfast, Karen Bell piled the children into the car and drove down the dirt track to collect her tormentor. Her stomach churned as she pondered the consequences of last night's call to the police. She fleetingly considered turning the car around and driving in an entirely different direction with the children. But there was no escaping Gary Bell. It would be just a matter of time before he came looking for her. The very idea of taking Gary's kids away made her feel guilty.

Karen found Bell trudging along the unmade road, staring glumly at the dirt. Few words were spoken as he climbed into the car.

'I can't stay here with you any more,' she told him, when they arrived at the farm. 'I'm taking the kids with me.'

'No way,' Bell snarled, playing his trump card. Karen could 'fuck off and never come back' but the children were staying put.

Their mother was torn. Still shaken, and badly bruised from her beating, Karen realised that if she stayed, she would be putting herself in grave danger. As much as she hated leaving her children behind, she had no reason to be concerned for their safety. They had never been on the receiving end of their father's violence. Karen Bell was in no doubt that Gary loved his children.

At lunchtime on Sunday 22 June, Karen Bell decided to save herself. She packed her bags and kissed and hugged her children. They looked upset as she promised she would see them all very soon. She had never left Bon before and hoped Gary might relent. But Gary wouldn't budge.

'Fuck off,' he snapped, tightening his grip on the little boy.

Karen reluctantly walked away from the farm, towards the dirt track.

'OK, we'll share custody 50/50,' she said. Bell made no reply.

A friend collected Karen from down the road, and drove her to her friend Tracey Wilson's place.

'Are the kids safe with Gary?' Tracey asked, looking worried.

Karen said they were.

During the afternoon, Karen rang Merimbula Police Station and spoke with Whitton, the officer who had arrested Gary.

'Are the kids safe?' the officer asked, repeating Tracey's concerns. Karen said they were fine. Bell had never hurt his children, she reiterated. Whitton said that since Gary had never hurt his children there was nothing more they could do.

Karen spent the Sunday night at Tracey's house. The following morning, Tracey dropped her off outside a local store. From there, she hitched a lift with a truck driver down to Bega, to her parents' home. This time there was no going back, she told them. Harold and Rosalie Bell looked doubtfully at their badly bruised daughter, and hoped that she meant it this time.

Sadly, leaving Gary Mark Bell was to prove the worst decision of her life. While Karen had come to fear that one day he would kill her, she had no idea there was a fate even more agonising waiting for her.

While Karen suspected that the AVO would mean nothing once Gary started drinking, she imagined that after a couple of days he would be in touch again, as he always had, playing the same mind games that always coaxed her back home. On Tuesday morning someone from a women's refuge rang to speak with the battered wife. Karen assumed she must have been contacted by the police. The worker told her that if she did not feel safe, she should not return to the farm. The next two days passed with passed with no word from the farm and Karen began to feel uneasy.

The young mother was not the only one who was worried about the silence from the farm. At Pericoe, Karen's Aunt Dianne and Uncle Ian were also growing anxious. They had heard every sound coming from the house next door, including the frequent 'domestics'. Yet there had been no sign of Jack, Maddie or Bon bouncing on their trampoline in the garden, or chattering or laughing as they played around the property. And Dianne had not seen or heard anything from Gary. This week the silence was deafening.

At first Mrs Auld wondered if the silence meant Karen had taken the three children to Bega with her.

By Thursday, Mrs Auld felt a flutter of anxiety when she noticed that even her niece's noisy generator had fallen strangely silent.

Later in the day, Mrs Auld received a troubling call from Gary's mother, Sheila Mills, who lived in Merimbula.

In the scattered coastal community where everyone knew everyone else, the children's paternal grandmother was well known to Karen's extended family and the Bells regarded the kindly Mrs Mills as a friend.

Sheila had already lost her husband Victor, and two of her four sons. Her eldest, Stephen, had been killed when his motorbike collided with a moving train at a level crossing in Inglewood, New South Wales, in 1977, a tragedy that had hit his family hard. Later, in 1997, another of her sons passed away from what the Bells understood to be a drug overdose. It must have broken the heart of the grieving mother to discover that her third-born, Gary, was a nasty drinker and known wife-beater. Former colleagues would observe that that relations certainly seemed strained between 'Gaz' and his mother.

Gary's mother had already telephoned Harold and Rosalie Bell's house that Thursday morning, wondering if they might know why her calls to her son's home had gone unanswered. Sheila had been surprised when Karen picked up her call. 'What's happened now?' Gary's mum asked, her heart sinking. She explained to her daughter-in-law that she had called the farm a few times during the morning, but had received no answer. Karen told her briefly what had happened. She suspected Gary was simply ignoring the phone again. But her mother-in-law was not so sure. She felt uneasy to learn that her volatile, heavy-drinking son was alone with her grandchildren. Sheila continued to ring the farm, panicking when Gary failed to pick up. She rang her daughter-in-law back again at lunch time, saying she was worried and was going to ask her friend to drive her up to Pericoe to find out what was going on. Karen told her to hold off, saying that this might aggravate Gary. The women agreed that Sheila should call Karen's aunt who lived next door, and ask her if she knew what was happening.

After lunch on Thursday the concerned grandmother shared her concerns with Dianne Auld, saying she was worried that her three young grandchildren were home alone with their troubled father. Mrs Auld admitted she was worried about them too. But with Gary Bell's violent history she had been too afraid of him to go up to the farm and check on things.

The women agreed that in view of the recent dramas they did not believe the children should be in the care of their alcoholic father at all. They should be with their mother, Sheila observed.

Karen's aunt hung up the phone and immediately rang her niece. From Bega, Karen explained that Bell had refused to allow her children to leave the house with her. After she had left Pericoe on the previous Monday, she had telephoned the police again from her parents' home, asking if they could help her remove the children from her violent husband's care. She had an AVO, she pointed out. But the police told her that since the children's names were not on the order, their hands were tied. She had left them with her husband voluntarily and there was nothing they could do.

But on Thursday, after hearing what her aunt had to say about the silence next door, Karen also began to panic. She called the police in Merimbula, reminding them about the assault and the AVO. She begged them to help her and she explained that nobody had seen or heard anything from Gary or the children since she had left. It had been four whole days and everyone was worried, she said.

The police told her again there was nothing they could do because the children's names had not been included on the court order. Karen urged them to send a patrol car up to the farm to do a welfare check and put her mind at rest. But the police said that since the court had not considered Bell a threat to his children when they granted the AVO, there seemed little point.

Again the police reminded the distraught woman that she had

voluntarily left her children with their dad, who had never been violent to them before. Karen couldn't believe her ears. It had hardly been a voluntary decision to leave them, she explained. Their violent father, now facing charges for assaulting her, had flatly refused to let them go. She hung up feeling more uneasy than ever.

Later that afternoon, Karen telephoned Tracey Wilson in Pericoe, telling her about her aunt's worried phone call. She told her friend about the conversation she'd had with the Merimbula police and asked if Tracey would mind driving to the farm to check on her family. The good-natured Tracey hesitated. She knew enough about her friend's husband to know Bell was not the kind of man you messed with. Tracey would later admit she felt a little scared of the drunken wife-beater. It was getting dark by now, and Tracey, nervous about the prospect of driving up to the farm, promised that she would call around first thing in the morning.

But Tracey shared her friend's concerns about the children and put the phone down, also feeling extremely worried about Jack, Maddie and Bon. Not wanting to trigger an angry confrontation with Gary at the farm, Tracey Wilson made a phone call to the police herself, to ask if there was anything they could do.

She reminded them about the violent scene at Two Creeks the week before and urged them to drive up to the farm to check on the children, who had not been seen or heard from since their mother was forced to leave them four days earlier.

'I almost begged them,' she would later tell Channel Nine's *Sixty Minutes*. 'I said to the policeman … "Please, I really think you should go. Something is not right. I do feel something is wrong."' In a premonition of things to come, Tracey made a throwaway remark that would later return to haunt her.

'I can't believe it,' she told the Channel Nine. 'I said to them … "I'm going to go out there and find dead bodies."' The officer tried to reassure her.

'Oh no, everything will be all right,' he said.

But Tracey was not convinced. She was stunned when the policeman went on to tell her that they did not want to send anyone out to the farm because they were afraid their presence might upset Gary Bell.

'You're worried about upsetting Gary?' Tracey replied, incredulous. 'What about the children?' By the time she hung up, Tracey Wilson's gut feeling that something really was wrong at Two Creeks was eating her alive. The police were concerned enough about the worried neighbour's call to telephone Karen back. But it was late, and she didn't see any point in the police waking the children up. The officers agreed. Pericoe was such a remote area and it was likely that they would get lost up there in the dark. They agreed that if Tracey did not feel safe driving up to the farm the following morning, then Karen should let them know and they would send someone around on a welfare check. Karen rang Tracey back to explain about the call. Tracey promised she would drive up to the farm with her partner as soon as they had dropped their own children at school next morning.

'Don't worry,' Karen said, trying to reassure her friend. 'Nothing will have happened to them.' Tracey didn't have to worry about getting there and finding anyone dead, or anything like that. All the same, Karen spent a restless night, panicking. She could not get that conversation with her aunt out of her head. With her three lively kids, Karen's house was never silent.

At some time after 10.30 a.m on Friday 27 June,, Tracey and her partner Peter Porada drove up Fulligan's Road and into the driveway, past the letterbox saying Hells Bells, towards the farm.

It was unusually quiet around the property they observed as they parked their car, leaving Tracey's four-year-old son, Lachlan, in the back in his child seat. Just as Karen's aunt had remarked in her worried phone call, there was no sign of Gary, or any of the children, who Tracey would have expected to see out in the garden.

She cautiously called Gary's name, hoping to alert him to her presence and avoid any dramas. But there was no response. Then she called out to the children: 'Jack, Maddie, Bon ... where are you?' Over the silence, her voice bounced back at her. Karen's neighbour gingerly made her way through the unlocked back door into the farmhouse. There was no sign of anyone inside and the place appeared deserted.

While his partner was looking around the house, Porada had spotted Gary Bell's four-wheel drive nearby. As Porada approached it, he noticed that two hose pipes had been connected to the car's exhaust. The car windows had been closed and it appeared that someone had taken the trouble to tape them. All around the vehicle, gaps had been carefully plugged with clothing. Peering inside, Porada was shocked to see the lifeless bodies of Gary Bell and his three young children. Wanting to spare Tracey the ghastly sight, Porada turned on his heel and went to find her.

When Tracey emerged from the house, she noticed Porada striding purposefully towards her. What happened next she would replay in her head for a long time afterwards; it took a few seconds before she registered the fact that Peter was actually screaming something at her, she told *Sixty Minutes*.

'Get the fuck back in the car,' he yelled. In tears, Tracey recalled her stunned response.

'They're dead, aren't they?'

Peter's face was stony. 'Just get in the car,' he urged.

The next thing Tracey remembered was falling to the ground and screaming endlessly into the sky as the enormity of the situation slowly sank in.

With no mobile reception at the farm, Porada just wanted to get out of there and alert the police to his gruesome discovery. He sped back to their house, with Tracey sobbing and shaking in the passenger seat.

'I wanted to rip the door off the car and just cuddle the kids,' Tracey told *Sixty Minutes*, reliving the harrowing ordeal on national TV. 'I let those babies down.'

Shortly after 11 a.m., the traumatised couple contacted the police to report what they had discovered.

The arrival of an ambulance crew in the tight-knit community provided the first hint of the unthinkable drama unfolding at Two Creeks. Due to the rugged terrain, the paramedics struggled to find the farm. Negotiating the windy dirt tracks would also prove a challenge to the detectives and forensic experts arriving from Queanbeyan and Sydney.

The paramedics had to pull over at the home of long-time Pericoe resident Rick O'Hara to ask for directions. O'Hara, who had lived in the region for 30 years, would later tell the *Sydney Morning Herald* that while he did not know the Bells personally, he knew plenty about the area.

The vast 400-acre property where the farm stood had once been an early cattle station, he told the reporters. But in the 'flower power' era of free love it had become a hippie colony. Its peaceful inhabitants had planted allotments on the land with a view to creating a self-sufficient paradise deep in the forest. But the crops had eventually withered and the hippies had abandoned paradise after sinking into a lifestyle of alcohol and drugs.

The colony's demise had earned the Pericoe Valley the unfortunate moniker 'The Valley of Failure'.

'The place is rotten,' he told other reporters, explaining that some of the more cynical locals dubbed the area 'deliverance' country due to the strange allure it still seemed to hold for single parents, itinerants and those seeking an alternative lifestyle away from the humdrum world.

As far as O'Hara was concerned, Two Creeks was just a 'dot in a dense, tall timber mountain wilderness'.

The paramedics no doubt agreed as they negotiated their ambulance towards what was now a crime scene. While calls flew between the local police and their colleagues in Sydney, Karen Bell was sitting beside the phone at her parents' home, anxiously waiting for a call from her friend Tracey.

Karen had telephoned every fifteen minutes since 10 a.m., getting more and more worried with every unanswered call. Perhaps Tracey and 'Pod' were on the farm having a big chat with Gary, she told herself.

Since the discovery, Tracey Wilson had been in such deep shock that all she could do was tremble and sob. A mother herself, Tracey had no idea how a doting mother like Karen Bell would cope with such a tragedy; and she had no idea how to break such terrible news. If Karen Bell had come to Pericoe with a dream of finding peace in paradise, all her dreams had been washed away in a single moment of madness. Tracey wasn't sure she had the words to explain it.

But news of the deaths had already begun to trickle onto the airwaves. Karen's Aunt Dianne's heart sank when she heard an early news bulletin about the grim discovery of four bodies, an adult male and three children, found in a car on the New South Wales far south coast that morning. When her own telephone rang, she answered it immediately, assuming it would be her niece. Instead, a reporter asked her what she knew about a murder–suicide at Pericoe.

Shocked, Mrs Auld immediately telephoned Harold and Rosalie's home cautiously asking if Karen had heard anything from Pericoe yet. Harold Bell answered the call, listening in stony silence as Dianne related the story she had just heard on the radio, and telling him about the call she had received from the reporter. His daughter hovered behind him, trying to read Harold's stunned face, assuming he was talking to Tracey.

'No, no, no, no...' her father gasped, tears welling in his eyes. 'Murder ... suicide ... no, no.' Trembling, Harold handed the phone to Karen, and sank into a chair. Again, her aunt repeated the horrible story. She said the reporter had asked her what she knew about three murdered children and a man who had committed suicide. Karen's stomach began to sink. In that instant, she knew instinctively her children had gone.

Shaking violently, Karen immediately phoned Tracey's home, her anxiety rising when the phone rang out again. Tracey was talking to the police. They had instructed her not to say anything about her grim discovery. As tragic as it was, they were trained to deliver such dreadful news. Karen telephoned three different police stations, but nobody was answering. She hung on the end of the line until the call was finally put through to the police in Bateman's Bay.

'We've had a lot of phone calls about this,' the officer said, as Karen hurriedly repeated what her aunt had told her. 'So it's true,' Karen sobbed. But the officer said he could not give her any further information. 'But I'm the children's mother,' she choked. The officer took down her name, address and phone number. Someone would be in touch, he promised.

Karen paced the backyard, chain-smoking and trembling as she dialled Tracey's number again. She finally answered. Karen fearfully asked her friend if she had been out to the farm yet to check on her children.

Tracey, numbly registering Karen's panic-stricken voice on the end of the line, was lost for words. She had been instructed not to say a word; but how could she lie?

'Is it true?' asked the terrified young mother, dreading the answer. Tracey admitted that it was. The children were all dead, she said.

Tracey would later tell *Sixty Minutes* that she would never forget that conversation or Karen's agony as she howled down the phone, drowning out her own sobs.

At 1 p.m., the Bells answered the door to find three policemen on their doorstep. 'I already know,' Karen said, in tears. 'We are so sorry,' said the police. They handed her the contact details for a Detective Kevin Coady, who was at the scene and would provide her with more information. Karen rang his number, but there was no answer. The telephone reception on the farm was terrible.

By Friday afternoon news of the shocking events at the farm had spread like wildfire. Karen's older sister Sandra had been driving home to Sydney from Canberra that day when her husband Alistair rang to tell her about a TV news bulletin he had just watched on Sky News. He related the story about the discovery of a man and his three children who had been involved in a murder suicide up at Pericoe. Sandra, paralysed by the news, had pulled over onto the side of the road to stop herself shaking, and compose herself. Even before she dialled her parents' number she knew who the young casualties of this murder–suicide were. Sandra immediately drove to Bega where the friends who Gary Bell had banned his wife from seeing now flocked to the family home to support the shattered mother.

At Pericoe, a police officer was posted to stand guard over the grim scene to preserve the integrity of the ongoing police investigation.

The young officer later told reporters converging on the scene that it was the worst thing he had ever seen. Journalists were turned away from the property and warned there could be no photographs until the forensic experts had examined the scene. That did not stop a TV crew in a helicopter filming the site from overhead.

Inside the deserted house, Maddie's little doll's house blinked emptily back at the detectives now combing the place for clues. Outside in the garden, the children's trampoline stood silently in the winter sun. The police and forensic experts later studying the scene wondered what could have driven a supposedly loving father to commit such an unthinkable act.

It seemed ironic to the locals that the former commune, founded so long ago on love and peace, was now the scene of what media quickly concluded was a triple murder–suicide.

It was, perhaps, a premature assessment, given that the New South Wales State Coroner's Office had only just been informed about the tragedy, and arrangements were yet to be made to transport the bodies to the mortuary in Glebe. There, toxicology tests would have to be performed and autopsies carried out on the four bodies.

But if it was a premature conclusion on the media's part, it was a reasonable one. The theory that this was a triple murder–suicide gathered momentum after Superintendent Michael Willing from New South Wales Police made a media statement confirming that they were not looking at any other suspects in connection with the four deaths.

The senior officer confirmed that the mother of the three children had been located and offered counselling. More disturbing still, he confirmed that the family had been known to the Department of Community Services and that the tragic discovery had occurred just days after staff had been notified about an AVO granted to the children's mother.

It would soon emerge that among the evidence collected from the property were two chilling suicide notes penned by the troubled father; one for his mother, and one for the mother of his dead children.

In those letters Gary Bell expressed his belief that he was set to go to jail for the assault on his wife, and would inevitably lose his children. He said he could not live without his children, nor they without him. A digital camera was also uncovered from the scene, containing a recorded voice message from Gary. Again he insisted that he could not live without his children 'and they can't live without me'.

'It's the end,' he wrote bleakly.

Detective Senior Constable Kevin Coady from Bega police, who joined ambulance crews and police officers at the scene on Friday 27 June, inspected the car with the four bodies still inside. He noted the hose that had been carefully run from a generator into tubing that in turn was taped to the exhaust. He examined the car's closed doors and windows and the clothing plugging every possible gap around the vehicle. This, and the dark messages left by the father, left nobody in any doubt that this had been a carefully and deliberately orchestrated tragedy. Someone had even taken the trouble to secure little Bon into his baby seat in the back of the car. An autopsy would later confirm that all four occupants had died of carbon monoxide poisoning as a result of the deadly fumes pumped into the car's interior after Gary Bell climbed inside and turned the engine on.

The violent husband had made good on his warning to his wife that he could not live without his children. He made sure that they would not live without him.

In Bega, in the arms of her parents, the real target of Gary Bell's anger was in pieces. Unable to comprehend what had happened, Karen Bell was so consumed by denial that at 3 a.m. on Saturday morning, she attended Bega Hospital where she forced herself through the ordeal of identifying her children. The painful task had had to wait until forensics had thoroughly examined the car and its contents, so that the bodies could be removed and transported to the nearest hospital morgue. For Karen, who could not believe her children were really gone, it was an agonising ordeal, but she had to see Jack, Maddie and Bon with her own eyes to accept it was real. Her friend Belinda drove her to the hospital, while her parents and sister Sandra followed in another car.

The grieving mother who had not been denied a chance to say a proper goodbye was distraught to be told she could not touch, or even kiss her children, because she might disturb vital evidence. She surveyed her three children through the morgue's glass window, taking in Maddie and Jack's small bloated faces which were tinged colours of red, purple and blue. She had been warned that they'd spent days in their father's car before their bodies were found, and the effects of the carbon monoxide poisoning would have changed their appearances. The nurse's warning was correct. Karen's two older children were unrecognisable.

But Bon looked like a small wax doll, with only a small bruise on his face. His mother noted sadly that he was wearing the same skivvy with cars and trucks on it that she had dressed him in that Sunday morning before collecting Gary. The top had once belonged to Jack. Karen was gripped with the realisation that the children must have died at some stage on Sunday after she left. That meant she would have been at Tracey's house when Gary snuffed the life out of her angels. Bon's clothing, along with other important evidence, would later allow the police to determine that the children's bodies had lain in the car for five days.

The nurse asked Karen if she wanted to see the face of the man who had robbed her of her whole world. 'Yes, I need to,' she replied. Bell's icy-blue eyes stared back at her from the slab. Karen felt so angry she wanted to charge in there and kill him all over again.

The following day Karen's brother Tom told journalists gathered outside the family home in Bega that identifying her 'three little angels' was the hardest thing she had ever done. But it was something she had to do, he told the *Sydney Morning Herald*, 'Because she really couldn't believe it, and had to see for herself that her babies were gone.' He went on to describe his grief-stricken sister as 'the best mum'.

'She loved her kids with all her heart,' he said. Karen, like their parents, was too distressed to speak.

In another story in the same newspaper, Karen's aunt described her niece's reaction to the news: she was 'devastated' and 'despairing',

Dianne Auld revealed. 'She's not in a state of talking about it ... she's not handling it very well at all, which is to be expected. Everything's gone ... she's not coping. I think you'd think that life's finished if you lost your three children in that way.'

The neighbours who had made the gruesome discovery described their own shock over the tragedy, which had hit their 20-strong community hard.

Tracey Wilson, who had been in tears ever since, blamed herself for not getting to the farm sooner.

'I got there too late,' she told the *Illawarra Mercury*. She described the heartbreaking conversation when she had to deliver the devastating news to her friend. Her heart had broken a little more, she said, when the shattered mother apologised to her for asking her to go to the farm.

'This is the type of woman she is,' Tracey told the *Mercury*. 'She said sorry to me ... I don't want her to feel guilt for that.'

If Tracey Wilson wanted to spare her friend the guilt that now consumed her, the Bells were convinced guilt was exactly what Gary Bell had wanted his wife to feel. He wanted her to be sorry for what she had made him do.

And Karen was consumed with guilt, repeatedly blaming herself for not being there when her children needed her most. If only she hadn't left them, she wept. Her family reminded her that there had been no warning signs to indicate that Gary would ever harm his children. How could she protect them from something none of them had ever imagined possible?

As far as the distressed Bell family was concerned, the blame belonged solely with the abusive husband who had, in the ultimate act of domestic violence, robbed Karen of her entire family.

Karen's brother-in-law Alistair expressed the anger of the entire family when he told journalists:

'Those three babies will go to heaven and that bastard will rot in hell forever. Those babies will be protected and looked after now. Simple as that.' Alistair said the family had come together to comfort the real victim of the terrible tragedy.

'Everybody was just very quiet and shocked,' he said as he left the house. 'The grief was there. It was a very surreal atmosphere ... there was not too many conversations, just a lot of silence.'

Meanwhile, pointed questions from the family and the media had sparked a political storm over the way New South Wales Police and the Department of Community Services had bungled the case. The New South Wales Premier, Morris Iemma, trying to calm the storm, responded with an announcement that there would be an inquiry into what went wrong and whether more could have been done to prevent the tragedy. DoCS would also be cooperating with that inquiry, he said.

'We need answers,' he told the *Weekend Australian*. Everything possible was being done to investigate the 'terrible tragedy'.

'We are going to find out what exactly happened and why. What action was taken will determine the course of action in the future.'

Meanwhile Opposition Leader Barry O'Farrell told the same newspaper it had to be established whether a phone call from social workers would have been adequate given the violent nature of the relationship.

Media later reported that the government was considering changing the recruitment process for DoCS workers if the existing special commission of inquiry into child protection found that qualifications were too strict. This followed earlier concerns raised in a Public Service submission, which highlighted the difficulty in recruiting social workers in remote areas of New South Wales because case workers were required to have a university degree.

DoCS was not the only agency under attack. Criticisms were levelled in the press at the New South Wales Police for its alleged mishandling of a case that had ultimately ended in tragedy.

Defending their lack of action in response to Karen Bell's pleas for them to check on her children's welfare, the police issued a peculiar statement claiming the children had been in the 'custody' of their father as part of some 'prior family arrangement'. Tom Bell was furious and publicly corrected the misinformation.

'They are using the wrong wording,' he said. His sister had been kicked out of the house, that's why the children were in Gary Bell's custody.

'I don't think that's an arrangement,' he said.

He argued that the police's comments about 'custody' implied this was a mutual legal arrangement between the parents. But this couldn't have been further from the truth. His sister had been forced to leave her children behind, and despite her discussions with the police, she had been led to believe that she had no legal recourse to have them removed. Neither the police, the courts nor DoCS had done anything to protect his sister's children, he said. Despite calls to the police from his sister and her neighbour, and the fact that DoCS already knew about the AVO the day it had been granted, nothing had been done by anyone until it was too late.

Tom Bell felt this illustrated the fact that even the police had not appreciated the risk Gary Bell posed to his family. Later DoCS would respond to the criticism, releasing a statement claiming that from the moment it had been made aware of the AVO, repeated attempts had been made by staff to contact the family. They claimed they had not been able to raise a response from anyone.

In another revealing comment, Catherine Gander, Executive Officer of the New South Wales Women's Refuge Movement, told Radio National's PM program on Monday 30 June that new laws meant that Karen Bell's children should have been protected by the AVO issued against her violent husband. Under the new DV laws introduced in March 2008, it was specified that in cases where an AVO had been taken out and children were involved in the domestic relationship, then each of those children should be included as protected persons under the order. Ms Gander told listeners that it was very clear from the stories surfacing that there had been a level of control in the abusive relationship, and that like a lot of abused women, the only way Karen Bell had been able to leave the property safely was without her children.

While the questions and criticisms flew, the focus of the coverage began to shift. Stories soon began to fill the press about the disturbed father at the centre of the tragedy. Since Friday's discovery, journalists had been converging on the tiny forested township in the Pericoe Valley and trawling neighbouring coastal towns to speak with those who knew Gary Bell best. They wanted to build a picture of the father who claimed he could not live without his children.

If the smiling photographs released by the Bell family of the once-proud mother posing beside her three bubbly children revealed no hint of her private hell, it appeared the public image of Gary Bell was also at odds with the violent man who tormented his wife behind closed doors.

What quickly emerged was a portrait of a troubled man with a double life. Not only had Gary Bell presented two different personas to the world — he had two different identities, too. The media leapt on the story.

Gary Bell was really Gary Mark Poxon, aka Gary Mills, the third son of UK-born parents Victor and Sheila Poxon, who had been among the hundreds of thousands of ten-pound Poms who arrived in Australia in the 1960s and '70s in search of a better life.

When Gary Poxon first met teenager Karen Bell, he was 29 and had recently separated from his first wife, a woman believed to be from the Tathra–Bega region.

He refused to talk about his former marriage, except to tell Karen that his former wife was a liar who had conned police into believing he had been violent to her, and had even threatened to kill her. It was all rubbish, he insisted. The police had taken him away on her say-so, and she had refused to have him back. Bell blamed her for the separation and accused her of preventing him from seeing his children. Everything was her fault, he told Karen.

Whatever the truth, the separation was certainly an acrimonious one because friends and former colleagues recalled Poxon bitterly referring to his first wife as 'the Bitch of Bega'.

While nobody really knew what had triggered the demise of Poxon's former marriage, most gathered it had been a turbulent relationship. The Bell family were later convinced his violence would have been a contributing factor to its eventual collapse. It was the general consensus around the traps, that after after the separation

Bell had apparently abandoned his first wife and left her to raise their four sons on her own.

The breakdown of his marriage appeared to have sparked some sort of identity crisis in Poxon, who began calling himself Gary Mills. Locals remembered him leaving Bega for a while before popping up again with his new, younger wife, Karen.

Former work colleagues thought it bizarre when Poxon suddenly announced his intention to adopt his new wife's last name. After his marriage he became known as Gary Bell, though nobody could understand what prompted the change. While some friends and co-workers felt this might have been an attempt to distance himself from ongoing family dramas with his first wife, others suspected there was a more Machiavellian motivation for his new identity. The general consensus was that Gary Poxon was attempting to dodge his financial obligations to his former family.

On Valentine's Day 2004, Karen had married Gary Bell at Tathra Headlands, NSW. The nuptials had been a small, private affair because Bell had refused to allow Karen's friends and wider family to attend the wedding ceremony, with the exception of her parents. He made no secret of the fact that he did not like Karen's sister. After Bell married Karen, he immediately began to systematically alienate his new wife from almost anyone who might have given her some perspective on the state of the violent relationship.

In 2005, when the Bells retreated to the more secluded surroundings of Pericoe, the 'disappearing' husband put even more distance between himself and his old life. In the remote wilderness, it was not difficult for a man to lose himself.

There, holed up in the farmhouse on the site of the failed hippie colony, Gary Poxon sank into an alcohol-induced haze. He brewed his own beer and there was talk that he'd even started making his own moonshine. He drank heavily, and became reliant on the marijuana that he cultivated for his own use. But mostly he kept himself to himself and he wanted his family to do the same.

At some stage in 2008, the Bells withdrew their two older children from the tiny Towamba Primary School. Jack and Maddie had been popular at the little bush school where all the young students were very close. But it had been decided, for financial reasons, that it would be cheaper and more convenient if the children were homeschooled. Their lessons were supplemented with the distance-education program run out of Queanbeyan.

With Jack and Maddie at home, Karen was busy. It was hard work educating two children and tending to a growing toddler and a demanding, unpredictable, hard-drinking husband. Karen now had very few friends, and her family had learned to keep their distance. She had even been forced to relinquish the beautician's job that she had loved so much. The turbulent nature of her violent relationship, and the constant time off as a result of her injuries, made it impossible for Karen to hold down a job. She gave away the position at the beauty salon in Merimbula, and made her mind up to focus on her children. Karen Bell's world slowly began to shrink.

It was clear from the things Tracey Wilson had to say about the man she knew as Gary Bell that Karen was isolated socially as well as geographically. In one story in the *Sydney Morning Herald*, Tracey described the abusive husband as a 'jealous' man who discouraged his wife's friendships and came to resent the bond she and Karen had formed. She was in no doubt that Bell knew Karen fled to her house when things got out of hand.

'He was cranky at me for helping her twice before,' she told the newspaper. As far as Tracey Wilson was concerned, Gary Bell was 'aggro'. Mostly they got along well enough, she said. She had no problem telling the guy he was an 'arsehole' when she felt he needed it.

But there were conflicting accounts of the man with two names and a secret double life. Journalists discovered that Gary Poxon aka Bell was also an affable sort of guy whose public persona was important to him. Bell was acknowledged locally as a talented, albeit unusually small, AFL player. He seemed friendly enough, observed some locals, but he had a large ego that belied his slight 168-centimetre frame. His inflated sense of his own worth and tendency to brag around town about where he'd travelled and what he had done rubbed more than a few of the locals up the wrong way. What Bell had actually done didn't really appear to amount to much.

In the three years since his arrival in Pericoe, Poxon had earned a reputation as a little man with a big mouth who enjoyed a few too many beers. Tracey Wilson's partner Peter Porada did not like him. After Bell's suicide, he told reporters the guy was 'a motor-mouthed legend'.

But if the motor-mouthed Poxon was more than happy to talk about himself, he was not so keen to discuss the fact that behind closed doors he was a wife-beater. But he didn't have to. Despite his embarrassed wife's attempts to keep his violence a secret, from the accounts gleaned by journalists, most of their friends and neighbours in the close-knit township were well aware of the violent 'domestics' taking place in the peaceful surroundings of Two Creeks.

Ironically, there was no creek at all at Two Creeks. And for Karen Bell, living deep in the forest, there was no peace either. The young mother's repeated absences from the family home as she fled her husband's attacks were noted by their neighbours, including her aunt who lived next door. Even neighbours who didn't know the family personally knew about Gary Poxon and his nasty streak.

Damian Foat, whose engineering company Sapphire Coast Engineering had employed Bell as a welder during the early 1990s, remembered him as a guy with a great deal of family melodrama.

In a story published on 30 June he told the *Sydney Morning Herald* that he had been under the impression that it had been Karen Bell who had first moved to the area, wanting to be closer to her family. Foat believed that Poxon had followed 'looking for her'. Foat said every so often Karen Bell 'took off' to escape the pressures of living with a guy who liked his beer.

'He was a pretty heavy drinker,' said Foat. 'As soon as he'd knock off he'd have a drink in his hand.'

Overlooking the fact that Karen Bell had been fleeing for her life, he attributed the battered wife's constant absences from the family home to her feisty personality. As far as Foat was concerned, Karen Bell 'took off' simply because she was 'a free spirit'.

'That was the reason he stopped working for me,' Foat concluded. But, 'Gaz lived for those kids', he told the newspaper. 'He was a great dad.' He just had a tendency to enjoy a drink and was clearly trying to 'distance himself from other people'.

Gary Bell's former boss admitted he had been 'blown away' after hearing about the tragedy, but explained it a little more generously than others who knew him: 'It obviously got all too much for him in the end.'

If Damian Foat remembered Gary Bell in a relatively positive light, others in the community did not. Another boss, Mitchell Heffernan, who employed the welder at his firm Wilton Engineering in Picton in the early to mid-1990s, recalled his arrival in the small town. Mr Heffernan suspected the then Gary Poxon had been running away from his family dramas when he left Bega for a fresh start in Picton.

'It was pretty drama-filled at the time,' recalled Heffernan, referring to the collapse of Poxon's first marriage.

At some stage he recalled Gary Poxon having a new wife and adopting a new identity. But Heffernan had a more cynical take on Poxon's motivation for the sudden name change.

'He didn't want to pay a cent in maintenance,' he said. As far as he was concerned, Bell was a manipulator who had adopted a new name to avoid his financial obligations to the family he'd abandoned. Heffernan remembered Bell as a good Aussie-rules player who showed some talent in spite of his small stature. But whatever name he gave himself, to Heffernan Gary Poxon remained an unpleasant, 'uptight' and 'aggressive' little bloke with a 'chiselled jaw' who suffered from 'little bloke syndrome'.

Not too many people appeared to like Gary Poxon or his alter ego, Gary Bell. Karen's relative Alistair told the *Sydney Morning Herald* on Monday morning that he had never liked Poxon, who he described as 'a piece of work'. He had been shocked when he discovered Poxon had changed his name to Bell.

'Don't ask me why. We all thought it was bizarre. It was his decision. We genuinely thought it was a bit strange.' But he said it was clear

Bell's public image was important to him, because he was so good at hiding his true nature.

'Every time when I was there, me or my wife, he always seemed to portray himself as just a normal character. He wouldn't show his anger in front of anybody. He wouldn't do it in public. He managed to hide everything from everybody. He was a good liar.'

Karen's brother Tom had never liked his violent brother-in-law either. He had personally witnessed Bell's violence towards his sister, and had restrained him from abusing her on one occasion. Tom could not understand why she stayed with him. Karen's father, who had once been on the receiving end of his son-in-law's violence, grew to dislike him too.

After the tragedy the Bell family vowed to distance themselves from the man who had taken their name and caused them such heartbreak. They would never again refer to him as Bell; he had tarnished their name and would never be linked to them again. To them, he would always be Gary Poxon, wife-beater and child-killer.

If Poxon's relationship with his in-laws had been strained, friends revealed things were just as strained when it came to his own family. Karen's relatives who had been in touch with Poxon's mother, Sheila, revealed she too was devastated by her grandchildren's deaths. Most wondered how painful it must be for the elderly grandmother who had now lost three of her four sons and had to grapple with the senseless deaths of three much-loved grandchildren.

So many lives had been touched by this tragedy. Since the discovery of their bodies in their father's car, Jack, Maddie and Bon had been keenly missed in the small Towamba community. On the Sunday after the news broke, Jack and Maddie's former classmates from Towamba Primary School banded together to create their own poignant tribute to their friends and their little brother.

The youngsters lovingly fashioned a heart out of the rocks on a sandy island in their local creek, and carved the initials J, M and B in stone. Then they spelled out the word 'love' beneath their unique tribute.

On the weekend after Poxon's car was found, his anguished wife, supported by her family, returned to the scene of her children's deaths. It was an agonising ordeal. The grieving relatives steeled themselves as they glimpsed the empty trampoline and Maddie's little doll's house sitting just where the outgoing seven-year-old had left it.

Karen had wanted to make the pilgrimage back to the property to collect the family's pets. She also wanted to retrieve some of her children's most precious toys and belongings, along with her own special mementoes, especially her photo albums and her digital camera, which had two years of undeveloped photographs on it.

Among her most treasured keepsakes were the three scrapbooks she had lovingly created, capturing the special milestones in her three children's lives. Each scrapbook contained snapshots and memorabilia including her children's ultrasound scans and their hospital tags. Karen had meticulously recorded every milestone she had celebrated during their first year of life.

The happy family snapshots looked so *normal*. There was not a glimpse of the bruises or split lips that Karen had endured. There was a photo of Jack with his front tooth missing, kids with their faces painted, and Maddie blowing out the candles on her first birthday cake. Another showed the two proud older siblings meeting their beautiful baby brother Bon for the first time. One touching photograph showed Karen proudly smiling with her three children, her happy smile belying her private heartache. To the outside world, beyond their neighbours and friends, they looked every inch the perfect happy family.

Gary Poxon, the man who had terrorised and beaten Karen, also featured in her scrapbooks. In a poignant scribbling, Karen tenderly referred to him as 'my beloved husband'.

After her painful trip to Pericoe, Karen agreed to talk to the *South Coast Register* about her heartache. Until then, she had not been able to contemplate speaking to reporters. They were like vultures, she concluded, through a haze of sleeping tables and pain. But among the surfacing stories there had been much misinformation and many discrepancies. Karen was so angry and upset when one of the

Sunday papers reported her children's ages wrong that she decided she would speak to the local paper to set the record straight.

Poring over the scrapbooks and the haunting photographs in her parents' lounge, journalist Steve Strevens noted the grieving mother's eyes were 'red from lack of sleep and tears'.

'I'm just trying to get through as best I can … trying to get through each day,' Karen said, looking around at the cards and flowers, many from total strangers wanting to offer comfort. She said she was grateful for the support, but just felt so empty. 'It's as though something as reached into my chest, grabbed my heart and ripped it out,' she told Strevens.

Karen's mother Rosalie spoke briefly about her grandchildren's visits and how she enjoyed watching them all playing in her garden. Maddie in particular loved her grandmother's home-made jelly. Rosalie could not believe she would never get to see them play at her house again. Throughout the interview, the children's shattered grandfather, Harold, sat behind his shed in the garden, too distressed to speak.

The scrapbooks were a legacy of three beautiful children and a mum who absolutely adored them, said Karen's brother Tom. The time that his sister had put into these mementoes was evidence of her great love for her babies.

Over the coming days Karen's scrapbooks and their haunting photographs would make their way onto the national news: a reminder of the senselessness of the tragedy. The newspapers all pounced on Karen's loving reference to the 'beloved husband' who had robbed her of everything she held dear.

Other stories were also emerging as the family and friends openly acknowledged the violent background to the relationship. Tom Bell spoke about the torment of watching his sister being manipulated by a controlling man who repeatedly abused her.

'All you could do was stand by her, support her,' he said. But this tragedy was a warning to other women in violent relationships. 'I don't think you should stay,' said Tom.

Nine days after the tragedy, Karen Bell appeared on Channel

Nine, telling *Sixty Minutes* about her violent relationship and the paralysing suffering this final act of family violence had caused.

'I'm very very angry, very hurt — I'm just disgusted,' she said. Karen spoke about the agonising phone conversation she had had with her friend Tracey when she learned her children were dead.

'I was screaming and she was screaming,' Karen recalled. She told viewers she had no doubt that Poxon's callous actions, as he meticulously planned and carried out the murder–suicide, were ultimately aimed at hurting her. And she spoke about his last harrowing communication with her, when he wrote her a letter telling her 'this is the end'.

Karen told presenter Liz Hayes she believed that when he wrote those words, he really meant this was the end of her life as she had known it.

'He was trying to make me feel guilty for the rest of my life — and I do,' she said sadly. Yet it made no sense, she said, because at the beginning her husband had been such a fantastic guy.

'He did love his children, he really did,' she reflected. She never doubted when she left the house that fateful Sunday in June, leaving her children behind, that they would be safe with their father. 'I never doubted that,' she said thoughtfully. 'And I still can't believe it.'

Karen's father Harold told how the young guy he'd once thought was 'such a nice bloke' had morphed into a violent bully. The shattered grandfather recalled how he had once made the mistake of 'backchatting' his arrogant son-in-law, who immediately turned on him.

'He just caught up, grabbed me — like … bang, bang, bang, bang … straight in the car and locked the door. It was over in what … half a minute?' said Mr Bell.

Karen described how she had survived the endless beatings by running away.

'But I always went back because he would never let me take the children,' she said. 'I wanted that family … you know, stick together. The children loved him, you know, I loved him, and we always worked it out.'

In a tribute to her children, Karen spoke proudly about her oldest son Jack's love of football. He was a smart kid who was popular with all the girls at school, she recalled. Karen's daughter Maddie was the noisy, more outgoing one — so funny and loving. Maddie had dreams of one day being a model, her mother proudly said. Her baby, Bon, had yet to make his mark on the world. But Karen would always remember him trailing around after her, and waking up several times a night for one of her special cuddles.

'The kids, they found it very hard seeing their mother hurt,' Karen said, thoughtfully. 'They were very torn, you know ... they wanted us to be together.'

Sixty Minutes noted that the deaths had sparked an investigation into the way in which police and social services had handled the case. But the true victim of Poxon's revenge crime told viewers that ultimately she did not believe anything or anyone could have prevented him from doing what he did.

'Not unless I had the children and he didn't see them,' she said. And that could only have happened if Karen had gone into hiding with her children so that he could never find them.

'I feel guilty that I was not there to protect my children,' she admitted in tears. 'Anybody who has a child would know that. You know that is all you live for. You live for your kids. You do everything for them you can. You try to make the best life you can and they've just been taken away.'

The heartbreaking interview, which gave valuable insight into the endless suffering caused by revenge-motivated crimes, was picked up next day in the national press who re-ran the grieving mother's comments that this was a tragedy that nobody could have predicted or prevented.

A few days before the interview aired, Karen had quietly attended Gary Bell's funeral. Because of the publicity surrounding the murder–suicide, it had not been advertised and was a small private affair organised by his surviving brother and his mother. Despite her anger towards Bell, Karen had spent 15 years of her life with him, and felt compelled to attend the ceremony. She was supported by her parents, her friend Jackie, and her partner Jason. Surveying the coffin and all the flowers, she felt angrier than ever. Karen hoped Gary would burn in hell for what he had done.

On 9 July, two days after her interview with *Sixty Minutes* aired, Karen Bell was back in the spotlight. Distressed and obviously exhausted, she cut a solitary figure as she wept among the crowds of mourners who packed into St John's Anglican Church in Bega to farewell her three children.

A congregation of hundreds braved rain and icy winter temperatures to pay their respects to Jack, Maddie and Bon Bell. A friend of the family, Seventh Day Adventist Pastor John Thompson, told the gathering that the entire community had to shoulder the burden of the tragedy. Everyone was responsible, he said.

'You are not guilty,' the pastor told the children's distressed mother, who was supported by relatives. 'How could you prevent an act like that?'

Pastor Thompson said that the grieving mother's courage in speaking out on national TV about the violent marriage that culminated in her children's deaths had already given other women the strength to leave destructive relationships.

Healing prayers were said for anyone experiencing abuse and tears flowed as the faces of the three children rolled onto a large screen. Among the montage was Karen's face, brimming with pride as she showed off her newborn son Bon, who would now forever be her baby.

Karen had written a eulogy to her children, which she was unable to read. Instead she lit three candles in honour of them and other victims of domestic violence and her brother Tom read her words.

Later, Karen watched bleakly as three small white caskets were lowered into the ground. Above her, balloons bearing touching messages from the children's classmates at Towamba Primary School bobbed into the clouds and disappeared from sight.

Ironically, on the day the funeral made headlines everywhere, the New South Wales Coroner's Office announced it could take up to 18 months before findings into the deaths were formally released.

Meanwhile, the local Bega newspaper announced it was coordinating an appeal to help the bereaved mother 'get her life back on track'.

It seemed like a hopeless prospect to a woman who had sunk to dark lows she never thought possible. The days that followed the children's funeral seemed to blur into one another in a fog of pain so deep that nothing could touch it. Karen chain-smoked and drank herself silly with bourbon in an attempt to numb the gnawing agony. But nothing worked. Karen's friend Jackie had taken her digital camera into a local store to have the photographs of the children developed for the funeral. Jackie had been distraught when the asssistant at Fletcher's explained that two years of photographs had been deleted. When Jackie explained how important these photographs were to the stricken mother, the technical team spent days trying to retrieve the lost snapshots. Karen was greatly relieved to learn that most of the photographs were eventually recovered, though some were damaged.

Jackie made the photographs into a beautiful album. She also handed Karen a disk that contained other milestones in the children's lives. Many showed them in snapshots with the father who had murdered them. There had been a few videos on the camera too, though none were retrievable.

Karen went to a friend's house to use her computer, in a last-ditch attempt to see if the video images could be retrieved. She was stunned when a single dark image flashed across the screen. The fleeting image was Gary Bell's face, which disappeared almost as soon as it appeared on the screen like an evil spectre. Karen was shocked to hear Bell's unmistakable voice speaking to her as if from beyond the grave.

From that dark, chilling image, Karen assumed Bell had tried to video a final message, which he wanted her to find after the murder–suicide. When the camera failed to work, he had spoken into the camera's microphone and left her a harrowing farewell message instead.

'This is it, this is the end ... it's all gone bad,' he said. In the background, Karen could hear the sound of the radio playing, and identified the voices as those of popular Australian entertainers, Roy and HG. The family regularly listened to Roy and HG show on Triple M each Sunday between 2 p.m. and 5 p.m. With her stomach sinking, Karen realised that the message had been recorded while the radio show was on, which offered a timeframe for her husband's crime.

The tape recording confirmed the police's view that the children must have died at some time on Sunday afternoon, after Karen left the farm and very shortly after their father recorded this message.

Feeling physically sick, Karen immediately contacted Detective Coady, and asked him to come and collect the ghastly tape.

The road ahead was agonising; there were days when Karen struggled to put a sentence together. She forgot simple things like names, and suffered debilitating panic attacks. Most mornings, she climbed out of bed feeling cold and numb.

In November that year she told *Woman's Day* that there was never any relief from the pain. There was no coming back from this horror, Karen said bleakly. After losing her three children, she would never be able to trust or love another man again.

But in the midst of her despair, Karen Bell was about to be proved wrong. Among the throng of family and friends who rallied around to support her through the dark days following the loss of her children, she found unexpected comfort in family friend Dean Gray. She had known Dean, a painter and decorator, for some time. Dean was the brother of a close friend, also called Karen. He provided a listening ear and became an understanding support for a damaged young woman with nothing left to live for.

By early 2009, the budding friendship between Karen and this gentle man of few words had turned to romance. Dean came to be the man who guided Karen through the saddest moments of her life: through Christmases devoid of children's laughter, through birthdays and important anniversaries like Mother's Day. She called Dean 'her rock' and experienced a kindness and gentle respect she had never dreamed possible in her former relationship.

If Karen Bell thought there was no coming back after such horror, she was glad to find she was wrong.

In 2009 Karen was delighted to discover that she was going to be a mother again. It had been agonising being a mother with no children. Nothing would ever bring back her first three children, and nothing would ever replace them. But her new pregnancy with a new gentle and caring partner had given her a chance to live again.

By the time the inquest into the deaths of her former husband and her three children prepared to open in Bega in mid-2009, Karen was eight months pregnant and news of her new happiness quickly found its way into the media.

In a frank interview with the *Bega District News*, the expectant mother spoke about her newfound happiness and how she had been driven to self-medicate her pain with alcohol. She said the love of her family, friends and community, combined with intensive counselling, had helped her survive the darkest moments of her life. She was glad to be happy again. She had not believed it to be possible.

Amid the joy of the new pregnancy came more unwelcome news. Shortly before the inquest began, Karen had met with Detective Coady who wanted to talk to her about a statement that had been made by a former associate of Gary Bell's. Coady wanted Karen to be aware of the contents of that revealing statement, in case it was raised at the inquest. Coady did not want this information to come from left field and preferred Karen to hear about it, directly from him.

Karen was stunned to learn about a conversation Bell had supposedly had with a man who had met him for the first time, several months before he murdered his children. In his statement, the man claimed Bell had told him he had brought his children into this world, and he would take them out. Bell had also told the man that he wished to be remembered as a martyr, not a murderer. What disturbed Karen most about this statement was that Bell had apparently made these claims a whole nine months before the murder suicide. So her children's deaths had not been a spur-of-the-moment decision after all, she concluded. Dark thoughts had filled his mind long before he carried out his final act of revenge to punish her for leaving him.

In August 2009, with her new partner by her side, an emotional

Karen filed into the Bega District Court house with her family to face the ordeal of hearing the graphic details of her children's final moments with their father. To Karen, reliving her children's final moments felt more like a funeral than a legal proceeding. Karen was grateful that the stranger's statement was never aired.

A toxicology report presented to New South Wales Deputy State Coroner, Hugh Dillon, revealed that traces of the drug Phenergan had been found in each of the children's stomachs. The evidence showed the children had been sedated shortly before being overcome by carbon monoxide fumes. Mr Dillon was told that the fact the drug had not yet made its way into the children's bloodstreams indicated it had not been administered very long before their deaths.

In another alarming finding, the inquest heard that a small amount of cannabis, along with some epilepsy medication, had also been detected in Gary Poxon's body. But it was impossible to determine what effect, if any, this may have had on Poxon's state of mind.

The coroner heard from police who examined the car that the doors, though closed, were unlocked. The windows were all closed and taped and all the gaps around the vehicle had been plugged with clothing. Detective Senior Constable Coady gave evidence about the hose he found running from a generator to tubing that had been fed through the exhaust into the vehicle's interior.

The coroner also heard about the dark letters Poxon had penned and the voice message he had left on a digital camera saying he could not live without his children. These were consistent with suicide notes, investigators concluded.

Given that the last-known contact with the disturbed father took place five days before the tragedy, it was estimated that the bodies had been in the car for up to five days before they were finally found, making the estimated time of death Sunday 22 June — the day Karen left.

It was the opinion of the police that the children must have already been sedated and placed inside the vehicle before their father connected the hose that subsequently pumped in the deadly fumes. All four occupants had died of carbon monoxide poisoning.

But despite the clear evidence that Gary Poxon had killed himself and his three children, Mr Dillon told the children's bewildered family that the *Coroner's Act* prevented him from stating this.

'And though it may sound strange, I can't mention his name in relation to the children's deaths,' he explained. Karen understood that Bell could not be named as the killer she believed him to be, simply because he was dead.

The coroner told the anguished mother he could not begin to imagine the pain she was going through and said that while she was not obliged to address the inquest, he would be 'most pleased' if she felt able to.

Battling tears, an emotional Karen Bell had plenty she wished to say. Her husband's actions had been 'selfish and cowardly', she told the inquest. 'I thought he would kill me, but never the children,' she said. But there had been 'no way' anyone could have seen this tragedy coming, or prevented it, she said, repeating what she'd told the media in the immediate aftermath.

Karen Bell said she was speaking out in the hope of highlighting the plight other victims of domestic violence. She wanted to bring the dilemma facing abused women to the government's attention so that ineffective laws, which failed to protect families at risk, could be changed and lives saved.

Again, she publicly described the dilemma that left her with no option but to leave her home without her children that fateful day. The law gave her no right to take her children, nor anyone else the right to remove them and keep them safe. It was a situation that continued to force abused women like her to either leave violent homes without their children or remain trapped in dangerous relationships.

'It is easier to go back,' she reflected sadly. But if the legal situation had been different, her children might be alive today. It was too late for Jack, Maddie and Bon, she said, but not too late for her to speak out in the hope that something good would come from her heartbreak. She hoped to highlight a serious issue and save other lives.

Assuring the grieving mother that he would ensure her recommendations were brought to the attention of the attorney-general, Mr Dillon observed there were some things that 'went beyond the law'.

'The death of children in horrible circumstances such as this raises concerns about the human condition,' he told the inquest. 'These stories affect anyone with children and they go to the mystery of the human heart.' The coroner said how anyone lived with the pain of losing three children was beyond his comprehension. 'I don't think any of us today would wish to go through what you are going through. Not ever in our worst nightmare,' he said.

But, noting Karen Bell's advanced pregnancy, he went on to say it was heartening that her loss had not destroyed her desire to live life again. He concluded that whatever it was that finally tipped Gary Poxon over the edge would forever remain a mystery. The deceased man appeared to have been a father who loved his children, yet in his 'distorted state of mind', and facing the prospect of a prison sentence, he clearly blamed his wife for all his problems.

The inquest found that Gary Poxon had died as a result of self-inflicted carbon monoxide poisoning, though prevailing legal constraints prevented the coroner from attributing the deaths of the three children to their father. Instead, the coroner could only say that all three had died from the effects of carbon monoxide poisoning 'from a known but deceased person'. Turning to the bereft mother in the public gallery, Mr Dillon said he hoped she would enjoy a long and productive life and that the lives of her children would remain a comfort to her.

The tragic story made headline news everywhere the following day. Under the headline 'Cowardly and Selfish', the *Bega District News* ran the coroner's findings, complete with his well wishes for the very pregnant young mother who had finally begun to heal and reclaim her life.

Mr Dillon's hopes that Karen's children would bring her comfort were not in vain. While her happy memories of Jack, Maddie and Bon continued to bring her comfort amid the unimaginable sorrow, the pending arrival of a new baby was a gift she had never dreamed possible.

Dean Gray was by Karen's side at Bega Hospital on 25 September to welcome their son, Connor Jack Gray. The baby's arrival in the early hours of the morning was welcomed with joy by his parents and made news around the country. On 23 November 2009, the delighted mother spoke to *Woman's Day* about her new baby.

'He is just awesome,' said Karen, showing her newborn to the world for the first time. 'Baby Connor is healing my heart.'

In the story by journalist Glen Williams, Karen admitted her new life with partner Dean had brought her the kind of contentment that she would never have imagined possible a year earlier. Back then she had cried tears of 'unimaginable sorrow'. It had been a horrific time and one she had believed there would be no coming back from. She was so happy to have been wrong.

'He's unselfish, he's thoughtful, he's a great dad. He is everything the other one was not. The fear has gone from me,' she said.

But in spite of her happiness, Connor's birth was tinged with memories of the births of her three lost children, who were never far from her mind. They would have been delighted with their new baby brother, she said sadly. The grief she still felt over the deaths of Jack, Maddie and Bon was unrelenting. But this was a new chance for her to do what she did best: to be a mum again.

The story was picked up by media outlets everywhere, most repeating Glen Williams' description of the new gentle giant in Karen Bell's life as 'a big-hearted bloke of few words'.

That same month, Karen received a letter from the Deputy Coroner, Mr Dillon, officially confirming his verdict. He had been true to his word. In another letter sent to Karen around this time, Mr Dillon attached a copy of correspondence he had sent to the NSW Attorney-General, conveying the issues Karen had raised during the inquest.

His letter to Karen said: 'I know that the Attorney-General has a real interest in the tragic problem of domestic violence, especially where it results in a victim's death. Because of the complexity of some of the issues, and of the law reform process itself, the committee, or working party which is being set up to look at the issues, will probably take some time over its work. I hope, however, that you will be patient with the process and that your patience will be rewarded.

'More than that, I hope that your new baby will bring you much joy and that you will have a long and fruitful life, enjoying most of it and treasuring the memories of the three lovely children you have lost. I hope those memories will always be a comfort to you. There is nothing purer than the authentic love of a child for its mother, or that of a mother for her child.'

If Mr Dillon was constrained by the laws which prevented him naming Gary Bell as his children's killer in court, he alluded to it in the letter he penned on Karen Bell's behalf to the Attorney-General. Summarising the case, he wrote that on 22 June 2008, Gary Bell had taken his own life and the lives of his three children, Jack, Maddie and Bon, at Pericoe in Southern NSW.

In his letter to the Attorney-General, the coroner briefly outlined the events leading up to Bell's arrest and the murder–suicide. 'It appears that in a disordered state of mind, Mr Bell came to the (probably correct) view that he faced going to gaol for this fresh offence and decided to bring his relationship with Karen Bell to a close in the most dramatic and final way he could, by suiciding and taking the lives of his children.'

The coroner said that while there had been nothing to predict the Bell children were at risk in their father's care, he was aware of the formulation of a working party to examine domestic violence homicides with a view to developing policy and statutory reponses to them.

'That committee is in a better position to consider the issues in detail than I was in Bega,' he wrote. He concluded that it was sad to note that the Bells' family tragedy was not 'uncommon' and that the children's mother's statement provided a voice for the victims of such awful incidents. Karen's voice was both a cry for help, and evidence of an 'altruistic desire' to help others avoid a similar tragedy, where possible. He said he hoped the committee would carefully consider the proposals she had made in her letter to the inquest. The coroner had upheld his promise to Karen who was encouraged to learn that her voice had been heard and that her children's deaths would count for something.

Karen Bell's ability to find happiness amid such pain has continued to be an inspiration to many other women wanting to escape years of violence and abuse. She has since told me that simply by living her life, it has been possible to find happiness again, even when you have lost everything you held dear.

On Valentine's Day 2011, Karen and the partner she refers to as 'her rock' welcomed a baby daughter, Eva Rose.

'Look at me,' Karen told Glen Williams, again in *Woman's Day*. 'I have a little boy and a little girl. Good things are happening.' Only three years before she had felt her life was over. 'How wrong I was and how glad I am that I was,' she said happily.

Karen Bell the survivor continues to fight back. Now re-married, she realises that by being happy again she has ensured that Gary Mark Poxon's chilling prediction that 'this is the end' will never be fulfilled. His dreadful crime marked the end of the life she had known, but her courage has helped her to start all over again and rebuild a new life with a new family.

'He did not end my life as he hoped to,' Karen told me, from her new home, a short drive from the Valley of Failure, where Poxon failed to achieve the destruction he intended to last her lifetime.

Ultimately, the aim of revenge crimes is to inflict a lifetime of suffering, to rob the true target of any future joy or happiness, to punish them into living with the guilt forever.

'There is no doubt that crimes like these really are the worst kind of punishment any man can dish out to his partner,' reflects Karen. 'From the moment these men commit such a terrible crime, they have won. The damage remains forever and there is no getting away from that. He's only lucky he killed himself.'

Karen's entire extended family and friendship network has

suffered, and continues to suffer. 'My father blamed himself for what happened; he always blamed himself for not doing more and he carried that burden of guilt until 2015 when he passed away from melanoma. Crimes like these affect everybody.' The pain remains as hard and as real as it was when the murders first happened. 'But that pain becomes a part of you. It's always there, but you can keep it on the backburner a bit.'

CHAPTER 7

'If he couldn't have them —
nobody else could.'

The story of Ingrid Poulson and Marilyn and Sebastian Kongsom

On 31 July 2003, newly separated mother Ingrid Poulson returned from work to find a menacing letter pinned to the windscreen of her car. The two-page note had been penned by her estranged husband, Thai-born Phithak (Neung) Kongsom. In it he threatened to kill her and then end his own life. It would be his former wife's punishment for ending their abusive relationship.

Ever since the final collapse of their eight-year relationship a few weeks earlier, the 31-year-old mother of two had been grappling with the emotional fallout and the histrionics of a man who refused to accept his marriage was over.

Kongsom had bombarded her with harassing telephone calls, sobbing and begging her hysterically for a reconciliation. He told his former wife how much he loved her and even tried to bribe her with clothing in the hope of persuading her to change her mind. When she refused to return, he angrily demanded to see his two young children, Marilyn, aged four, and Sebastian, aged 23 months. Ingrid, not wishing to upset him, tried to accommodate his often unreasonable demands. Her family took turns driving the children to see their father, only to have him refuse to see the youngsters when he discovered their mother had not come with them.

When his emotional manipulation failed to bring about the change of heart he wanted, Kongsom's mood grew darker. As the weeks passed he became more angry and aggressive and threatened ominously that Ingrid would suffer 'big hurt'. When Kongsom threatened to take his children and disappear back to Thailand, the frightened young mother organised for a stop to be put on Marilyn's and Sebastian's passports.

As Kongsom's rage continued to simmer, he began to threaten to kill himself. Later his threats became more menacing and he warned that he would not only take his own life but would take Ingrid with him.

Kongsom's sister-in-law, Rebecca Poulson, would later describe him as a 'clever and restrained' man. He must have been fully aware that his suicide threats would strike a particularly painful note with Ingrid and her family. For the past decade the close-knit Poulsons had been tormenting themselves over the inexplicable suicide of Rebecca's younger sister Ingrid and their older brother, Adrian, who had died of self-inflicted shotgun injuries at the age of 24. Rebecca would later reflect on the guilt her family had suffered over the heartbreaking tragedy. It was no accident her manipulative brother-in-law had chosen to threaten suicide, knowing the reaction it would be likely to generate in a family already grappling with its own grief.

Initially Rebecca put the threats down to Kongsom's dramatic personality, which had revealed itself in his grandiose dreams of becoming a Formula One driver. She suspected his death threats, like the fantasy dreams of being a famous driver, were just a part of his own personal 'landscape'. Nevertheless it was obvious to Ingrid and her concerned family that Kongsom, whom they called by his Thai nickname 'Neung', which means 'number one son', was clearly not coping with the separation he had not wanted.

Just like Arthur Freeman and Robert Farquharson, the once 'sweet and gentle' man Ingrid had fallen in love with was not someone who coped well with change. The couple had met in the mid-1990s at the American University in the northern Thai city of Chiang Mai, where Ingrid was teaching English. When they married on Neung's family's property, his mother had been delighted with her intelligent and thoughtful new daughter-in-law. She would later tell reporters she thought Ingrid, who she referred to as 'Inga', was more like a Thai girl. The older woman was brimming with pride when her neighbours congratulated the new bride on her choice of a husband: Neung was a 'mild mannered', peaceful young man. Ingrid Poulson was a lucky girl, they said.

The couple remained in Thailand after their marriage, but decided to return to Australia in 1999 ahead of the birth of their first child. At first they lived with Rebecca in Sydney but, requiring more space for the new baby, they moved before the birth to live with Ingrid's father, Peter, and his second wife, Cheryl, at their house in semi-rural Wilberforce, 60 kilometres north-west of the CBD.

In October that year they welcomed a baby daughter, Marilyn. The proud parents affectionately nicknamed her 'Malee' — Thai for 'beautiful flower'. Two years later, Ingrid gave birth to a son, Sebastian (Bas), and her happiness was complete. But after their son's birth, cracks began to appear in the once harmonious marriage and the relationship quickly began to flounder.

With Neung's racing dreams now on indefinite hold, the indulged economics graduate found himself drifting from one menial job to another until he finally settled into work he enjoyed as a trainee postman with Australia Post. But with every passing month the 31-year-old appeared more distant and more resentful about his life. His simmering anger saw him become increasingly argumentative, his once peaceful behaviour now erratic and unpredictable. When they moved into a place of their own, the heated exchanges turned ugly and aggressive, and Ingrid glimpsed a frightening side of her husband's personality that she had never seen before.

During one particularly explosive outburst in June 2003, Kongsom began violently hurling things around the house in front of their two frightened young children. Ingrid, observing her children's anxious faces as they witnessed their father's violent tantrum, felt so afraid that she barricaded herself with the children in a room and waited for the storm to subside. Not wishing to expose her children to further violent abuse, she decided enough was enough. The following day, she told Neung to pack his bags and leave their flat. He did as she asked, but the nightmare for Ingrid had only just begun.

If the disillusioned young wife was ready to move on, her husband was not ready to let her go. Living alone in a gloomy one-bedroom apartment and facing life as a single father, Kongsom grew increasingly depressed. His mother in Thailand observed that in his weekly phone calls home he had become convinced that he was losing his children. She later told reporters that Neung, her only child, was a man who lived for his children. He was devastated about his restricted role in his children's lives and resented the new access arrangements that allowed him just two days a week with them. He failed to mention that the restrictions had been put in place to protect the children from his violence. But he did tell his mother it had been Ingrid who wanted the separation, and that she had rejected his constant pleas to rekindle their marriage.

Mrs Kongsom would later admit she felt upset and helpless as she listened to her son. There had been no signs of trouble in the marriage when she had visited Australia the previous December to spend time with her grandchildren. The older woman admitted she had been stunned when Neung telephoned her a few months later, instructing her to postpone the next trip she was planning and explaining that his marriage was on the rocks.

By June 2003 it was clear from the tone of the phone calls that Neung was no longer coping. He was so despairing over his situation that he had been taking sleeping tablets to combat his insomnia. He intimated to his mother that he would have liked to leave Australia and bring his children home to Thailand, but this was impossible because Ingrid would never allow it. Neung did not tell his mother that his father-in-law had become so concerned by his erratic behaviour that he had offered to pay his fare back to Thailand in the hope that he would benefit from counselling and the support of his friends and family there.

By the middle of June 2003 Neung's anger had begun to fester. In this dark, brooding state of mind he began to blame his wife for his misery, and the genesis of a murder–suicide plot slowly took root in his mind.

In the menacing two-page suicide letter he was to leave under

Ingrid's windscreen wipers on 31 July 2003, he wrote: 'These [sic] night, I had mad [sic] a decision. I am going to kill you and myself.'

But the letter and its chilling contents followed such a relentless number of phone threats and vile abuse that Ingrid was almost desensitised to his rants. When the angry calls failed to illicit the response Neung hoped for, he began turning up outside his children's childcare centre, where he angrily abused his former wife and caused ugly scenes.

Ingrid concluded that his suicide letter, like the menacing calls, was just another of her estranged husband's emotional mind games — more high drama aimed at intimidating her into returning to a marriage she no longer wanted. She chose to ignore the note, hoping that with time Neung would come to accept that the marriage was over and that he would eventually calm down. Instead, things got worse.

He demanded to see his children at whim, frequently leaving his in-laws to change their own plans to meet his irrational requests. In the lead-up to the Father's Day following the separation, Kongsom refused his former wife's offer to have his children over for a visit. Then, on Father's Day morning, he changed his mind and wanted the access visit. Abandoning his own plans for Father's Day, Peter Poulson drove his grandchildren over to their father's, where he waited in the car for hours to take the youngsters home.

As the weeks passed, Kongsom became so enraged that he threatened to take his children and flee to Thailand, only to call again a couple of days afterwards, begging Ingrid for a reconciliation.

But by August, the emotional roller-coaster that had culminated in the suicide note appeared to be subsiding. When Ingrid called around at her estranged husband's flat during the first week of August to collect her children from an informal weekend access visit, Kongsom appeared affable and invited her inside.

He claimed he had just prepared an evening meal and asked Ingrid to join him. Not wishing to provoke a scene, she followed him into the flat, where it quickly became obvious that his promise of a meal had been a ruse.

To Ingrid's amazement, Neung suddenly fell to his knees and began crawling around on the floor, sobbing loudly in front of their two children. He pleaded with her again for a reconciliation and claimed he had even set the flat up in readiness for her return.

Observing the children's frightened faces as the drama unfolded around them, Ingrid made her way towards the telephone with the intention of calling her father to drive over to mediate.

But Kongsom had disappeared into the kitchen where he pulled off his jacket and grabbed a kitchen knife. With his terrified daughter clinging to his leg and sobbing with fright, and his small son looking on bewildered, he began to wave the knife around. He finally pointed the blade at his throat and threatened to kill himself in front of them.

'Well this is it then,' he told their shocked mother. 'There's $6000 in my bank account. You can use it to pay for my funeral.'

Alarmed, Ingrid raced around the kitchen where she wrestled the knife from his hands and attempted to calm him down. But when Ingrid began to gather the children to leave, the storm erupted again. Neung became hysterical, warning her darkly that he would not allow her to take Malee and that if she tried to take their daughter, he would kill himself.

'I'll do it,' he raged. 'I'll die right now.'

Terrified, Ingrid fled from the flat with Bas in her arms and immediately telephoned Triple O to report the matter to police. But while the loving mother could not fathom any parent behaving in such a dangerous manner in front of their own children, she was unprepared for the indifference of the female police operator when she tried to describe the violent background to the relationship that had culminated in the suicidal threats.

The operator noted that the only person who appeared to be at risk of any real harm was the irrational father himself.

'He hasn't hurt you, has he?' she asked pointedly.

Ingrid told the operator about the death threat her former husband had left under her windscreen a couple of weeks before, and went on to describe the weeks of harassing phone calls when he had made repeated threats to kill himself. Since then Neung's behaviour had grown more unpredictable, she explained. Now he was armed, unstable and alone in his flat with their four-year-old daughter, who he had refused to relinquish after an access visit.

Despite the disturbing background and the threats of suicide, the police operator did not consider the complaint to be of a domestic-violence nature. Oblivious to the red flags Ingrid was waving, the operator treated the frightened mother's call as a welfare concern rather than a report of escalating family violence perpetrated by an out-of-control, angry and manipulative man.

Instead of being handed over to the police's Domestic Violence Liaison Officer (DVLO), who was responsible for handling complaints with a history of abuse, the report found its way to the uniformed branch of the New South Wales police, and four officers were dispatched to accompany the alarmed mother back to her ex-husband's flat to collect her little girl.

But the officers also failed to inform the frightened young wife about the existence of the DVLO, or to explain that she had the option of taking out an apprehended violence order to protect herself from her former husband's violence.

Instead, they determined that the best way to diffuse the tense situation was to send Ingrid back into her ex-husband's apartment by herself to retrieve her daughter. While a traumatised Ingrid ventured cautiously inside, not knowing what kind of scenario she might find, the police officers waited patiently outside.

Fortunately, Kongsom had not carried out his threat to kill himself and she eventually persuaded him to allow her to leave with Malee. But there would be no follow-up call from the police, either to inquire about the abused mother's welfare, or that of her children. And there was never any suggestion that she should consider applying for a court order to protect her family. The incident was still not classified as a domestic-violence case and, despite the history of violence, was never flagged for further investigation by the DVLO, who was skilled in handling such matters.

Despite the police decision to take no action over the dramatic scenes at Kongsom's flat, his former wife was so shaken by the incident that her concerned parents insisted she go down to the police station to find out if anything more could be done. Leaving her children in the care of their aunt, Ingrid's mother Janice Poulson accompanied her daughter to the police station, certain that the response of the police in such a serious case did not sound right. The women were finally referred to the DVLO, who was helpful and immediately issued a preliminary apprehended violence order on the young mother's behalf. The order prohibited Kongsom from further threatening or harassing his estranged wife and, as a result of his violence, his access to his children was restricted to protect them from their father. It would take a few weeks, she was warned, before the order reached the courts where Kongsom had the right to contest it. But this temporary order offered her some protection, and served as a warning to Kongsom, who could be punished if he breached it. Until then, Ingrid and her family had bent over backwards to ensure that Neung's every demand had been met. No more.

The full order would prohibit Kongsom from making further threats or harassment for the next 12 months and halted his access to his children. It was a tough decision for a young mother dealing with the emotional pain of a messy separation. After weeks of torment, Ingrid felt emotionally drained. She was torn at the prospect of having to take such drastic long-term action to protect herself from a man she had once loved. But observing the devastating impact of her ex-husband's behaviour on their two small children had been enough to convince her that there was no other way. Unfortunately, it would be at least three weeks before the AVO reached the courts.

On 27 August 2003, while Ingrid waited in court for her AVO application to be granted, the *Hawkesbury Gazette* ran a desperate message in the Personals column. In a last-ditch attempt to mend the failed marriage, Kongsom professed his undying love for his former wife.

'*You are the most wonderful lady in my entire world,*' he wrote. '*You are my love and my life, thank you for being a good wife to me and a good mother to my children ... from all my heart I love you always.*'

But it was too late for Ingrid Poulson, who was already leaving the Magistrates' Court armed with the order she believed would protect her from further violence from a husband who still refused to accept that his marriage was over.

Ingrid's relief as she headed around the supermarket that day was short-lived. The ink had barely dried on the court order when Kongsom rang her mobile phone, again begging for a reconciliation. The call constituted an immediate breach of the AVO, which prohibited him from harassing or approaching his wife. But Kongsom was undeterred. Later that same day he arrived unannounced at Ingrid's home and barged in and began playing with his children. When her stepmother, Cheryl Poulson, told him to leave he refused.

'I don't care what they do to me,' he said defiantly. 'I'm just going to come and play with my kids.'

After he left the property, Kongsom rang Ingrid again. Before the day was out he had breached the apprehended violence order four times.

Later Ingrid Poulson claimed she reported these breaches of her AVO to the police, a fact hotly rejected by the police who denied they had received any such report from her.

However, a check of telephone records would later confirm that a call had been received from Ingrid's father, Peter, reporting his son-in-law for breaching the AVO, which was not yet a day old. Whatever the truth, it appears the breach had been reported. In 2006 Ingrid would tell Andrew Denton on the ABC TV show *Enough Rope* that while she firmly believed she had been the one who had made the report to police, she had been so distressed at the time it was possible her father had made the report on her behalf.

In any event, the report resulted in two officers attending Peter Poulson's home to talk to the disgruntled father and his alarmed daughter. An inquest later heard from the Poulsons that they had been told there were two ways they could handle the violation. The 'official' way, according to the Poulsons, involved sending a couple of police officers to Kongsom's flat, where he would be arrested and thrown into jail for the night. The 'unofficial' way would be a stern warning about the consequences of breaching his AVO, which might result in him being charged and punished.

Faced with the responsibility of making such a major decision, the distressed young mother found herself in a dilemma. After months of harassment and intimidation, Ingrid Poulson felt too traumatised to have to make such a painful choice. She was aware that being arrested and charged with a criminal offence might cost Kongsom the only job he had enjoyed since their return to Australia. This might only aggravate an already tense situation for a man whose mental state appeared to be unravelling, and create further animosity and resentment.

But what was so bewildering to Ingrid and her family was that the whole point of taking out the AVO was to remove the burden of having to deal with her estranged husband's ongoing violence from her and place the responsibility onto the authorities. With a court order in place, they had anticipated that any breach would constitute a criminal offence that would automatically be dealt with by the police and ultimately the courts.

But even with the order in place, the responsibility for making the final decision still fell on Ingrid's shoulders. Faced with an impossible situation, she agreed to the 'soft' option and Kongsom was warned about the consequences of further breaches of his AVO. The stern talking-to would make little difference to Kongsom, who would go on to breach his order a staggering 19 times between 27 August 2003, the date it was served, and 15 September 2003. The lack of action following her initial report of the breaches discouraged Ingrid from reporting the subsequent ones. In evidence later tendered to the inquest, Ingrid would recall that the officers dispatched to speak to her about the breach had remarked that dealing with domestic violence amounted to a pile of 'crap paperwork' and was hardly worth all the trouble. The police denied this.

On Sunday 14 September 2003 Ingrid Poulson spent the day with her children and Rebecca, who adored her young niece and nephew. The sisters spent most weekends together doing enjoyable things with the two youngsters who also adored their Aunty Becky, who spoiled them. The women spent their Sunday afternoon at a Wiggles concert where they watched the children singing and dancing along to the songs. Rebecca would later recall her delight as she watched Bas dancing and running around while his big sister Malee chased her Wiggles ball. When Rebecca kissed the children goodbye at 4 p.m. that day she had no idea that this would be the last time she would ever see her nephew and niece alive.

If that beautiful Sunday afternoon spelled a perfect end to a perfect day, the new week was about to start on a far more horrifying note. During the early hours of Monday 15 September, Kongsom broke into his estranged wife's home armed with a knife. Ingrid woke in the darkness, suddenly aware of her former husband moving over her on the bed. To her shock, she felt the blade of a knife pressing against her throat. Kongsom had taken the trouble to bring along a length of cabling which he used to bind her hands to the bed. Then he brutally raped her.

After the assault, Kongsom handed her a knife and instructed her to stab him.

'Well, I have broken in here and done this so that you will kill me,' he told her.

But Ingrid, surveying the weapon, refused.

'I'm not going to kill you,' she said. 'I'm not going to jail. I'm never going to have my children not have a mother because of you and what you have done.'

When Kongsom finally fled the house, Ingrid sat on the bed contemplating the horror of what had just happened and wondering how she could protect herself. Her immediate instinct had been to put her two children in the car and simply flee. But Kongsom had repeatedly warned her during his outbursts that if she ever tried to leave, he would 'hunt' her down. She had no doubt now, after what he had just done, that her AVO meant nothing and that he would be capable of carrying out his threat. Neung was clearly spiralling out of control and his terrified former wife telephoned the Rape Crisis Centre and reported the rape. The person she spoke to immediately advised her to contact the local police station and ask for the Domestic Violence Liaison Officer.

At 6.30 a.m. on the Monday morning, Ingrid telephoned her local police station only to be informed that the liaison officer was not working on that day. Instead, her call was put through to another officer, who listened carefully as she related her story again. At this stage Ingrid was not sure if she wanted to have Kongsom charged with the rape, though she did want him arresting for breaching the AVO. With Neung at large she was now more fearful than ever for her safety and wanted the police to find him quickly.

She told the officer she was worried about her former husband's deteriorating mental health and had no idea where he was or what he might do next. He had expressed suicidal thoughts before, and she was afraid he might be working up to the murder–suicide he had threatened her with.

'With all due respect, ma'am,' interjected the concerned policeman, 'I don't care about him. I care about you and what I can do for you right now.'

The policeman offered to visit her home with a female colleague. Later, he and a female officer arrived on Ingrid's doorstep to discuss what had taken place and to consider what action needed to be taken. Ingrid's relief was palpable as the policeman informed her this was a very serious matter that required specialised handling and investigation.

The conversation was a turning point, Ingrid would later tell Andrew Denton. It was the first time her fears had been heard and validated. The officer advised Ingrid that they needed to take her to a hospital to collect medical evidence to support her allegation of rape. They would also need to document her account of what had taken place at her home. Ingrid agreed to accompany the officers to the hospital, leaving her two children in the care of her father at his home in Wilberforce.

While Ingrid made her way to the hospital that morning, her sister Rebecca was on the phone to her father. Rebecca was celebrating her thirty-third birthday and her dad had telephoned to wish his oldest daughter a happy birthday. Hearing Marilyn and Bas in the background, Rebecca asked her father what was going on. It was unusual for Malee and Bas to be with their grandfather on a Monday morning and Rebecca was concerned. Peter explained that Ingrid had gone to the police station to report another breach of the AVO. Afterwards, a concerned Rebecca rang back four more times to find out what was happening. When she made her final call the phone just rang out, though she would not know why until later.

Ingrid was still at the hospital when tentative police inquiries into Kongsom's whereabouts revealed he had gone to work as normal that morning, but had since left. Whether Kongsom had been alerted to the police inquiries and guessed his wife had reported the rape remains unclear, though it would later be apparent that after leaving work he had been captured on security camera at a nearby supermarket, buying packing tape and a 30-centimetre knife.

At the hospital, concerns were mounting for Ingrid's safety. She would later tell Andrew Denton how police tentatively suggested the possibility of placing her in protective custody during the rape inquiry. If Kongsom had posed a threat to her before, he might become an even bigger one once he discovered she had reported him for a sex crime.

More than six hours after Ingrid made her initial rape report to police, the detectives indicated that they were poised to arrest Kongsom. But first they offered to drive the traumatised mother back to her father's home to see her two children. At around 1.30 p.m. on that Monday afternoon, Ingrid Poulson sat in the back of a police car as it headed back to Wilberforce. But as the car pulled onto the driveway, Ingrid observed a sudden change in the tone of the chatting detectives. Moving her gaze from their now serious faces to the driveway, she glimpsed her father's body sprawled on the ground. Ingrid found herself numbly wondering where her children must be if her dad, who was supposed to be minding them, was out here. Gripped by a horrible realisation, Ingrid leapt from the police car, taking in the image of her blood-covered father, who lay where he had fallen across a broom.

On the driveway to his right lay the blood-soaked bodies of her two children. Their father hovered over them, still clutching the murder weapon, which he moved in a striking motion over his small son.

As he prepared to stab Bas again, a detective pulled out his handgun and shot Kongsom. When Ingrid reached the children, both Marilyn and Bas were dead. The father who had fatally stabbed them was clinging to life; his body showed signs of stab wounds.

Detectives at the scene were in no doubt that the grandfather had been desperately trying to protect his two grandchildren from their father's frenzied stabbing by using a broom to fend him off. The 60-year-old had paid for his bravery with his own life.

Kongsom, who was still alive, was taken under police guard to the Windsor Hospital where he died a few hours later. An inquest would later find that he had not died from the gunshot fired by police, but had succumbed to his own self-inflicted knife wounds.

The children and their grandfather had all died after being fatally stabbed by Kongsom.

After months of menacing threats, and in spite of an AVO that had been breached countless times, Neung had finally carried out the murder–suicide he had been brooding over. But he had not snuffed out the life of his estranged wife; he had killed his own flesh and blood instead.

Inside the house detectives uncovered a suicide note in which Kongsom vowed he was about to do something that would destroy Ingrid and her family. There was little doubt in the minds of the police that the crime had been motivated by revenge and had been deliberately planned to punish the mother of his children for leaving him.

While Ingrid wouldn't know it for another three weeks, the entire attack had been over in a matter of minutes. She had arrived with the police four minutes too late to save her family.

Neung Kongsom had committed his last act of family violence, and in doing so he intended to inflict a punishment that would last a lifetime.

But Neung Kongsom had not counted on the formidable strength and courage of the Poulson women. Ingrid would later reveal in her 2005 interview with Channel Nine's *Sixty Minutes* that she had 'stood among the souls of the dead' that afternoon. But as she'd hovered over the bodies of her family in the silence, slowly processing every tiny detail from the blood to the smallness of the murder weapon that had caused such catastrophic damage, she had heard a voice 'whispering through her'. The voice told her that she would not allow herself to 'be brought so low', and in those seconds, as everything became sharp and clear, Ingrid vowed she would somehow rise above her devastating loss and deny Kongsom the lifelong suffering he had intended for her.

Ingrid's sister Rebecca would later reflect that there were times in the aftermath of the murders when she felt Kongsom had almost been granted his wish. By inflicting such suffering, her brother-in-law had managed to manipulate her shattered family from 'beyond the grave'.

In a later television interview with *Studio Ten*, she would recall how she had learned that her family had been murdered. Two officers had arrived on her doorstep later that afternoon to tell her what had happened, and that's when she realised that when she'd been on the phone wondering why her father wasn't picking up, Kongsom had already embarked on his killing frenzy.

The shocking triple murders of Peter Poulson and his grandchildren Marilyn and Sebastian Kongsom sent shockwaves throughout the close-knit community of Wilberforce. The 60-year-old was a popular figure and an active member of the local rural fire brigade. It was a heartbreaking story and it made headline news everywhere around the country.

Three days after the murders, Rebecca Poulson addressed the media outside Penrith police station. Her sister Ingrid was too distressed to speak, she explained.

'As you understand, this has been very traumatic for her,' Rebecca said. 'She is devastated, as is our whole family by this awful tragedy. While none of us could ever have seen this happening, we lost three stars on September 15, which was my thirty-third birthday.' The stars were her sister's beautiful children, and their grandfather who had lost his life trying to save them. Rebecca said that Ingrid had asked her to pass on a message to parents around Australia.

'Hold your babies tight,' she told journalists. 'Just love them a little more. They deserve it.' Battling her own tears, Rebecca Poulson went on to share her memories of the three stars in her life.

Malee was a 'popular, bright, outgoing little four-year-old girl who brought much happiness to our family like everyone she came into contact with,' her aunt said. 'She was so beautiful. She was our little flower.' But Malee was also a tomboy who loved to play in the mud and stay in the swimming pool until she turned into 'a prune'. The little girl had reached an age where all she wanted to do was protect her younger brother, Bas, whom she adored.

'Bas was a cuddly and curious little boy,' his aunt recalled. He would have been two on 7 October. A typical boy, the curious tot loved his grandfather's tractor and had a growing fascination for machines of all sorts. He particularly liked pressing the on and off switches on the computer and had just learned to say his first words like 'no' and 'Mummy, Daddy and Becky'.

In her statement, Rebecca paid tribute to her sister's strength, describing Ingrid as an 'amazingly strong beautiful woman'. She told reporters that Ingrid would get through this terrible time with the love and support of her family and friends and by 'taking it minute by minute'.

The following day, 19 September, the story made headline news again. Under the headline 'A Mother's Plea' in the *Sydney Morning Herald,* an article by reporter Les Kennedy relayed the family's gratitude for the outpouring of love and support they had received in the wake of the tragedy.

'Thank you all the people who have shed tears for my father, my family, me and my babies,' Rebecca had said, passing on her sister's thanks.

The article included the heartbroken aunt's tribute to her niece and nephew and to her father Peter, whom she described as a loving grandfather who took his two adored grandchildren on excursions to pick up horse feed.

'He would do anything to protect and look after his family,' she told reporters. The newspaper reported her saying Peter Poulson was a vocational trainer with an 'amazing ability' to lift people around him to extraordinary heights.

This would be the only public statement from the grief-stricken family. In her formal statement, Rebecca Poulson urged the media to respect the family's privacy when they mourned their loved ones at a funeral to be held the following day. Significantly, there was no mention of the man whose actions had robbed the Poulson women of so much.

Five days after the tragedy, a private funeral was held in the Blue Mountains for Peter Poulson and his grandchildren Malee and Bas Kongsom. Mourners gathered among the gum trees under sunny spring skies in the Springwood Memorial Gardens where the devastated mother remained on her feet with the help of her family. Janice Poulson, a university psychologist and counsellor, read the eulogy penned by Ingrid in honour of her children.

'Thank you for giving me so much joy,' their mother wrote. 'I have lost part of myself. But I will never lose the love you gave me. I hope you will take care of each other wherever you are; not too much hair-pulling, my darlings. I miss you.'

In her eulogy, Rebecca paid tribute to a father whom she said 'had such faith in us':

'You had the biggest pair of rose-coloured glasses when it came to us. You gave so much to everyone and in the end you gave your life for Malee and Bas, thank you.' She said her father would be remembered as a lab technician, a soldier, a coalminer, a teacher, a bungee jumper, a lover of classical music and a respected firefighter. Peter Poulson would also be remembered as a man who tore through life at the same speed — in top gear.

'He fitted so much into his life,' his daughter recalled.

Afterwards, mourners wearing three different coloured ribbons in honour of Peter and his grandchildren watched as three white doves were released overhead. The song 'Hush A Bye Don't You Cry' was played as the coffins were lowered into the ground.

Ingrid Poulson bent over the grave and threw a flower onto the single coffin bearing her two beloved children. The media, as requested, kept their distance. But the funeral and the deaths still found their way into the press in the days ahead as pointed questions were asked about how such a tragedy could have happened.

But while criticisms were levelled at the New South Wales Police for failing to prevent the deaths, the grieving mother at the centre of the storm refused to lay blame. Blame was not going to bring her children back, her family would later tell the media. Ingrid felt there were important lessons to be learned from her loss, and she hoped awareness and education, rather than blame, might spare another family her own worst nightmare.

The weeks that followed were paralysing for the Poulsons. Ingrid would describe the physical agony that came with such grief. Her loss was so consuming that she found herself curled into a ball, unable to heal the ache of being unable to smell, touch or hold her two children. Like Cindy Gambino, whose three sons were murdered by their father two years later, Ingrid described her emptiness as feeling hollow; like an alien living on a foreign planet where all notions of normality had been inexplicably turned on their head. Her family's deaths had left such a gaping void that nothing felt real and everything now felt 'unnatural and nonsensical'.

Ingrid described being haunted by debilitating nightmares filled with images of knives, of being pinned down by some strange force and having her eyes gouged out. In her dreams she glimpsed her children drowning, and saw herself frantically trying to reach them as they slipped slowly from her grasp and disappeared.

Rebecca Poulson would later tell *Studio Ten* how she had forced herself to return to her father's home in the days following the tragedy to collect some clothes for the children's funeral. It had been 'excruciating' glimpsing Malee's bed. The fairy quilt was ruffled and pulled back, just as the little girl had left it that morning. She could barely bring herself to look at the children's height chart on the wall.

'There were not going to be any more heights there,' she told *Studio Ten*. It had been torture, she told viewers, seeing the pretty dresses she had bought her niece still hanging in the wardrobe where she'd put them. They had been too big for Malee, but Rebecca had told her niece she would soon grow into them. Now Malee would never wear those dresses and her aunt's heart was broken.

'I had a few moments where I couldn't stand it any more and I had to get out of the room,' Rebecca said. She paused in the laundry to grab one of Malee's soiled tops from the laundry basket and inhale her niece's scent one last time. The house that had once been the hub of so many family celebrations was now shrouded in bad memories for Rebecca Poulson. Kongsom's terrible crime had swept away all the good memories. For a long time, all Rebecca felt was pain.

'It comes down to pure revenge,' she told *Studio Ten*. 'Our suffering was more important than the lives of his children.'

But while the Poulson family mourned their loss, in northern Thailand another mother was also heartbroken. Neung Kongsom's 50-year-old mother collapsed in shock when a local journalist arrived at her farm to deliver the shattering news that her only son was dead and that he had killed himself, his two children and his Australian father-in-law in an act of vengeance.

On 21 September 2003 the *Sun Herald* gave the shattered mother's reaction.

'I lost my only child and two beautiful grandchildren and nothing I can say will bring them back,' she said. Neung was a father who 'lived' for his children; the thought of not being able to see them had obviously become 'too much' for him to bear. 'In the end I think he was so wound up, taking too many sleeping pills and just thought that if he couldn't see his children, then nobody else could,' she concluded sadly. On her last visit to Australia the family had seemed so happy, she recalled, and she related the story of how the couple had met and fallen in love.

According to Mrs Kongsom, her son had become so distraught following the separation that he had made the desperate suggestion that the siblings be separated so each parent could raise one child each.

'He was a doting father and was extremely close to his son,' she said, in tears. 'He talked about nothing other than his children. He wanted a lawyer to grant one day access a week but they said it was impossible.'

Mrs Kongsom said her son had been so stressed after the separation that he had been taking sleeping pills to help with his insomnia. She had tried to help him by selling some land and sending him $18 000 for a deposit on a new home. Now she did not even have the cash to bring his ashes home because she had given him everything.

Acknowledging that her son's crime had brought great shame on her family and her country, Mrs Kongsom told the newspaper, 'He must have just snapped because he was missing his children so much. He was driven over the edge, I think, more because he didn't understand the system in Australia.'

Amid her own anguish, the distraught grandmother expressed her sorrow for her former daughter-in-law and her Australian family. They would always be in her prayers, she said.

Battling their own grief in Australia, the Poulson women — Rebecca, Ingrid, their mother Janice and stepmother Cheryl — embarked on a crusade to ensure lessons were learned from their tragic loss. They lobbied for changes that would address the laws that had failed to protect a loving grandfather and two innocent children. There needed to be greater protection for women and children living with or fleeing from family violence. One of the biggest challenges meant removing the responsibility for dealing with violent men from their abused partners onto the authorities, who they felt were ill-equipped to deal with violent offenders who flouted the law.

Their tragedy highlighted the need for greater education and training within the police force, and greater community awareness about domestic violence. With better understanding they hoped there would be an improvement in the way the police responded to complaints from abused women such as Ingrid, who were struggling to deal with a dangerous and erratic husband.

The responsibility of dealing with Kongsom's threats should never have fallen on Ingrid's shoulders, they argued. Red flags had been ignored by the authorities and the consequences had been deadly. It could not happen again.

In July 2005 an inquest into the deaths of Peter Poulson and his grandchildren highlighted failings in the police investigation, which might have prevented the tragedy and spared a family a lifetime of heartache.

In the Westmead Coroner's Court, New South Wales Deputy State Coroner Carl Milovanovich told the inquest that police may have had 'a window of opportunity' to prevent Kongsom returning to his estranged wife's home and murdering his two children and their grandfather. He noted that Kongsom's wife had telephoned police at 6.30 that morning to report him for sexually assaulting her the previous evening. Yet at 1.33 p.m. he remained at large and free to commit the murders.

While the police insisted they had acted appropriately, requiring time to investigate the complaint before making an arrest, the coroner concluded the public had a 'reasonable expectation' that the police would have arrested Kongsom sooner.

'I have raised the issues, not for criticism of officers, but to draw attention to a possible window of opportunity that may have existed to in turn, change the course of events,' the coroner said.

Mr Milovanovich further recommended that the New South Wales Police Commissioner review the case and consider new guidelines that would compel early arrests. He observed that while the complainant had been kept safe, and nobody could have predicted the children were in any danger, it ought to have been clear to the police that Kongsom was at least a threat to himself. For this reason, he recommended that the police commissioner should consider forcing police officers to participate in regular and improved training in domestic-violence matters. The findings were welcomed by the Poulson family, who supported one another through the much publicised inquest.

Afterwards, Rebecca Poulson spoke for the family when she said this was a step in the right direction and that the coroner's recommendations would lead to further improvements in a system that had 'so terribly failed' her own family.

'We believe there appears to be a systemic aversion to dealing with the domestic-violence issue within the police force,' she told journalists.

In its coverage of the inquest in the *Sydney Morning Herald* on 16 July 2005, journalist Geesche Jacobsen noted that the coroner had praised the actions of the police while acknowledging that resources for education and training for the police was a prevailing problem.

But the coroner had also said that one of the lessons that could be taken on board before the murders was that when Ms Poulson contacted the police to express her fears, there had been a failure on the part of the officers to 'look outside the square'. Police needed to investigate more deeply and thoroughly when dealing with situations involving domestic violence, Mr Milovanovich found. He also felt it was important for police officers to record their actions in their notes, if only to head off future criticisms.

In this particular case, the coroner said, the children's mother could have rightly expected the police to take a harder line when she reported the breaches of the apprehended violence order.

Rebecca Poulson said that the family wanted improved training for all police, and a broader recruitment process to help other women and children trapped in the cycle of family violence in the future.

'We are survivors,' Ingrid's mother Janice, reminded the media. 'We are strong women.' The story ran with a photograph of Janice, Ingrid, Rebecca and Cheryl Poulson supporting one another.

One month after the inquest issued its findings, the mother behind the heartbreaking tragedy gave her first interview to Channel Nine's *Sixty Minutes*. Ingrid spoke about the paralysing shock and grief and the anguish of being stripped of her very identity.

'When it first happened I'd have to look at myself in the mirror on some mornings and say ... you know, "My name is Ingrid. ... who used to be a mum and I'm not any more,"' she said. 'I was stripped of everything I had been.'

She described the bloody scenes that greeted her on her father's driveway that fateful afternoon in September 2003.

'I just remember lying on the police seat saying "Oh it's all too late,"' she said. 'I kind of had the feeling even when we drove onto the driveway. I thought it's all too late.'

Ingrid went on to relate the demise of the marriage that had begun as a romance in a foreign land. She recalled the arguments, and her husband's resentment, and ultimately the violence that finally caused her to leave.

It was very hard, she explained, coming 'to grips with somebody that you really loved and you know has been so much part of your life, but has changed in such a radical way that they are threatening to kill you', she said. More poignantly, Ingrid spoke with affection about her role as a mother.

'I really loved being a mum. You get so much love back,' she said. 'I think you can't recognise that you have this capacity to love so much and then, you know, you're getting that love back as well. It's a very incredible relationship to have.'

Chief Inspector Malcolm Lanyon, the officer in charge of investigating the tragedy, defended the police's decision to send the traumatised mother back into her husband's flat after he had threatened to kill himself following a family access visit. Lanyon said this had been an 'operational decision' based on trying to produce the best results with the least risk to all parties involved.

'He was only threatening to self-harm at the time,' said Lanyon. 'That is not a criminal offence.'

Speaking about the three-week lapse between the time she was granted the interim AVO and the time the full order was finally granted by the court, Ingrid told viewers she felt 'like a sitting duck'.

'It was horrible,' she said. Throughout that entire period, Kongsom had continued to threaten and harass her and there was nothing she could do to stop him.

Even after the AVO was served, he had immediately breached it and the responsibility of dealing with him still fell upon her. The presenter asked Lanyon why the police hadn't taken control.

The policeman replied that the decision had been based on the circumstances at the time.

Ingrid said that she hoped her tragedy would bring about changes in the law, including greater awareness about domestic violence, improved training for police officers and in particular, more recruitment of policewomen. In the end, she just wanted to make sure people learned from her loss.

But how does any woman recover from such an enormous loss? Ingrid Poulson answered the question simply: by not giving up.

'That's not me at all,' she told viewers. In order to demonstrate how much her father and children meant to her, she had to live life. 'So I have chosen to live as well as I can and make my life the best that I can — kind of an honour to them.'

It was a philosophy that each of the Poulson women had come to embrace.

Ingrid and Rebecca both became tireless advocates for women and children at risk of family violence. They were vocal as they lobbied for changes in the law and an improved response from the police. They felt the entrenched attitudes of the police towards 'domestics' needed changing and this could only be brought about through education and greater awareness.

In June 2006 Ingrid's presentation at the three-day Australasian Police Conference on Family and Domestic Violence reduced many high-ranking officers to tears. Hosted by the New South Wales and Victorian police forces, Ingrid was keen to put a human face to the issue and draw attention to the numbers of casualties of domestic violence. In almost three years since her family had been murdered another ten innocent children and three mothers had lost their lives as a result of domestic violence. This was just the tip of the iceberg. Ingrid Poulson pulled no punches in her presentation.

'Your statistics,' she told the gathering of 27 senior police chiefs, 'equals my family. And I want you to meet them.'

There, on the big screen at the Australian Police College in Manly, appeared the faces of Ingrid's father Peter and her children Marilyn and Sebastian. This was her happy family, she said, full of life and promise before her former husband killed them all.

Ingrid went on to remind everyone that the night before this terrible crime, her former husband had broken into her home — breaching the AVO yet again — and had bound and raped her. His final crime had claimed the lives of real people; people she had loved. Her father had been an inspirational man and a mentor; her daughter, Marilyn had been a giggler, a vibrant little girl full of life; her son Sebastian had been learning his first words. She loved to hold him close to her at night. Her life had been happy and filled with dreams. Now her family had gone.

In its coverage of Ingrid's presentation, *The Age* described the silence that fell upon the room as the pictures of these casualties of domestic violence filled the screen.

Tears had flowed among the attendees, who included five Australian assistant police commissioners and their colleagues from New Zealand and Hong Kong. The newspaper reported the bereaved mother saying that only a consistent, rigid application of the law against perpetrators would make domestic violence unacceptable, in the same way that anti-drink-driving campaigns had made drunken driving unacceptable.

'It wasn't accidents that reduced drink driving,' Ingrid pointed out. 'It was the law.'

She went on to say that in the aftermath of the murders all the media had wanted from her were photographs of 'a distraught shattered woman … tears, hysterics, accusation'. She would not give them that. Neither would she condemn apprehended violence orders when urged to do so. She argued that even though they had failed her, they still worked for other women.

She would never consider herself be 'a victim' of domestic violence. 'Victim' was a term she despised for all its suggestions of 'passivity and complicity'. Ingrid Poulson saw herself as a fighter and survivor; a crusader committed to change. She urged the police to be a part of that.

'I stand among the souls of the dead,' she told the gathering, using a phrase she would use many times in the years ahead, 'to ask you for help in protecting those who are yet to die.'

She recalled the words of the detective who she claimed had told her that dealing with domestic violence cases was too hard and meant 'a bunch of crap paperwork'. That same attitude still prevailed in the police force, she observed. Too many police officers continued to view domestic violence as an 'annoyance' that got in the way of real policing. But this attitude was part of the problem. The other problem was the lack of proper police training in domestic-violence matters, and their reluctance to examine failures in the system. This had to change if lives were to be saved, she said. She was not bitter about these failings in relation to her family. But she was impatient to see changes.

Her determination to ensure such changes were put in motion prompted Ingrid's appearance on the ABC show *Enough Rope* in October that year. Presenter Andrew Denton introduced her by explaining that one in four relationships in Australia was scarred by domestic violence.

Ingrid began by describing the romance that had blossomed in Thailand with the 'sweet' though 'persistent' young economics graduate who went on to become a 'lovely father'. Neung had been such 'an unassuming person', she reflected. But then the cracks began to appear in the relationship, and he morphed into someone completely different.

Ingrid described the obstacles facing women escaping from violent partners, and the entrenched attitudes of the police when dealing with family violence.

'It's people caught in a situation they don't feel that they can really get out of,' Ingrid told viewers. 'It's kind of this hidden sort of secret and if the police start to take a stance on it, like this is a crime, and if you report this crime you will be protected ... you will be looked after, we will do the right thing and this person will be punished ... If that comes in then that will be fantastic.'

Ingrid explained that the interval between when a violent partner is served with an AVO and when it reaches the courts for approval is a dangerous period. That is when women are unprotected and at great risk.

This was why there was an urgent need for changes in police training to allow officers to be better equipped to handle situations when women who had been abused remained at risk.

'They [police] need to learn to sit down and listen, and validate and understand what you are experiencing ... that your fears are real and true. And at least be aware of the fact that this is a serious crime and violent behaviour very very rarely is redeemable,' Ingrid said. 'If someone uses violence once they are not going to go back to not using violence ... things can escalate.'

Andrew Denton asked Ingrid if she felt in hindsight anything might have prevented her former husband 'in the frame of mind he was in' from doing what he ultimately did.

Ingrid paused before answering. 'There was some talk at the time of putting me in protective custody when they realised what had happened to me,' she said. But Neung would have found her just as he had threatened. 'He was absolutely so determined,' she said thoughtfully. 'So I don't know really what would have stopped him.'

Still, police needed to be taught to pass on the concerns of women reporting violence, or at least they needed to be shown how to use that knowledge and 'to better exercise their powers' when protecting women at risk. Ingrid felt that even in cases when women did not want to press charges, the police had a duty to follow up.

'If you are in that situation it's very difficult to be objective,' she reflected. 'I was motivated out of care, I was motivated out of love; I was motivated out of trying to protect him. I am sure a lot of other women are as well,' she said. The police needed to have more of an understanding of this.

'It's not like you are motivated out of hatred or the need for revenge to report your partner. So that's what you are dealing with ... it's very messy.'

Ingrid's mother Janice told Andrew Denton of her dismay

and frustration at the recent inquest when she heard the police's explanation for the way they had handled the case.

'I thought it was one bumbling episode after another,' Janice said frankly. 'From the wrong classification at the first incident to the time when the two [policemen] came to interview Ingrid and her dad at the house the day after the AVO had been taken out.'

She described her former son-in-law arriving at the flat to play with his children hours after the AVO had been granted, and flatly refusing to leave when Cheryl Poulson asked him to do so.

'This was all reported to the police who seemed to think that they could get away with saying that they were just going there for an educational talk, to explain to Ingrid and her dad what an AVO was all about, even though there was a record at the station saying it was an AVO breach by Pete. They obviously hadn't followed any of the correct procedures,' she said.

Given an AVO had been reported she was amazed the police had not taken the situation more seriously and were simply going to talk to Neung, who had shown a complete disregard for the law. She felt this slack attitude on the part of the police demonstrated that they felt dealing with domestic violence was just too hard.

'I also think it is what one of the police officers said to Ingrid: "It's just a bunch of crap paperwork."' She explained that the detectives who had come around to the house after Neung had breached his intervention order four times on the same day had not been happy at the prospect of doing 'lots and lots of paperwork'.

But they had not looked into the history of her daughter's violent relationship, which would reveal a situation of escalating violence that had culminated in the breach and Neung's total lack of regard for the law.

This was why the process needed educational rather than punitive solutions, said Janice Poulson. The family wanted to see a focus on training and changing attitudes.

Her daughter had been 'a stunning mother' and a 'wonderful wife', Janice reflected. Despite the fact it had ended 'so badly', her daughter had worked hard to pick up her life and continue to make something of it. Ingrid's vow to honour her children and her father for the rest of her life had given her the strength to keep going and keep 'doing amazing things'.

This raised the obvious question from Andrew Denton. 'How do you put your life back after it?' he asked Ingrid.

'I don't know if you ever do,' she replied. 'I certainly think you just grow around it a bit. You can't ever fill in the space or pretend it didn't happen or disregard the lives that were.' But Ingrid said she could make sure that lessons were learned from her tragedy and that changes were made to protect other casualties of family violence in the future. She urged other women in violent relationships to break their silence.

'Speak out, and make sure that your voice is heard,' she said. 'If you do have an AVO make sure that the police come around and enforce it. The only way people are going to respect this instrument is if they are punished for what they do with it.'

It was a sentiment shared by Ingrid's sister. In her 2015 book *Killing Love* Rebecca pointed out that in spite of the countless threats and persistent harassment Ingrid had endured from her former husband, the red flags alerting everyone to Neung's escalating violence were dismissed, even after his repeated breaches of his AVO were reported.

She revealed that when Ingrid reported the knife incident that had occurred in front of her two small children at Neung's flat, she was made to feel like 'a drama queen getting in the way of real police work'. This, Rebecca said angrily, amounted to a 'giant brush-off'.

What is important about Rebecca Poulson's own moving account of her family's journey through suicide and murder is the prevailing danger that continues to exist for women and children living with family violence.

Family homicides claim many more casualties beyond the mothers who are the primary targets of these revenge crimes, she observes. These crimes affect the wider family and the friends who are close to them. They reach beyond the fleeing wife whom the perpetrator wants to punish for the remainder of their lives.

In her later interview with *Studio Ten* Rebecca described the 'crippling guilt and pain' she felt for being alive when her father and her sister's small children had been murdered. It tormented her that she had not been there to protect Malee and Bas.

In her book Rebecca revealed that while she had supported her sister, her mother and her stepmother through their pain, she had denied herself counselling, convinced she was not entitled to feel the same 'big grief' that the others had been forced to endure. Time was not a healer for the anguished aunt, who lived with daily reminders that her father and niece and nephew were gone forever.

'But this does not mean that I have dedicated my life to one of sadness and grief,' she told me. 'I have grown outwards.'

The tragedy had sparked a crusade for the grieving Poulson women, and the Poulson Family Foundation was established to prevent further child homicides. Rebecca became its CEO. She argued that at a time when 85 per cent of all child murders in Australia were known to be committed by a parent, alarm bells are often ringing before family violence escalates into murder. Many of these deaths are more preventable than those child murders perpetrated by strangers.

Yet despite the introduction of mandatory reporting of children at risk, and a shift in police attitudes towards domestic-violence procedures, tragedies like the ones suffered by Ingrid and Rebecca Poulson continue to happen.

The way ahead, they reason, lies in cultural change within the police force from the top down, along the lines that Victorian Police Commissioner Ken Lay advocated in 2015 when he made his 'we believe you' speech. It was imperative that women reporting family violence were believed and supported, he said.

In October 2015 Rebecca Poulson launched a Facebook campaign again calling for the same changes her family had advocated over a decade earlier, among them immediate prison sentences for violent men who breached intimate-partner AVOs. Her petition to Prime Minister Malcolm Turnbull, New South Wales Premier Mike Baird, New South Wales Police Minister Troy Grant and New South Wales Police Commissioner Andrew Scipione demanded greater public awareness and better education for police, who need to be taught domestic-violence procedures and shown how to follow them. Other changes the petition called for included mandatory police follow-up on all AVOs, even in those cases where abused women drop them.

The petition attracted more than 1200 signatures in just three days. By February 2016 more than 27 816 people had signed it and were continuing to share it around social-networking sites.

Rebecca Poulson continued to call upon the Department of Social Services to allocate more case workers to children at risk. She also urged the media to report the 1800 RESPECT number whenever they highlight cases in which women and children are murdered as a result of family violence.

Another way the government could help is to reopen the emergency shelters closed by the Abbott government, and provide more safe houses for women and children fleeing family violence. Abused women, she points out, are still the biggest single group of homeless Australians. And since more than half of women in violent relationships have children in their care, their children are without homes too.

Today Rebecca and Ingrid continue to be vocal advocates for other women and children living with or escaping from family violence. Both are inspirational public speakers and both have written books about rebuilding their lives after terrible adversity.

After the murder of her family, Ingrid returned to study, embarking on a masters degree in cognitive science at the University of New South Wales and nurturing her own resilience to help her rebuild her shattered life.

When Ingrid's book, *Rise*, was launched in 2008, she was determined it would not be a 'sob story' but a book of hope and inspiration. The result is partly memoir, but mostly a self-help guide on how to overcome adversity through resilience.

But writing the book meant revisiting the most painful and harrowing time of her life. In an interview with Melbourne's *Sunday Herald Sun* in August 2008, Ingrid admitted that she had had to steel herself to write about the torment of being continually harassed and threatened, and to describe the horror of surviving being raped and seeing her family murdered.

Ingrid wrote that her best support during those early days came from people who simply allowed her to grieve. Her family and close friends did this by closing ranks around her, allowing her to weep when she needed to without trying to comfort her or to stop her tears from flowing.

'A lot of people felt uncomfortable around me,' Ingrid revealed. 'So I admire the people who came forward in spite of their discomfort and said "I don't know what to say but I am here".'

Despite this, there were many bleak periods when she felt overwhelmed by anger, sadness and grief. But she discovered coping skills that included playing soothing music when she felt sad, going for a brisk walk when she felt angry, and surrounding herself with colour and flowers on days when life felt dark and empty. But what really buoyed her through those terrible times was the voice that continued to whisper in her head, reminding her she would not sink 'so low' and that her life was not over.

Ingrid identified four key areas she believed were vital to fostering resilience and surviving unimaginable grief. These included resolve, identity, support and everyday resilience (RISE). From this insight came the title of her book.

Identity was of prime importance, since Ingrid recognised that possessing a strong sense of who you are is vital in helping survivors find their own identity and ultimately tap into resilience.

In a few moments of madness Ingrid Poulson was robbed of her identity as a mother. In her book she describes the experience as being 'unmummed'. As she had explained to *Sixty Minutes* two years before her book was launched, the experience was so disabling that she had found herself staring at her reflection in the mirror, wondering who she was now she had become a mother without children. This loss of identity has been described by other mothers whose children have suffered sudden violent deaths.

Ingrid says through fostering her own resilience, she has been able to rediscover her identity. She explains that she owes this in part to her ability to retain her core values: compassion, empathy, love, kindness and generosity.

'Someone once asked me if I was proud of myself and it sounds odd to toot your own horn, but if I do feel proud of myself in any way, it's because I have managed to retain those values that were important to me through this experience,' she wrote.

With resilience came the desire to keep going. In her book Ingrid revealed that in the early days following her family's deaths, she was amazed by her body's physical ability to keep on going. In her interview with *Studio Ten*, Rebecca recalled how grief caused her and Ingrid to lose their appetites. They were fading away, almost willing themselves to disappear from the agony of their loss. Yet their physical bodies just kept getting up each day and going on with life.

For Ingrid, it was an uncomfortable experience learning to smile again; she later said she felt that rediscovering happiness was somehow dishonouring the important roles her father and children had once played in her life. In the end she realised she was simply surviving.

Through Ingrid's work with other survivors, and the cathartic writing experience, she came to understand that her survival not only lay in her refusal to drown in the deep sorrow Kongsom intended for her, but was also due to a promise she made herself after he murdered her family.

In her book she recalled sitting beside her children's grave early one morning and glimpsing the image of a woman. The woman was her future granddaughter who was writing a story of how Ingrid had survived the tragedy of losing her family and had gone on to live a full and positive life. As she glimpsed the young woman, Ingrid felt her father's presence strongly around her. When she returned home she made a promise to him that she would rise above her tragedy and honour their lives. In the end, the book did not wait for her future granddaughter; Ingrid decided she would write it herself.

'I could have refused to honour the people I lost by never rising; never reaching my goals and by cultivating misery,' she wrote. 'But

I chose to honour my family by living well and demonstrating how much they meant to me by being the best I could be in spite of everything.'

This is why her story became one of resilience and hope. She says she found that hope by holding on to the good memories and developing skills to help her through the empty days.

Ingrid survived painful anniversaries like birthdays and Christmases by surrounding herself with people she loved and by performing rituals that brought her comfort. On birthdays she took gifts and cards to her family's graves, and on special milestones she lit candles to honour them. A far greater challenge was finding a place for her memories of the man who had cost her so much.

On Neung's first birthday after the murders, Ingrid wrote him a card expressing her pain and confusion over what he had done to her. She later burned the card at the cemetery. She also burned the clothes he had bought to bribe her back into the marriage.

Ingrid Poulson's life has moved on. When her book was released in August 2008, she had just become an aunt for the first time, and shared her delight at her sister's baby boy in publicity for her book. It was a wonderful gift to have a child in the family again, she told Melbourne's *Sunday Herald Sun*. Perhaps more significantly, the intensely private Ingrid revealed she had recently embarked on a new relationship, though she declined to elaborate. What was important, she told the newspaper, was that her experience had not left her with a morbid distrust of men.

'I could have gone down that path, but I didn't because I had had such wonderful men in my life,' she said. 'My best friend is a man, my father was fantastic and my sister's partner at the time that all this happened was also fantastic.'

But despite her achievements as an educator, campaigner and anti-family violence advocate, it is as an inspirational speaker raising awareness about domestic violence that Ingrid Poulson has perhaps gained greatest recognition.

Among the many issues she has highlighted is the subtle secondary victimisation frequently described by survivors of family homicide.

She raised the subject in a speech in Wollongong to the Police Anti-Violence Committee on White Ribbon Day in 2011. Describing herself as a 'pretty average' sort of person who had a face that appeared to blend in, she said her story was not an average one.

'It is a big event,' she said. 'It got into the media; it got into people's hearts and minds and even now it sometimes still gets discussed.'

The downside of being in the spotlight and being so well known, she revealed, was that her life story was often scrutinised by strangers in online forums and chat rooms. Those discussions had given her some 'interesting insights' into people's reactions to her story and attitudes to victims of domestic violence in general. It was alarming to discover that people appeared to be more interested in the way she looked, her age, her work, her educational background, her character, her actions — everything except the actual crime that had been intended to destroy her. While she had received 'a tonne of sympathy and support, compassion and love' after the murder of her family, the questions and comments from the public that followed showed very little insight into the true nature of family violence.

She said that after her appearance on *Enough Rope* she was blasted by one angry male viewer who slammed the segment on her family's murders as 'crap', claiming it was the most biased story he had ever seen.

'Women can lie their ass off and men are not believed,' he claimed, and accused mothers of holding children to ransom just to upset separated fathers.

A woman in an online chat room naively asked why Ingrid had not packed her bags and left the moment Kongsom showed his 'true colours'. The woman also wanted to know why she had left her daughter with Kongsom the night he threatened to stab himself. Other misguided supporters, focussing solely on her appearance and education, suggested 'helpfully' that Ingrid might be a perfect spokesperson for domestic violence issues simply because she had all her own teeth!

She said that judgements like these showed that people were

still missing the point about family violence. Worse still, the more punitive judgements only served to compound the guilt she already felt over the death of her family; their questions were ones she had tormented herself with many times over the years.

'I already felt guilty,' she told the White Ribbon gathering. 'That it was my fault that they had been killed for daring to leave the man who was starting to act violently towards myself and my children.'

Yet there were so many judgements about what it meant to be a victim of domestic violence.

'We are all judged,' she said. 'And we are judged differently. I have no doubt, no doubt at all, that my character, my actions, my life would not have come under such scrutiny had it been that a branch fell randomly from a tree and killed my family.'

She told the conference that when she first came under public scrutiny her own feelings of guilt convinced her that people were looking for reasons to blame her.

'But what I have come to realise is that what most people are looking for is difference ... How is she different from me? People don't want to be anything like me, because then it's possible that something like that might happen to them. So the fear has always been on how am I different as a person and how my story is completely different from theirs. Because things like this happen to people like her, not people like me.'

It would be easier, Ingrid concluded, to look at the similarities rather than the differences. Just being born female means women are statistically more likely to suffer from acts of family violence than males. Because in the end how you look, where you are from, whether you are educated or not, is irrelevant.

'What I do, or what I said, or why I left or didn't leave, are irrelevant,' Ingrid said. 'Because it's just simply not about me at all. It's about him and his choices. It's always about him.'

Being told she would be a great spokesperson for domestic violence because she was educated and well presented not only missed the point, it illustrated how much community attitudes needed to change. Domestic violence had nothing to do with education or looks or talent or character. It was about power, control and violence against women.

She told the gathering it was encouraging to see men in the White Ribbon movement condemning intimate-partner violence, saying violence is never the solution and telling men who use violence that their behaviour is wrong. It is about showing respect and support for women.

Today Ingrid continues to honour the promise she made in 2003 when she stood among the 'souls of the dead'. She has refused to be destroyed. Instead, she has continued to rise to new heights by living her life as well and as positively as she promised herself she would.

Ingrid Poulson is now in a respectful relationship with a supportive and loving partner, and has experienced the joy of being a mother again. She is also a doting aunt to her sister Rebecca's three children and lives a quiet life in a small town, out of the public spotlight. Her sister says Ingrid prizes her privacy and is reluctant these days to agree to interviews or talk further about the tragedy.

Today Rebecca Poulson continues the fight to raise awareness and generate attention for a crime whose impact reverberates forever.

'The pain is always there; you just learn over time to add new layers to your life so that you can live it in the best way you can. But it's always there,' Rebecca told me. 'The sad thing is that Ingrid and the family tried to support Neung after the separation. We bent over backwards to help him, but in the end it made no difference. It was not about us, or the children, it was always about him.'

Today Rebecca and Ingrid continue to demonstrate that it is possible to survive terrible adversity and rediscover hope. But as Ingrid Poulson revealed on White Ribbon Day in 2011, her biggest hope is yet to be realised: that one day there will be an end to family violence.

'For the end of violence, although remarkable in and of itself, is just the beginning of what life can really be like,' she said.

Family and Domestic Violence Support Services

1800 RESPECT National Helpline 1800 737 732

Women's Crisis Line 1800 811 811

Men's Referral Service 1300 766 491

Lifeline 24 Hour Crisis Line 131 114

Relationships Australia 1300 364 277

Sources

Introduction

Destroy the Joint, Counting Dead Women Facebook initiative: at https://facebook.com/DestroyTheJoint (2015, June 05) The Minister for Women. Facebook update, retrieved 13 May 2015 from http://www.facebook.com/DestroyTheJoint

Manchester University Institute of Brain Behaviour and Mental Health, 'Study into Filicide and Filicide–Suicide' *Journal PLOS One*

'Findings from most in-depth study into UK parents who kill their children', sciencedaily.com, 4 April 2013

'Analysis, 32 Years of US Filicide Arrests: "First Comprehensive Statistical Overview of the Tragic Phenomena"', conducted by the Alpert Medical School at Brown University, Providence, US, lead author Dr Timothy Brown

'First comprehensive statistical overview of tragic phenomena', sciencedaily.com

New South Wales Ombudsman, media release into *Report of Reviewable Child Deaths in 2012 and 2013*

Dr Debbie Kirkwood, *Just Say Goodbye*, Discussion Paper No. 8 2012, published by Domestic Violence Resource Centre Victoria.

Jane Hansen, 'The Family Annihilator', *Sunday Telegraph*, 15 February 2014

Anastasia Powell and Kristin Diemer, '2014 National Community Attitudes towards violence against women' survey

Dr Carolyn Harris Johnson, *Come with Daddy: child murder–suicide after family breakdown*, University of Western Australia Press

E Yardley, D Wilson, A Lynes, Birmingham City University's Centre of Applied Criminology, 2013 UK study, 'A taxonomy of male British family annihilators, 1980–2013,' *The Howard Journal of Criminal Justice*, August 2013

Wiley CDA press release, 'Characteristics of family killers revealed by first taxonomy study', on Science Newsline, Medicine/Social Sciences, 14 August 2013

Adam Cooper, 'Luke Batty's death was not foreseeable', *The Age*, 28 September 2015

Rachel Blaxendale, 'Luke Batty had "trusted" his father who killed his son before being fatally shot by police', *The Australian*, 13 February 2014

Dr Jenny Mouzos and Ms Catherine Rushforth, *Family Homicide in Australia*, Australian Institute of Criminology, Canberra

Miki Perkins, 'Royal Commission into Family Violence: what you need to know', *The Age*, 30 March 2016

Kirsten Veness, 'Family violence report: Rosie Batty calls for federal support for Victoria's Royal Commission's recommendations', ABC News, 30 March 2016

Jeremy Pierce and Paul Weston, 'Tara Brown's cries heard in grim recordings moments before she was allegedly bashed to death', *Gold Coast Bulletin*, 11 November 2015

Chapter 1 Michelle Steck and Kelly East
Based on interviews with Michelle Steck conducted by the author
Layla Tuck, ABC *Stateline WA*
'Sins of the Father,' Channel Seven *Sunday Night*, 13 October 2013

Chapter 2 Dionne Fehring, Patrick and Jessie Dalton
Interviews with Dionne Fehring conducted by the author over several years.
Further material from:
Liz Jackson, 'Losing the Children', ABC *Four Corners*, 16 August 2004
Kate Kyriacou, 'Family, friends, experts search for answers on Brisbane bridge tragedy. How could a dad do this?' *The Advertiser*, 25 February 2012
Joanne Gibbons, 'Little angels will not die in vain', *Gold Coast Bulletin*, 24 July 2004
Daryl Passmore, 'Mother plans lawsuit over murdered tots', *Sunday Mail*, 4 July 2004
Melissa Ironside, 'When good parents turn bad', *Sunday Telegraph Magazine*, 5 June 2011
Jen Jewel Brown, 'Suffer the little children', *Sydney Morning Herald*, 3 May 2009

Chapter 3 Cindy Gambino and Jai, Tyler and Bailey Farquharson
Chapter based on author's notes from court cases and interviews with Cindy Gambino and her husband Stephen Moules, and his children, along with eight years of research in the courts. Other material from court transcripts, Cindy's private letters and journal records. All material included in Cindy's heartbreaking account of the tragedy in *On Father's Day* by Megan Norris, published by Five Mile Press.
Further material:
'A little town's heart bleeds', *Geelong Advertiser*, September 2005
Karen Kissane, 'A town farewells three small brothers', *The Age*, 15 November 2005

Chapter 4 Peta Barnes and Darcey Freeman
Court coverage from author's notes and Victorian Coroner's report.
Paul Anderson, 'Darcey Freeman thrown from the West Gate Bridge in the horrifying murder that still haunts Melbourne', *Herald Sun*, 24 January 2014.
Patrick Carlyon, 'No, it will never be all right', *Herald Sun*, 8 October 2009
Patrick Carlyon and Paul Anderson, 'The death of Darcey: a dad's monstrous act', *Herald Sun*, 30 March 2011
Andrea Petrie, 'This Little Girl Lost', *The Age*, 29 March 2011
Paul Anderson, 'Accused West Gate Bridge throw dad Arthur Freeman told Darcey's mum to say goodbye to kids — court told', *Herald Sun*, 7 October 2009
Pia Akerman, 'Man weeps in court as dead girls' injuries are described', *The Australian*, 16 March 2011

Paul Anderson, 'Arthur Freeman, accused of throwing daughter Darcey Freeman off bridge, appears in court', *Herald Sun*, 21 May 2009

Andrea Petrie, 'Mother testifies in Darcey murder case', *The Age*, 17 March 2011

Katie Bice, 'Darcey Freeman's mum Peta Barnes to sue over bridge saying barriers could have saved her child's life', *Daily Telegraph*, 27 January 2012

Stuart Rintoul, 'Time won't heal the grief', *The Australian*, 12 April, 2011

Angus Thompson, 'Inquest hears of moments leading up to Darcey Freeman's murder', *Herald Sun*, 16 July 2015

Adam Cooper, 'Mother of Darcey Freeman addresses inquest, praises emergency services workers', *The Age*, 16 July 2015

Wayne Flower, 'Victorian coroner grants inquest into the death of Darcey Freeman', *Herald Sun*, 5 February 2015

AAP on SBS News, 'Coroner delivers Darcey Freeman findings', 30 October 2015

Angus Thompson, 'Doctor didn't believe Darcey Freeman was at risk, inquest told', *Herald Sun*, 16 July 2015

Further material from court transcripts, victim impact statements, State Coroner's findings

Chapter 5 Rachelle D'Argent and Yazmina Micheline Acar

Research taken from court transcripts and coroner's findings.
Further material:
Amelia Harris, 'Yazmina will never leave me, says mother', *Herald Sun*, 22 November 2010

Amelia Harris and Mark Butler, 'Tears flow for little Yazmina Acar', *Herald Sun*, 20 November 2010

Andrea Petrie, 'Murdered daughter Yazmina my everything, says mum', *The Age*, 16 June 2011

Adrian Lowe, 'Calls, texts and Facebook updates reveal girl's final hours', *The Age*, 5 May 2011

Norrie Ross, '"Bout 2 kill ma kid", guilty father Ramazan "Ramzy" Acar's chilling Facebook updates', *Herald Sun*, 4 May 2011

Anthony Dowsley, 'Murdered little girl's grandmother gets horror call from jail', *Herald Sun*, 4 July 2011

Olivia Lambert, 'Coroner investigates the murder of Yazmina Acar', news.com.au, 4 December 2015

'A Mother's Heartache', Channel Nine *Sixty Minutes*, 1 July 2011

Anne Wright and Anthony Dowsley, 'Meadow Heights man Ramazan Acar charged with murder of daughter', *Herald Sun*, 19 November 2010

Chapter 6 Karen, Jack, Maddie and Bon Bell

Based on discussions with Karen Gray (Bell), along with coroner's findings

Glen Williams, 'Bega mum's miracle family; I can finally smile again', *Woman's Day*, 25 October 2010

Glen Williams, 'New baby for Karen Bell mother of murdered Bega Trio', *Woman's Day*, 23 November 2009

Glen Williams, 'I've found joy again,' *Woman's Day*, 1 August 2011

'Karen Bell gives birth to baby boy,' *Daily Telegraph*, 23 November 2011

'Karen Bell pines for the three children her husband murdered,' *Herald Sun*, 7 July 2008

Liz Hayes, 'A mother's story,' Channel Nine *Sixty Minutes*, 6 July 2008

Steve Strevens, 'Cowardly and selfish', *Bega District News*, 27 August 2009

Steve Strevens, 'Karen's new beginning', *South Coast Register*, 19 July 2009

Yuko Narushima, Les Kennedy, Jano Gibson, 'Violent past of murder–suicide father', *Illawarra Mercury*, 29 June 2008

Evelyn Yamine, 'Killer dad Gary Bell feared loss of kids, left suicide note', *Herald Sun*, 6 July 2008

Steve Strevens, 'Children drugged before they were gassed', *Bega District News*, 28 August 2009

Connie Levett, 'Children killed to punish me, says mother,' *Sydney Morning Herald*, 7 July 2008

Yuko Narushima, Peter Veness, Kately John, 'Mother's grief turns to anger over loss', *Sydney Morning Herald*, 29 June 2008

Les Kennedy, Jano Gibson, Yuko Narushima, 'Father was arrested before murder–suicide', *Sydney Morning Herald*, 28 June, 2008

Les Kennedy, '"Valley of failure" murder suicide: father and three children found dead', *Sydney Morning Herald*, 27 June 2008

Yuko Narushima, 'We are all responsible for children's deaths', *Sydney Morning Herald*, 9 July 2008

Steve Strevens, 'Family torn apart by tragedy', *South Coast Register*, 1 July 2008

'Bell Children farewelled with balloons', ABC News, 9 July 2008

Peter Veness, 'A mother's farewell', *Illawarra Mercury*, 10 July 2008

'A mother's grief turns to anger over loss', *Sydney Morning Herald*, 28 June 2008

Gemma Jones, 'Karen Bell's scrapbooks of Jack, Maddie and Bon', *Daily Telegraph*, 1 July 2008

Yuko Narushima, 'Brother in torment for abused sister', *Sydney Morning Herald*, 1 July 2008

Narushima, Kennedy and Gibson, 'Killer's past: liar who abandoned his first family', *Sydney Morning Herald*, 30 June 2008

John Bateman, *Ten Pound Pom: Victor Poxon Goes to War*, Google Books, 2012

Chapter 7 Ingrid Poulson

Author's interview with Rebecca Poulson.

Further material:

Ingrid Poulson, *Rise*, Macmillan, Sydney, 2008

Rebecca Poulson, *Killing Love*, Simon and Schuster, 2015

'In harm's way', Channel Nine *Sixty Minutes*, 21 August 2005

Enough Rope with Andrew Denton, ABC, October 2006

'Survival Instinct', *Sunday Herald Sun*, 17 August 2008

Tim Elliot, 'I live for those who cannot', *Sydney Morning Herald*, 9 August 2008

Geesche Jacobsen, *Sydney Morning Herald*, 16 July 2005

Geesche Jacobsen, 'A mother's tale of murder reduces police to tears', *The Age*, 14 June 2006

Candace Sutton, 'Rebecca Poulson on family's story of survival after triple family tragedy', *Daily Mail* UK, 29 August 2015

Eammon Duff and Andrew Drummond, 'Killer the perfect son — mother tells', *Sydney Morning Herald*, 21 September 2003

Acknowledgements

The stories in this book have been as painful for me to process and write as they have been for the mothers who have been courageous enough to share them and reveal what it is like to live with the knowledge that their children were murdered simply to punish them.

There have been times during the writing process when some of the mothers have had to stop and ask themselves if they really wanted to relive these harrowing events. At other times I have asked myself whether I am able to do these stories justice in a single chapter.

In the end we all agreed that these tragedies, heartbreaking and confronting as they are, were too important not to be told. I hope that by sharing these experiences we may shed some insight into a little-understood crime that appears to be on the rise.

So a heartfelt thankyou to Michelle Steck and Dionne Fehring, who have spoken to me many times over the years about their experiences and whose stories I have touched on in my magazine work. Your insights as you fight to raise awareness and educate the community about family violence have given me a valuable understanding about the lifelong suffering such crimes cause. Your stories have been as confronting to write as they were for you to read in print.

A particular thanks to Karen Gray, who though I struggled to locate her, was so generous with her time. She answered my constant questions at very short notice, and talked me through the events surrounding her children's murders at a time, when she was reliving her loss on the anniversary of their deaths. In spite of this, she was still willing to share her story in the hope of generating a greater understanding about such crimes.

Thank you, too, Cindy Gambino and your husband Steve Moules, whose journey I followed for eight long years both in the courts and beyond. I saw first-hand the impact of Robert Farquharson's revenge crime on your lives and those of your families. Your courage, like that of Michelle and Dionne, continues to inspire and amaze me.

A special thanks to anti-family-violence campaigner Rebecca Poulson for sharing her own journey about the brutal murder of her father Peter, who battled valiantly to save his two beloved grandchildren from their father's vengeful attack. If Neung Kongsom set out to destroy your sister Ingrid and the rest of your family, the Poulson women's inspirational survival story only demonstrates that evil never succeeds. The Poulson Foundation remains a legacy to your father and his two small grandchildren. It is to be hoped it can save other young lives in future.

Though I have never met them, I hope the tragic stories of Peta Barnes and Rachelle D'Argent will also generate some new understanding of the nature of these revenge crimes in highlighting what can happen to children when domestic violence turns fatal.

A special thanks to Debbie Kirkwood, whom I met some years ago and whose research and ongoing work in this field has made her the authority she is today. And to my long-time friend, criminologist Judy Wright, whom I first met in the courts 26 years ago. Her straight-shooting take on these sorts of murders and the men who commit them has always kept me focused.

Thank you to my commissioning editor, Julia Taylor, for her patience and her insistence that this is a book that must be written, and to my eagle-eyed editor Linda Funnell, whose constructive advice has helped shape this book into one that I hope will make a difference. Huge thanks to Luke Causby for his superb cover design, to Shaun Jury for his excellent internal design and typesetting, and to Jackey Coyle for brilliant proofreading under extraordinarily difficult circumstances.

And finally, a really big thankyou to my long-suffering husband Steve, who struggles to read the tragic subject matter of the books I write, but who believes in me anyway.

After she read her chapter, Michelle Steck pondered whether anyone would want to read about such a sad and confronting subject. If you have got this far, then I hope you will remember the stories of these little children and their mothers, and join Rebecca Poulson's campaign for change.